PROS
AND CONS

Book Two in the
Silver Shores Series

Acknowledgements

My thanks to:

Deborah Pointer Larson
Horses Healing Heroes

Vito Carbone

And my 'first readers'

Stephanie Fiddler
Yvonne Miller
Carolynne Petrie
Stephen Polli
Charlene Steving
Lauren Wasserman

In memory of:

MLKMini
and
"my" Patrick,
J. Richard Wilkinson

-1-

"Please Mommy...no more singing!"

Danica Rossi glanced in the rear view mirror at her five year old vocal critic; her son, Robbie.

"What's wrong, you don't like the song?"

"NO! And I don't like your singing!"

Dannie laughed and reached to the controls for the satellite radio, switching to a kid-friendly station. She had to admit Robbie wasn't her only detractor when it came to singing; she herself knew she would never win any contests. As a matter of fact, singing alone in the car, the shower, an empty house; those were her best bets with the operative word being "alone".

She glanced once more at Robbie strapped safely in his child safety seat, contentedly nodding his head and tapping the arm of the seat in time with the music; such a happy little boy.

Dannie and Robbie had just traversed the twisting road of a mountain pass that divided the California coastal area where they lived from the agricultural mecca that was the great Central Valley, more specifically their current destination in the

San Joaquin Valley. It was a vast area that cut through the center of the state from just below Sacramento and finished at the Tehachapi Mountains.

On this blustery spring Tuesday, Dannie and Robbie were heading for nearly dead center in the valley. Dannie was hired to work as a starter at the Jamaican Farms Spring Classic Horse Show from Wednesday through Sunday. The following week, Easter week, she would go north one hundred miles or so for five days of work at the Gala Horse Shows Spring Egg-stravaganza and then finish the three-week stint back down the valley at the Coast with the Most Horse Show, the one and only event each year headed by show manager, Langston Rubicon, Esq.

She had only left home a few short hours ago yet Dannie was already questioning whatever had led her to agree to work these shows. Last summer, she was determined to finish the shows at the Silver Shores Equestrian Complex and then take her life in a different direction. A single mother, her desire to improve her life and the life of her young son was palpable. She thought she had everything figured out...until she didn't.

By the time the last horse trailer pulled out of Silver Shores that summer, longtime show manager and all-around jerk, Jumpin' Jimmy Bittler had been murdered. Dannie had nearly met the same fate as Jimmy's assistant manager and his killer, Darlette Simon, had almost succeeded in throwing Dannie off a cliff to the rocky beach of Pacific Ocean below.

Dannie had discovered, in actuality more like stumbled upon, the fact that Darlette was Jimmy's killer but she came to the realization in Darlette's presence and it almost cost her everything. In the end, it was Dannie's desperate act of self-defense that took Darlette's life as she had taken the fall planned for Dannie.

It was her personal life however that had truly been turned upside down last summer. When Dannie was working at Silver Shores her father, Joe Hoffman and her stepmother, Judith, had been killed in a tragic accident while on vacation. Almost nine months later, it was a loss Dannie could scarcely allow herself to contemplate; not a day went by she didn't think of them and miss them terribly.

But the deaths of Joe and Judith had also changed Dannie's financial situation forever. Dannie, an only child, had inherited the couple's beach house in Silver Shores, all their material possessions and Joe's copious investments valued at roughly twenty million dollars. Additionally, Judith's sizeable portfolio had been earmarked for Robbie's education. It was Joe's final gift to his daughter and grandson but Dannie primarily felt tremendous guilt at receiving such a bequest only because of a death.

The final life-changing event of the previous summer brought a smile to Dannie's face and caused her heart to swell just at the thought of him...Jeff. Detective Jeff Barnes had been assigned to investigate the murder of Jimmy Bittler. After his initial meeting with Dannie, Jeff had sought her out as his translator of sorts as he delved into the world of horse shows and horse people while working to solve his case.

Jeff was gorgeous; young Paul Newman gorgeous, and their attraction had been immediate. But with so much happening in that short window of time, Dannie had wondered if they could really have a lasting relationship or if it was based more on the drama of the moment. Happily not only had the relationship lasted, Dannie and Jeff's feelings had deepened. He had moved in to the beach house in the early fall and on Thanksgiving morning, Jeff brought Dannie breakfast in bed on a tray with hot coffee, a warm, buttery croissant with blackberry preserves and a beautiful linen napkin with an exquisite engagement ring serving as a napkin ring. It was perfect and just what Dannie would have chosen for herself; tasteful, classic and simple. No ostentatious, garish "glass-cutter" would have made her nearly as happy as the ring Jeff had chosen.

She loved him. It overwhelmed her to think how much she loved him and caused her to wonder if her first ill-fated marriage to Brian Rossi had ever involved love at all. Jeff was smart, funny, kind, and an amazing role model and mentor for Robbie. He always put Dannie and her son first and showed them all the thoughtfulness, respect and devotion she could ask for.

It had not escaped Dannie that though the last nine or so months had presented her with great drama, turmoil and loss it had also bestowed an irreplaceable gift.

She was shaken from her thoughts by a noise in the back of her SUV. It was her black Lab, Jake, adjusting and readjusting his position and seemingly restless; in short, very "un Jake- like". He probably could use a pit stop.

Dannie glanced at the screen rising from the center of the console to see the time; she still had about an hour to reach Jamaican Farms yet she wasn't due to meet her mother for another two hours.

Beth Hoffman, Dannie's mom, was driving down to meet her and pick up Robbie. Robbie would spend the remainder of the week with his Nana, and then Dannie would drive up next week to work the show for Gala. The show grounds were only about ten minutes from Beth's house, so Dannie would stay with her mom for the week. That Sunday, Easter Sunday, Jeff would drive up so they all could enjoy Easter dinner when the show was over and the following day Dannie would head back down the valley for Langston Rubicon's show and Jeff would take Robbie home to Silver Shores.

"Feel like a girly cheese sandwich, buddy?" Dannie asked Robbie, using his five-year-old word for grilled cheese.

"Yes!" said Robbie enthusiastically, "can I have fries too?"

"Well, a few I guess," Dannie smiled.

She activated the hands-free device in her SUV and called Beth to let her know her plans, assuring her she would still arrive at Jamaican Farms in plenty of time.

Five minutes later she pulled in to a truck stop right off the highway. Dannie began by hooking a leash to Jake's collar and letting him stretch his legs and take care of business though neither dog nor owner were overjoyed with the cold, blustery north wind. Then, with Jake safely back in the SUV, Dannie and Robbie had a quick meal; grilled cheese and fries for Robbie and a turkey burger and small salad for Dannie. Robbie insisted on a visit to the eclectic gift shop where he convinced his mother to buy a fierce, plastic T-Rex he found and they finished their visit, once more braving the wind, by walking to the truck wash with Jake in tow to let Robbie look at the many rigs; big and bigger.

An older, somewhat grizzled driver invited Robbie up to see the inside of his cab. It was a gesture that would have made Dannie much more nervous had eagle-eye Jake not guaranteed the old gentleman knew he was being watched. The short tour was such a hit it was all Robbie talked about from the time they left the driveway of the truck stop until they parked, an hour later, at the beginning of the dirt and gravel road leading to Jamaican Farms.

She had purposely not driven on to the show grounds, preferring to meet her mother privately. There was nothing untoward about what Dannie was doing, but she was intensely private and felt the less people knew about her and her family the better. Her years in the horse world had taught her that gossiping about each other was mere sport to horse people and before you knew it, the most benign event could take on an outlandish life of its own.

Beth arrived not more than ten minutes after Dannie had parked. Dannie watched as she piloted the new compact SUV toward them. For years, Beth happily drove wherever she needed to go in an aging soccer mom van with a sticker in the rear window proclaiming "I love my granddog". While Dannie was sure Jake appreciated the sentiment, with the beach house as her new home she knew Beth would be driving many more highway miles back and forth for visits and Dannie was insistent Beth agree to the gift of a new car.

Beth parked along the side of the road behind Dannie and Robbie, who had been waiting impatiently and the young boy flew to hug his Nana as soon as she stepped out of the car.

"Nana! Look, I got a T-Rex and I had girly cheese and then I got to see a big truck, then..."

"Whoa," Beth laughed, "I want to hear all about it, every bit, but let's get your car seat and your suitcase in my car so we can let your mom get to work."

Robbie acquiesced and ceased his story for the moment, but he held tight to Beth's hand as she walked forward to help with the transfer.

Dannie had already opened the lift gate and Beth was greeting by a madly-wagging Jake. She took a moment to greet the dog and then lifted Robbie's suitcase with her free hand and returned to her car to stow it away for their trip back to her house.

Dannie was right behind with the car seat and when it was safely installed, she and Beth shared a huge hug.

"Thanks, Mom, I really appreciate you meeting me here."

"Oh honey, anything for more time with Mr. Robert here," Beth said, ruffling the hair atop Robbie's head.

Dannie knelt down in front of her son. "Give me a hug, buddy, I'll see you on Monday." She wrapped her arms around the little boy and held on for dear life. "I'm going to miss you so much."

Robbie squirmed in the embrace and said, "Mommy, you are going to em-brass me in front of Nana!"

Dannie released him as Beth howled with laughter. "Don't worry, Robbie," said Beth, "your mom's been em-brassing me for years."

Dannie kissed Robbie on the forehead and helped secure him in his seat and then hugged Beth one more time. "I'll see you Monday, Mom. I'll call when I'm on the road."

"Love you, honey," answered Beth.

Dannie watched as Beth fastened her seat belt, started the car and began her three-point turn to return to the freeway. As she executed the second part of the turn and backed toward Dannie, it did not escape her that in the lower left of Beth's rear window was a shiny, new sticker proclaiming, "I love my granddog."

-2-

Once Dannie was back in her SUV, she proceeded up the dirt and gravel road to Jamaican Farms; up because the show grounds were on the highest part of the property, a sort of plateau. The road itself was poorly maintained and she drove slowly to avoid the many potholes in her path.

Her slow progress allowed the opportunity to take in her surroundings. The field grasses, tall and still green with the April rains, were being buffeted so by the wind they were almost parallel to the ground. As the wind gusted, then subsided, the long blades fluttered somewhat piteously near the soil as if they wished to stand tall again but lacked the energy to do so.

The spring sun shone brightly, glared in fact, with no trees and very little else to absorb or divert the rays. Dannie was so happy for her sunglasses and made a mental note that a hat was in order for work tomorrow so she could cut even more of the brightness.

From the entrance to the show grounds the road was a little over three-quarters of a mile and as she climbed higher more of the facility came into view. She studied it and realized the arena and office area resembled the hub of a wheel, with the remainder of the grounds set up as the spokes; all jutting out in different directions down the hill.

At a man-made flat area at the end of a narrow road down one side was the spot designated for equipment; jump standards and rails, tractors, water trucks, front loader, and various implements such as drags, blades, and harrows.

One hundred and eighty degrees on the other side of the hill was another man-made flat section, larger than the first, housing rows of portable stalls. Further down, below the stables and at nearly the same elevation as the entrance, was the designated parking for cars and horse trailers. At the entrance where Dannie had met Beth, you could take the road straight up the hill as Dannie had done, directly to the show grounds and office. There was also the option to turn left as you entered and drive straight to the parking area.

This was not the show to attend without access to a golf cart, scooter or bicycle of some sort thought Dannie. If exhibitors, trainers and grooms were afoot, copious amounts of time would be spent climbing and descending the hill to the barns.

As she pulled up to the show office and parked, her scan of the arenas and warm-up rings produced evidence of frenzied activity that could rival any beehive. One beautiful horse after another was being schooled by a trainer, lunged by a groom, or just out for a walk around the grounds to stretch their legs, but no matter what they were doing the blustery wind was an issue.

Horses and wind were often not a good combination, but for the trainers schooling in the arenas, all were working hard to keep their mount's mind on their job and reinforce the idea that when they were under saddle it was time to go to work.

As she opened her lift gate to attach Jake's leash, she became aware of the music sailing on the wind from the facility sound system. Reggae. Of course, she was standing in front of the horse show office at Jamaican Farms. Her previous visits here had taught her that for the next five days, the prevalent music would be the aforementioned reggae, as well as ska, and other Jamaican folk music heavy on the steelpan and full of African rhythms. Dannie enjoyed the music, but not a five day, force fed diet of it.

She stepped aside to allow Jake to jump out of the car and turned toward the show office only to see a brightly colored golf cart speeding in her direction. The driver, show manager John Bowman, stomped on the brake causing the cart to slide in the loose dirt for the last few inches of its journey.

"Dannie! Wah gwaan mi sista!"

"I'm sorry.... what, John?"

"Naw, naw, naw. I be J-Bo," he replied.

"You be an idiot!" laughed Dannie, though in truth she wasn't kidding.

"Oh come on, Dannie, play along. I said, 'what's going on', you know, Patois."

"I don't understand Patois, nor do I speak it and frankly, I don't think you do either."

Patois, also known as Jamaican Patois, is an English-based Creole language with influences from West Africa. It is native to Jamaica and linguists have also tagged it Jamaican Creole. But repeated attempts at Patois were only one of John Bowman's Jamaican "idiosyncrasies". An arriving trainer approached John with a question regarding their stall placement for the week and as he consulted his copy of the stall chart it gave Dannie time to reflect.

John had come to the horse world as a dad. His young daughter showed and John embraced the horse world, all of it. He went to every show with his daughter and cheered her on, organized and sponsored hospitality events where she was showing and even tried to involve himself in some governance issues with the different horse show organizations.

When his daughter was just a few years from college, John decided to leave his chosen career as an accountant, buy the property that currently housed Jamaican Farms and become a show manager. The facility also housed a boarding stable to generate additional income and the permanent barns that held the boarders were down the hill behind the horse show office.

As far as Dannie could tell the problem with John Bowman, horse show manager, was that he didn't know one thing about managing a horse show. John was a party guy, and it was a commonly-held thought that John threw a horse show to go along with his parties. He had never bothered to learn the rules of the sport nor did he care, but woe be to anyone that neglected to have the barbeque hot or the beer cold.

To date, John had managed to have reasonably successful shows in spite of his lack of knowledge by hiring an 'assistant' to perform the tasks of the manager. He had been through many and Dannie wondered who had been chosen for this year's Spring Classic.

She pulled her thoughts from the show and returned to the self-appointed Rastafari. As he sat in the cart addressing the stall inquiry, Dannie looked at him and smiled ruefully, shaking her head.

John Bowman was a paunchy, balding, fifty-one year old former accountant. The incarnation of "J-Bo" sat before her in a crocheted Rasta cap, a sort of tam with circles of green, yellow, red and black. Dannie was sure he would have dreadlocks protruding from the cap if at all possible but his DNA was making it difficult to have much hair at all. He wore sandals and khaki pants and his shirt was a tie-dyed monstrosity of the same colors as his hat.

He had paid to have a wild vinyl wrap done on his golf cart with the same colors as his outfit minus the black…it was a sure thing no one on the show grounds could miss him.

One thing Dannie knew for sure was that John Bowman was harmless. She was fairly certain, as was everyone else, he had never even been to Jamaica. All this was just some sort of oddly-designed theme, what John considered a hook. Dannie knew he meant no disrespect to anyone or anything and as ridiculous as she found it, it hurt no one.

The trainer of a few moments before had wandered off to find her stalls and John noticed a group near one of the arenas that he wanted to greet.

"Dannie, mi deh guh, si yuh latah."

Dannie simply raised her eyebrows in reply.

"I said, 'I'm going to go. See you later.' You're no fun." John waved a dismissive had in her direction and sped off.

Dannie waved at the retreating golf cart and said, "Yeah, thanks John, good to see you too."

The horse show office looked like one of those sheds shown on TV and touted as super strong, but it was probably twice the size. The outside was tidy, but nondescript. A glass slider served as the front door and there was a small window on either side for light and air circulation. Today, because of the wind, everything was shut tight.

Dannie and Jake stepped through the slider into a space that could only be described as cramped. Her friends, show secretaries Michelle Carpenter and Jennifer Brooks, were sitting elbow to elbow behind an eight foot long, molded plastic table loaded with two computers, two printers, pens, pencils, paper clips, tape, staplers, scissors, sticky notes, and yet-to-be-assigned show numbers for the rider's backs.

Just to Chelle's right, against the wall, was a smaller table stacked with clipboards, reams of paper, and binders. In an inconvenient and unlikely position under the table were two large radio charging stations plugged into the outlet there.

Behind this table, also against the wall was a simple wood desk where it appeared some sort of explosion had occurred. There were papers, notebooks, coffee cups, self-inking stamps, pens, permanent markers, file folders, receipts, envelopes; all scattered haphazardly across the surface leaving no area in evidence for actual work.

On the wall behind the desk there were lists, flyers, sticky notes, take-out menus, photos of small, fluffy dogs, and two wall calendars; one for the previous year permanently flipped to December and one for the current year that had not advanced past the month before. Everything on the wall hung at disjointed angles having clearly been stabbed into submission with push pins.

In the midst of this chaos sat Barb Snowden, John Bowman's assistant for not only the shows but for the day to day running of Jamaican Farms.

Barb stood as soon as she noticed Dannie and headed for the door. As an afterthought, she grabbed a small stack of papers from her desk to accompany her. Dannie wasn't sure if she was truly on a mission or if the papers were her excuse to get out of the office. On Barb's list of friends and favorite people, Dannie didn't even rate an honorable mention.

As Barb threaded her way through chairs, extension cords, power strips and computer cables on her way to the door, she acknowledged Dannie in her practiced monotone, "Danica."

"Hey, Barb," Dannie replied noncommittally.

Then, as Barb rounded the table occupied by Chelle and Jen she looked down at Jake and sneered, "Is it necessary for you to bring *that dog* in here?"

Poor Jake. It seemed he became part of the fallout whenever the people that didn't like Dannie were around.

"Yes. Yes it is, Barb," Dannie replied as Barb swept past her and out the sliding door and Jake viewed the retreating figure with what Dannie was sure was disdain.

Barb closed the door behind her and turned into the wind, her imperious demeanor disappearing as a gust caught the papers in her hand and they flew away from the building like a startled flock of birds. She was immediately reduced to running sideways while bent down to the ground as she tried to retrieve the errant papers.

Dannie clapped her hand over her mouth to avoid roaring with laughter. All she could visualize was a crab scurrying across a sandy beach.

She turned to see Chelle and Jen stifling chuckles as well and only then did she notice the desk up against the other wall and directly behind Jen. It was as stark and pristine as Barb's was chaotic. There was an open laptop, dead center, and a small pencil cup holding any necessary office supplies. In front of the pencil cup was a business card holder. The only other things in evidence on the desktop were the rule books of the various sanctioning organizations, standing on end between two carved wood bookends that if placed together would create one garishly painted red balloon.

Sitting at the desk was a man that seemed familiar to Dannie but she couldn't place him. At that moment, he looked up from his computer and at Dannie as if he had just become aware of her presence in the office though she doubted that was the case.

He stood quickly, a huge, yet insincere smile spreading across his face. "Dannie! I'm so happy you're here. Do you remember me?"

"No...no, I'm sorry, I don't."

"I'm Kent Mallory. We met several years ago when you and your husband... Brian, I think, were attending a Silver Shores show. I am a friend of Tootie Bittler and Sunshine Forrest. I've done events for them."

"Horse shows?" Dannie asked.

"No, no." Mallory turned and pulled a business card from the holder on his desk, handing it to Dannie.

It proclaimed "KENT'S EVENTS" with brightly colored foil balloons on either side of the business name. Below that, along with contact information was the slogan, "we put the hearty in your party".

Dannie could find no appropriate words so she looked blankly at Kent.

"I'm an event planner," he said as if she had lost the ability to think.

"Yeah, I got that," Dannie said, "so what are you doing here? John's no stranger to throwing parties."

"I'm J-Bo's assistant. I'll be managing the show."

"You've produced horse shows before?"

"No, but plenty of events; charity dinners, weddings, bar-mitzvahs, same thing, right?" Kent said dismissively.

"Um, no," Dannie said and it was now her turn to stare at Kent as if he'd taken leave of his senses.

He continued, undeterred. "Anyway, you'll be doing Hunter 2 this week. I've paired you with Mikey Gregory. You'll be training him for a job as a starter. Know him?"

"No," Dannie said, "should I?"

"He's Payton Gregory's brother," said Kent.

Payton was a junior rider but Dannie was unaware she had a sibling.

"OK," said Dannie. "So, has he shown?"

Kent snorted. "Certainly not."

"Worked on crew, local shows, ever done a gate?"

"No, but how hard can it be?"

Dannie bristled and fought the urge to snap back but instead, drew a deep breath and slowly released it. Her job as a starter was certainly not on par with that of a nuclear physicist, it was instead in a field that featured people jumping animals over large sticks. The important thing to Dannie about serving as a starter, announcer, or both was that as any job worth doing, it was worth doing well. And done well, the job of a starter combined elements of organization, attention to detail, patience, teamwork, a small knowledge of psychology both human and animal, and a boundless talent for multi-tasking. Oh, and the ability to sit in one place for hours on end with no opportunity for a bathroom break was a plus too, she thought.

She was long accustomed to people offering their opinion regarding how simple and trivial her job was and without exception, they were people that had never done the job, or any job, at a show. Ultimately, she had decided not to rise to Kent's bait and to just move on.

"How old is Mike?" she asked.

"He prefers Mikey," replied Kent.

"Oh, so he's five...six?"

Kent gave her a condescending smile and said, "He's nineteen, cute, and the girls will love him. He's perfect!"

"No doubt." said Dannie skeptically.

"Hunter 2 starts at eight, please be here at seven."

"No problem, does Mike know the starting time?"

"You needn't concern yourself with what Mikey knows," said Kent, "he answers to me."

"Perfect," said Dannie, not meaning it.

She turned to Chelle and Jen and said, "Any info on the motel for me?"

Chelle tapped a few keys on her computer. "Printing directions," she explained. About a twenty minute trip, I think."

"You think?" asked Dannie. "Haven't you been there?"

It was the frequent practice of show secretaries to arrive a day before check-in to set up their office and be ready to go first thing the next morning. As such, Jen and Chelle would have spent the previous night in the staff hotel.

"No," Jen chimed in, "we came down early this morning. I left home at four AM."

Chelle passed Dannie the paper with the name and directions to...

"Are you kidding me?" asked Dannie. "The Inn and Out Motel? Sounds a bit like porn. Well, no matter, c'mon Jakey."

As she turned to go, Kent Mallory spoke again. "Oh, Dannie, it looks like you and I will be seeing a lot of one another this spring and summer."

She turned slowly, not warming to the idea, "Oh? Why's that, Kent?"

Well, I won't be working at the Egg-stravaganza next week but my wife, Muriel, and I will be there, then I will be helping Langston with his Coast with the Most Show."

"Uh-huh," grunted Dannie.

"But I'll be at all three weeks of the Silver Shores Summer Shows this year. Tootie and Mary Jane Bittler have hired me to manage and you are going to be my assistant."

"I see," chirped Dannie, "lucky me. Guess we'll cross that bridge, well, you know the rest..." With that she made her exit from the office and walked purposefully to her car.

She quickly secured Jake in the back and then got into the driver's seat, happy for the cocoon-like feeling the inside of the SUV supplied.

Her previous exposure to Kent Mallory was beginning to return. What she remembered most could only be described as oily. He seemed to ooze from place to place leaving only a small, unpleasant residue behind. He gave her the creeps.

And now to add to the dilemma, she was to be his assistant manager at Silver Shores? Admittedly, though Dannie, Tootie and Mary Jane had shared multiple discussions regarding the possibility of Dannie being the primary part of this year's management team, no contract had been signed. Maybe Kent was just muddying the water. Was she expected to assist an event planner that knew nothing about horse shows?

Dannie started the car and punched the address of the Inn and Out Motel into her GPS. Kent had to be wrong. She wasn't going to react until she had more information. She turned up the heater in the SUV, cranked up her stereo to drown out the Bob Marley she could hear from John Bowman's sound system and pointed her car to the Jamaican Farms exit.

-3-

Dannie followed the directions to the Inn and Out Motel and felt dismay, but little surprise, when she pulled up in front of the office.

It was a three-story building built in a virtual rectangle and comprised of stucco that may have once been white but now was dirty and yellowed. Entrance to the rooms on all floors was from an exterior catwalk which appeared only to be accessible by stairs. Dannie could see no evidence of elevators; a fact she filed away as she gathered her things to check in. Being someone that tried to discourage thieves by leaving nothing in her car and sharing her room with a dog that needed a potty break now and then, the lack of elevators became a notable feature.

The doors to the rooms were a faded red and though each room appeared to have a window, on every floor there were several that either had large cracks with duct tape preventing expansion, or some that had been broken out altogether and sported a large piece of plywood covering the opening.

Dannie left Jake in the car as she headed to the office. She took note that there was not a bit of vegetation to be seen. Every area not used as a sidewalk or parking lot was covered with faded red lava rock. Well, at least it matched the doors, she thought.

She pushed through the glass door of the office entrance to find two men. At a desk sporting the sign "Security" was a man that likely couldn't guard a candy bar from a ten year old. Dannie knew looks could be deceiving but she surmised he was over sixty-five and had clearly never missed a meal. Even sitting at the desk he was breathing as if he'd just run laps.

Manning the check-in desk was a boy appearing to be eighteen or nineteen whose nametag identified him as Nathan. Nathan would prove not only to have a bad complexion but a bad attitude.

"Hi," said Dannie, "I'm checking in, I'm with the Jamaican Farms Horse Show. My name is Danica Rossi."

Nathan glanced at a piece of paper next to his computer for a least a nanosecond before declaring, absent eye contact, "You're not on my list."

"Could you check again?" Dannie asked, but she had already begun to dial Jen at the show office.

Nathan didn't look down, but again repeated, "Yeah, not there."

Jen had answered her phone and Dannie quickly explained the situation before handing the phone to Nathan. Jen would verify that Dannie did indeed need a room.

While the two talked, Dannie leaned over the counter and peered at the show room list. Even upside down she spotted the name that was likely meant to be hers.

"Nathan, what about this one?" she said, pointing to a name on the paper.

"Nope, that's for Daniel Ross."

"There's no Daniel Ross working for the show," said Dannie, "but Daniel-Danica, Ross-Rossi…get it?"

"If you want me to change that room," Nathan said into the phone, "I'll have to have permission from Mr. Ross."

"THERE IS NO MR. ROSS!" Not only did Dannie yell in frustration but she heard the same five words come through the phone from Jen.

Finally after what seemed an eternity, Nathan agreed to give Daniel Ross' room to Danica Rossi and he and Jen ended the call.

"Would it be possible to have a first floor room?" Dannie asked. "I have a dog."

"You know that's extra," Nathan said sharply.

"Sure, what's the pet deposit?"

"Twenty dollars."

Dannie pulled a twenty out of her purse and placed it on the counter. Nathan glared as if she had spilled coffee on his paperwork.

"I need a credit card."

"The horse show pays for the room and I don't leave my credit card number for open transactions."

"What if the dog causes damages?" challenged Nathan.

"Then I'll pay for them...but he won't. Look, how about I leave one hundred in cash for a deposit, but I'll need a receipt."

"We don't accept cash," said Nathan.

"Of course you don't. Well, we have a problem then because I'm not supplying my credit card for this."

The standoff would have likely continued had the security guy not intervened. "Take the cash and give her a receipt, Nathan."

Nathan was petulant and seemed ready to actually stomp his foot but in the end thought better of it and said simply, "OK, Grandpa."

Dannie stopped herself from laughing but was sure her face spoke volumes. Unfortunately though the two words from Nathan explained a lot, it gave Dannie less confidence in the state of motel security.

She was almost free but Nathan had one more road block for her.

"There are two bath towels in the room, if you need more just let us know."

"Two per day is plenty for me," Dannie said.

"No, that's two for your stay. You can pick up more here between 10 and 2 if you need them."

"I'm at work then."

"Too bad," said Nathan, not thinking it was 'too bad' at all.

Dannie paused, about to say something else, but in the end just said, "Never mind. What room am I in?"

Armed with her key, Dannie emptied her SUV and stowed her belongings in a room that could only be described as depressing.

While placing her toiletries in the bathroom, Dannie picked up one of the bath towels she had been told about. It was small and threadbare; not much larger than a normal hand towel.

She returned to the main part of the room and grabbed her keys, summoning Jake. She would go to the Target she had glimpsed from the freeway several miles back the way she had come and pick up a couple of towels as well as some snacks and fruit.

She followed up a successful Target "run" with the purchase of Chinese take-out from a nearby chain and then returned to the motel.

It was just past four-thirty but Dannie was starving so she dug in to her Orange Chicken as if it were the last meal of a condemned man. When she had finished, she fed Jake and took the trash from her meal to the outdoor garbage can. She retrieved Jake from the room and walked with him to a small area of dead grass next to the chain link fence that separated the motel from the freeway, waited for him to 'do his thing', then they both returned to the room and she shut the door and locked it, securing the deadbolt as well.

She sat down at the small round table that was steadied by a folded piece of cardboard under one side of its base. It was a particle board slab covered by a cheap wood veneer that had seen better days.

Dannie pulled her phone from her pocket and called Jeff. He might still be on duty, but she wanted to hear his voice.

"Barnes," he said when he picked up.

"Hey, are you still working?" Dannie asked.

"Still at the station but wrapped up for the day. How's it goin'? I miss you already, D."

Dannie smiled. Jeff had begun calling her "D". She liked it but was aware she hadn't suggested the nickname to anyone else. She just liked to hear Jeff say it.

"I miss you too."

"How was your day?"

Dannie told him the highs and the lows; the wind, Robbie's tour of the rig at the truck stop, and Nathan of the Inn and Out Motel. She finished with Kent Mallory and his revelation about her serving as his assistant at Silver Shores.

"I have to be honest," said Jeff. "I don't know why you're even there, or any horse show really. You no longer need the money."

"I promised to help for one more season," Dannie said. "You know, some of the managers said they hadn't the time to make other arrangements or find another gate. I felt I owed it to them."

"Why? They're just using you to make their life easier. Do you actually think they have the same loyalty to you that you feel you owe them? Except for the few you've told me about on occasion, these managers would drop you like a hot rock if it suited them and never think twice. I think for many, loyalty is expected yet rarely given in return. What you owe them is to show up; on time, ready to work, and to do the best job you can. I know you and I know you have done that and then some."

"I have no idea why I agreed to these three weeks," Dannie sighed.

"Then come home," Jeff said softly.

"I can't. I made a commitment."

"I know. But it's just a stupid horse show," he sighed.

They spoke for a few minutes more and then Dannie and Jeff ended their call. While they'd been speaking, Jake had come to the table and placed his big head on Dannie's thigh, pushing hard to let her know he was there. She had been rhythmically stroking his ear during the call, but now she took his warm face in both hands and looked into his soft brown eyes.

"You understand, don't you, Jakey."

The dog closed his eyes in rapture and thumped his huge tail.

"I knew you did!" she exclaimed and hugged him tightly.

But if she was honest with herself even she didn't really understand it. She was at a loss to know what compelled her to leave the beach house and the man of her dreams to follow the horse show carnival from city to city. She had the vague, uneasy feeling she had left something undone and that there were still things she was meant to accomplish but she caught herself and shook her head, chiding herself in the next moment.

C'mon Danica, how dramatic can you be? You sit at a gate and push riders into the ring to compete for a two dollar ribbon and five minutes of bragging rights. It's nothing more than 'adult Disneyland' and you and your fellow carneys are no more than background noise.

But then, just as quickly, the words of her father came to her; words from a letter she had received from the attorney after Joe Hoffman's death. It said, in part:

> I need you to know how strong you are, how smart you are, we don't tell our children things like that nearly enough. However, you can't just know it, you have to believe it. We all have doubts, but damn it, Dannie, don't wallow. Have your doubts, have your moment, then get on with it. Do something! Be a wonderful daughter, mother, make a difference in this life, however big or small.

You always could cut to the heart of it, Dad, thought Dannie, and indeed she was wallowing. She sat up, drew a deep breath and promised herself, 'No more'. Her life was changing and her focus at the shows had to change too. She had agreed to work as a starter at a handful of shows this year to help out a few managers. She wasn't making this her life's work and if they told her to take a flying leap tomorrow it wouldn't change the trajectory of her life. It was time to change her approach.

She spent the next half hour making sure everything was ready for tomorrow; her backpack and Jake's bag, and then she pulled out the two lightweight sleeping bags she had purchased several years ago.

Dannie never slept in a hotel bed; not in any hotel, not anywhere. She had seen just one too many expose's on the horrors of what lurked in a "cleaned" hotel room, not to mention the ever-present possibility of bedbugs. She and the rest of the staff never had the opportunity to choose their lodging; show management made deals with local hotels or motels and staff was directed where they would stay. But in truth, she knew infestations and lack of cleanliness could happen in even some of the finest hotels so it was no one's fault, just something she chose to address by opening the two bags and laying one on the bedspread and using the other as a cover. She also brought her own pillow.

After her bed was set up and Jake had taken his position in one lower corner, Dannie took a quick shower, laid out her clothes for the following day, and snuggled within her sleeping bags to watch a movie before falling asleep with the din of the howling wind in the background.

Wednesday morning dawned with no cessation of the cold, biting wind. Dannie and Jake stepped through the office door at ten to seven and had to stand in line behind other staff members as they struggled to negotiate the cramped space and collect clipboards, radios, copies of courses and whatever else they may need in the next nine to ten hours. Fellow starter, Logan Peters, was on hands and knees under the small table against the wall pulling radios out of the charging bank and handing them up to outstretched hands.

When Dannie got close enough she gratefully took a radio from Logan and grabbed the clipboard with her name on it. She turned and worked her way back to the door against the surge of bodies all trying to reach the same twelve square feet, greeting friends as they squeezed past each other.

When she finally made her way outside again, she stopped at a picnic table placed just outside the office to reorganize. Jake, toasty warm in his fleece-lined jacket, waited patiently, tail wagging madly as he looked at Dannie with unabashed adoration.

Before she stowed the clipboard in her backpack, she checked the staff radio list to verify this week's panel of judges. Happily, the first was her horse show BFF, Patrick Collingsworth, and second was another personal favorite, Rebecca Kirtlan. The third judge was definitely not in the same class as the other two, at least when it came to personality. Beatrice, or Bea, Thomas, was in her early seventies and operated with a permanent chip on her shoulder. She believed herself to be above 99% of the people she encountered in a day and had no problem trying to prove that fact as often as she could.

As Dannie slipped her arms through her backpack once again she hoped the rotation would only find Bea Thomas in her ring just once in the five day show.

Leaving the office, the three competition rings presented themselves left to right across the large, flat plateau; Hunter 2, Dannie's ring, on the left, Hunter 1 in the middle, and the Jumper ring on the right. Three warm-up rings; one dedicated to each competition ring, were directly behind, hence further from the office. As she walked toward her gate, Dannie noted that with the back gates on the office side of the rings and the warm-ups on the other the "flow", as the managers liked to call it, was severely hampered.

A show grounds with flow had a design that helped trainer, riders, grooms, spectators and horses get from place to place at the show with ease and good managers made the show flow effortlessly. There was no flow to be detected here at Jamaican Farms, thought Dannie wryly, but they were dealing with John Bowman and Kent Mallory; two names not known to be uttered in the same sentence with the term "good manager".

Dannie surveyed her back gate area as she drew nearer. Under a flimsy, EZ-Up-style tent was a plastic table, about four feet long and covered with a plastic tablecloth. Holding down the tablecloth was sound equipment; an amplifier and microphone, and a large water cooler similar to what was utilized at construction sites. Next to the table was a folding plastic card table chair. This could prove to be a problem as she would have Mike Gregory sharing the small table area while he learned. In addition, she also had concerns about two of the four legs of the tent moving up and down, in and out of the ground with the wind gusts.

She used her radio to call the office and request another chair and some help with the tent while she watched the part of the plastic tablecloth not held down by equipment flapping frantically and creating rapid, staccato, snapping noises. Right where horses are expected to walk in the ring, Dannie thought, this will never work.

Placing her backpack in the chair, she proceeded to remove the plastic cloth from her table and then folded it as neatly as she could while fighting the wind. She tucked it under the water cooler then set about organizing her work space for the day.

When she made her thirty-minutes-to-start barn page, it occurred to her she had not seen Mike Gregory. Granted, she had never met him, but as she and Jake were the only breathing beings within fifty feet of the gate she was confident she hadn't missed him.

Movement caught her eye and she looked up to see a golf cart with two occupants; Kent Mallory and a woman unknown to Dannie.

"Morning, Dannie!" said Kent expansively. "Have you met my wife, Muriel?"

"No", said Dannie, extending her hand, "a pleasure to meet you, Muriel."

Muriel Mallory didn't move a muscle except maybe to put her nose just a little higher in the air. "I would very much appreciate it if you addressed me as Mrs. Mallory."

Dannie dropped her hand back to her side and stared. She did not however, address Muriel further and made a pact with herself that from this moment forward she would not address her by any sort of title at all.

"Where's Mikey?" asked Kent.

"How should I know? I don't even know what he looks like and you told me not to concern myself with when he arrived." She felt churlish. She knew she shouldn't but lack of manners had that effect on her.

"A bit early to be a smart-ass, even for you, don't you th..." Kent stopped mid-sentence. "Dannie, where is the tablecloth?"

She pointed to the folded plastic under the water cooler. "I took it off. It was flapping in the..."

"Put it back," said Kent quietly.

"I won't be able to get a horse in the gate," Dannie protested.

"Put it back. The ambiance this show presents is of absolute importance. The attendees must feel this atmosphere is special and we pay attention to detail. Put. It. Back."

"Fine." Dannie retrieved the cloth from under the water cooler. She was fairly certain that a plastic tablecloth from the nearest party store didn't qualify as ambiance or represent any attention to detail but decided not to mention it.

As she fought the wind to spread the tablecloth, a tall, blonde, good-looking young man walked up to the table and plopped a huge backpack right on top of the crumpled cloth. He didn't give Dannie a look, but instead turned to the golf cart with a million dollar smile.

"Mikey!" exclaimed Kent. He rose and walked forward and the two proceeded to execute a prolonged "bro shake".

Oh brother, thought Dannie, what's next, the melding of their secret decoder rings? But Mikey wasn't done, he followed the male-bonding with a patronizing kiss on Muriel's cheek; a move that rendered her positively giddy.

Only then did Mikey turn back to Dannie. She extended her hand and said, "Hi Mike, I'm Dannie Rossi."

For the second time in less than five minutes her offered hand was ignored. "I prefer to be called Mikey," he said.

"Well, good for you. I hope that works out for ya, Mike," she said. Does no one ever just say, 'Hello, nice to meet you' anymore, she thought irritably.

Dannie was itching to do the last of her organizing and get the first few riders lined up to begin her day. She let the Mallorys chat with Mike while she returned the tablecloth to the tabletop, made a barn page, and checked her sign-in sheet against the actual riders in the warm-up ring. The trainer at the top of her list, Michaela James, seemed to be wrapping up her warm-up and satisfied, Dannie turned to find John Bowman arriving in the golf cart that served as his homage to Jamaica. He had the chair for Mike and a few tools on the seat to anchor the tent.

"Mikey mon! Happy to si yuh. Glad yuh here, bredda!"

To no one's surprise, Mike replied, "Dis a great! Tank yuh, J-Bo."

More male bonding and another "bro shake" followed. Dannie imagined this to be not much different than attending a bad frat party. She noticed Michaela James trying to get close enough to the board that held the jumping courses and spoke up.

"OK, old home week is over. I have a horse to get in the ring."

At that very moment a huge wind gust caused the tablecloth to begin wildly flapping again and Michaela's horse shot backwards, ears erect and pointed at the offending cloth. Only the fact that she was rock solid in the saddle kept her from finding herself on the ground.

After circling her horse and moving back six feet or so to calm him, Michaela turned to Kent and John. "Seriously? Kent, what gave you the idea those tablecloths were a good idea in this wind? This is the Future Hunter class, the greenies!" 'Greenies' was a nickname for horses just learning their job in the show ring and usually denoted young and inexperienced animals.

"Good call, Michaela," oozed Kent. "Dannie, you should have noticed this would be a problem for these horses."

Dannie stared for a moment in disbelief, but remembering her vow to alter her approach, in the end, simply removed the plastic nightmare from the table once again.

Michaela returned to the warm-up ring for a moment to get her horse's mind back in the game. Dannie thought the opportunity presented itself to start laying out her job to Mike Gregory but just then her judge for the day, her friend, Pat, stopped by the gate on his way to the judge's booth.

"Are we ready to do this?" he smiled.

Dannie smiled back and hugged him tightly. "I've missed you, so glad you are here today. I have an apprentice of sorts this week. I'll be teaching the job to Mike Gregory." She turned to find Mike about ten feet away face buried in his phone. "Mike? Let me introduce you to today's judge. MIKE!"

The second time his name was spoken, Mikey looked up from his phone but made no move to come nearer and be introduced. Instead, he tilted his head sideways and gave it a quick jerk back as he uttered, "Hey," then returned to his phone without waiting for a response.

Pat rolled his eyes but gave no further response. "Dinner tonight?" he asked Dannie.

"Love to," she said. "We'll talk when the day is over."

With that, Pat headed to his booth and Dannie settled down to the start of her very windy day.

-4-

Dannie struggled to avoid the chance of a speeding ticket in her effort to get back to the motel and thus put the first day of the Jamaican Farms show behind her. Pat was following her down the freeway as the pair had decided to opt out of John Bowman's "Welcome Wednesday" wine and cheese extravaganza. In actuality, it was little more than a plate or two of grocery store crackers and cubed cheese but the wine flowed freely enough that no one cared.

Dannie had always spent enough time with trainers and exhibitors by days end that the parties held no allure for her and Pat maintained that his ethics as a judge precluded him from socializing with people he may be judging the following day. Instead, the friends had decided to regroup briefly at the motel and then take Dannie's SUV to dinner so Jake could relax comfortably in the cargo area while they ate.

As she headed south, she squinted against the bright sunlight coming in from the passenger window as the sun dipped ever closer to the horizon. Her shades were no match for such intensity from that angle and she was happy to pull off the freeway and into the motel parking lot.

Pat piloted his small sedan into the space next to Dannie and, while extracting horse show gear from their respective vehicles, they agreed to meet outside again in just five minutes.

Ducking into her room, Dannie threw everything in her arms onto the bed and headed for the bathroom. Her plan had been to splash some water on her face, take the wind-resistant braid out of her hair and then give it a quick brush. However one look at the brown water running into the sink from her face and she was convinced soap was in order.

Her face felt raw and burned from the day's incessant wind and if there was a silver lining to be found, Dannie thought she had probably received an absolutely free dermabrasion that many would pay dearly for.

After combing her hair and pulling it into a quick ponytail she returned to the main room and removed a couple of the layers that had saved her today. Glancing briefly around her, she took note that the area had probably not been touched by any motel staff since she left that morning. But, she thought, if they weren't going to give her fresh towels there wasn't much else that could be done to improve the situation anyway.

With Jake at her side, Dannie opened her door and returned to the parking lot to find Pat waiting, leaning against the fender of his sedan.

"Better?" he asked.

"A bit," Dannie smiled.

After securing Jake in the back of the SUV, the two friends settled in for the short trip to their chosen restaurant, a casual burger and brew joint. Their conversation was fast and full of animation, just what could be expected of two friends that had not been in each other's company in months.

Arriving at the restaurant they stopped talking just long enough to return the greeting from the hostess. Once seated, they found it necessary to ask the waitress to return for their orders as they were so engrossed menus had not yet been consulted. They did manage to sneak in drink orders; an IPA for Dannie and a sparkling water for Pat, before she left.

"OK," Pat laughed, "moratorium on talking until we make a dinner choice."

Dannie made a face but complied and when the waitress returned with the drinks they were ready.

With the order complete, Dannie drank deeply from her glass and followed with a huge sigh, feeling the tension abate in her shoulders.

Pat said simply, "Soooooo...Mikey."

"Ugh," replied Dannie. "That one's going to be a challenge."

Pat's raised eyebrows urged her to continue.

"In the first place, we didn't hit it off and that's a hindrance for sure. He's very young, pompous, knows nothing about horses or horse shows, is way too fascinated with his phone, has no work ethic, and has to this point, clearly skated through life on his winning, surfer dude smile."

"Oh, I see, but what do you really think?"

"Oh, Pat. I know, I'm whining after just one day. I keep telling myself the situation has changed. My very reason for doing shows this year is to help a few managers out and begin training some new starters. But my ring hadn't even started and the BS began all over again." Dannie continued, telling Pat about Kent; his news about being selected to manage Silver Shores, and the ridiculousness of the tablecloth in the wind.

She finished by saying, "Then, they send me this smart-ass who believes nothing of value can be learned from someone with two X-chromosomes. I don't know, I guess my heart just isn't in it."

"You are one hundred percent wrong about that," Pat countered. "Your heart is in it, in fact, the very reason it bothers you is because your heart is in it. You care too much. I know you love the horses and many things about this crazy business. I also know you want people to care about the starter job as you do. You want the people that own show dates to hire a manager, or coordinator, or assistant or whatever name they wish to call it, that has something of a working knowledge of how best to serve exhibitors, staff, and the animals at the show. You want a complete reversal of the absurd direction this business is headed as does anyone that has been in the industry for more than a year or two."

At that moment, the waitress returned with a monstrous burger and a mountain of fries for Pat and a grilled salmon Caesar salad for Dannie. When she left them to their meal, Dannie bestowed a warm smile on Pat.

"Wow, how is it you know me so well?"

"Because you want what I want." He paused and drew a deep breath. "But we're not going to get it. We're all sitting on a runaway train and anyone with the power to stop it has jumped off long ago."

"I hope that's not supposed to make me feel better," said Dannie.

"No, how could it. And regarding your X-chromosomes, surely it has not escaped you this is a man's world."

"No, I'm well aware, are you saying I should just be good with that?"

"C'mon Dannie, you know me better than that. But it's no secret that in this industry the percentages of women to men run in the high nineties for women and the single digits for men. Yet overwhelmingly, men run the show...no pun intended. And we've both seen time and again when women have a chance to step up and take that leadership role, they defer to the men."

The thought of Darlette Simon, figuratively bowing and scraping to a far less competent Jimmy Bittler last summer at Silver Shores crossed Dannie's mind. "Aren't you afraid they'll revoke your "man card" for such blasphemy?"

"Not likely. I've worked for many knowledgeable, competent guys in this industry, hell, so have you; Gary Desmond, for one."

Dannie nodded. Gary was one of the best managers she had ever worked for and she believed a large part of that had to do with his experience in the business. By the time he became a show manager he had done stints on ring crew, back gate, and as an announcer and judge. He had done nearly every job at the horse show, so when he asked you to do something you respected his knowledge and knew it was a reasonable request. Gary had always been fair with her and that was all she could ask.

Pat went on. "Even Gary left management because he couldn't take the foolishness of it anymore. Managers spend more time being a smarmy event planner a la Kent than they do worrying about schedules, footing, and rider and horse safety. And the time that it takes keeping up with the Jones's is enormous. At the same time, today's horse show patrons have been convinced a great party makes a great show, but I was around when a great show was enough and everyone made their own parties. You didn't ask for my opinion, Dannie, but I'm going to give it to you anyway. It's hard to fight a fight that can't be public. You can't take this to the exhibitors. Most of them are blissfully ignorant of what goes on behind the scenes, as they should be. This is their recreation...their fun."

"Agreed," nodded Dannie.

"And if you take it to other staff and certainly many, but not all, managers, they'll give as much resistance as you can take, and more. But I watched you last year with the Jimmy "situation" and you're up to it. You're smart and you may not change the world, but you will effect change. Your financial autonomy puts you in a perfect position. They can't touch you. Just think about it."

And think she did. Long after she returned to her room and prepared for bed it seemed she thought of little else and tossed and turned for what seemed an eternity until she fell into a fitful sleep.

The following morning Dannie drove to the show grounds after a disappointing start to her day. She thrived on routine and that routine was interrupted when she missed her morning shower due to no hot water in her room. She hoped this wasn't commonplace at the Inn and Out Motel.

Even though the morning had dawned without a breath of wind, the temperature was in the mid-thirties and off to the west there was a huge bank of ominous, black clouds. Dannie shivered just thinking of her exposed position at her gate and felt gratitude for her many layers and other cold weather protection that years of experience dictated.

In another fifteen minutes she had parked, organized herself and Jake and was approaching the front of the horse show office. It was there she saw one of her favorite people, man or woman, in the horse industry; Rebecca Kirtlan.

Rebecca was nearing sixty and was always effortlessly impeccable. She opted for the natural look, not a lot of makeup and no attempt to hide the slowly encroaching gray hairs. On the other hand, her hair was always neatly cut and styled, her clothes classic in design; expensive yet not ostentatious. She had a smile that would light up a room and a roguish sense of humor.

Rebecca had been a hunter and jumper judge when Dannie first began riding at age nine; which calculated to a minimum of twenty years though Dannie knew it was much more. Rebecca had lived all over the country but currently hailed from Montana. That was an interesting choice in Dannie's opinion, but Rebecca did what she wanted and she seemed to be mostly comfortable in her solitary life so who was Dannie to judge, she thought.

"Bec!" Dannie exclaimed.

Rebecca turned to see Dannie and a huge smile spread across her face as she threw her arms wide. "Dannie! It's been too long. How are you?"

Dannie hugged her friend warmly, stood back and held up her left hand, wiggling her ring finger.

"GET OUT!" laughed Rebecca. "We have some catching up to do."

"Want to have dinner tonight?" Dannie asked.

A momentary shadow crossed Rebecca's face but disappeared in a flash. "I haven't been very hungry in the evenings lately... been eating monstrous lunches. Are you at the Inn and Out? Maybe I can just come by the room and visit."

"Anything you want. I'd love to," Dannie replied.

Rebecca greeted Jake and made a tremendous fuss over him. The black dog reveled in the greeting though Dannie knew he thought it was nothing more than his due.

"I have to snag my clipboard and radio," said Rebecca, indicating the office door with a jerk of her head.

"Me too. Let's do it," Dannie smiled.

The pair entered the office to find Chelle and Jen at the front tables and behind, Barb Snowden at her desk with Kent's wife, Muriel and the third judge for the week, Bea Thomas.

"Mornin' ladies," said Rebecca.

Chelle and Jen returned her greeting amiably, while the three crones at the back desk glared with the zealousness of a pack of coyotes sizing up options for their next attack.

Barb spoke first. "I understand there were a couple of mistakes found on your judge's cards from yesterday, Rebecca."

Judge's cards were the papers with which judges registered their observations and comments about a horse and/or rider in a class. Judges used these notes to place the class from best performance down to the also-rans. They were customarily only available to show secretaries and the judges themselves, everyone else had to go through channels to see one and even then could only see how they themselves were marked and not the comments on anyone else in the class.

Muriel Mallory's face registered pity and she shook her head as Chelle spun in her chair. "What the hell are you talking about, Barb?"

"I heard you ask her about it myself, Michelle. Don't pretend you didn't."

"I did, just as I asked Bea about her cards." Bea Thomas managed to look somewhat sheepish. "What I'm asking, Barb," Chelle continued, "is what possible business is this of yours? Any paperwork corrections are between me and the judges and none of it has anything to do with you."

A smart woman would have backed down, but no one ever used "smart" and "Barb" in the same sentence.

"J-Bo needs to be aware of information like this," she countered.

"Information like what? Transposed numbers? John doesn't care, he pays me to care," snapped Chelle. "Whatever it is he pays you to do I suggest you do it. This discussion is over." Chelle, forever consistent, was always adamant that people should stick to their jobs and not insert themselves into hers.

Dannie so wanted to high-five her friend but decided against it…for now. At that moment as if scripted, the sliding door opened and in came John Bowman, Jamaican Farms knockoff Rasta.

"Rebecca mi sista, weh yah ah workin tideh?" he asked, a huge smile spreading over his face.

Rebecca looked frozen in place so Jen jumped in, "She's in Hunter 2 with Dannie today, John."

"Dat ah great. Yuh reddi to dweet? Com pon, I'll gi yuh a ride to de arena." And without waiting he turned and headed out the door to his golf cart.

Rebecca paused, clipboard and radio in hand and said to Dannie. "I never have any idea what he is saying. I find it best to just smile and nod. Have a great day ladies!" And with a hearty laugh and a wave to the room she was out the door to catch a ride to her judge's booth.

Dannie glared in Barb's direction momentarily, decided against escalating the matter further, and left the office to start her day at Hunter 2.

It became evident that Dannie's morning with no shower was just an indicator of the day to come. Mikey Gregory again waited to arrive until just minutes before the ring was to start and through the morning, continued to show no interest in learning any part of the job for which management was grooming him.

Just before lunch, Dannie hit on an idea she hoped would change the trajectory of things. "So, Mike...tomorrow I'm going to have you run the gate here. I will be available for questions and such but it will be your baby."

"About time," he grumbled.

"You'll have to be here at seven," Dannie continued, "to get your check-in lists started and begin your barn pages."

"Can't you do that? I'm really not a morning person," said Mike, following with another of his winning smiles. At any moment Dannie half-expected to see a quick glint of light sparkle from his ultra-white teeth.

Dannie didn't return the smile but said simply, "Then you're in the wrong line of work. And no, I won't start the day for you."

Undaunted, Mikey went on. "Will this same judge be here tomorrow?"

"Rebecca? No, judges rotate rings every day here. Why?"

"She's such a bitch!"

Dannie bristled. "What the hell are you talking about? You've not spoken one word to her all day; you know nothing about her."

"Barb and Muriel said she is."

"Of course, the two women on the show grounds without a vicious bone in their bodies. I should have guessed. Trust me, they don't have a clue what they are talking about and I would find their motives a little more than suspicious. I don't want to hear you say that again."

"Oh. OK....Mom!"

Dannie ignored him and returned to her paperwork readying to begin another class. She looked at her list of riders as two fat raindrops plopped in the middle of her class sheet. The clouds from the west had finally arrived.

Since the morning had been so cold, Dannie was already sporting her coveralls; waterproof and flannel-lined, that she'd purchased for days just like this and Jake was toasty in his fleece lined coat. Water on her paperwork was a problem though and as the frequency of the raindrops increased she glanced up to see why her tent offered no protection. She felt foolish to realize she had not noticed the tent above her was covered with shade cloth and hence porous.

She reached into her bag and retrieved a collapsible umbrella, opened it and then leaned it against her shoulder so it could cover her clipboard, radio and a portion of her workspace while she sat at the table. She only had a few hours left in her day and barring a deluge, this would suffice. She was sure she looked a bit silly, but she'd learned long ago this job was about functionality and comfort, not 'the look".

Dannie glanced at Mikey with amusement as he had arrived this morning with nothing *but* the look; plain jeans and a fitted, lightweight designer windbreaker complete with strategically placed logo. She wondered if he would look as good soaked to the skin. She picked up her radio and called to the judge's booth.

"You OK over there, Bec?"

"I'm dry, but I am a little cold."

"I'll see what I can do." Dannie prepared to turn her radio to the management's channel but stopped when she saw John Bowman and Kent Mallory arriving in a mini-convoy of golf carts.

"A bit dramatic, Dannie, wouldn't you say?" questioned Kent eyeing the umbrella.

"Well, you'd think so wouldn't you, until you realized the tent has holes in it."

Kent's lips compressed into a thin line but John laughed loudly.

"I was just going to call you, John," continued Dannie. "Rebecca's a bit cold. Do you have something to help?"

"She's just a whiner, she's fine," Kent interjected before John could respond.

"Nonsense," said John. "I be bak."

He sped off toward the office and Dannie relayed the message to Rebecca. John really doesn't have a mean bone in his body, she thought. Maybe he wasn't the brightest bulb but he did want everyone to be happy.

Mikey had started to shiver and Kent invited him into his golf cart. "Let's go get something to keep you dry."

"Or you could always bring him something," needled Dannie.

Kent glared in response and drove away with Mikey huddled beside him and it was no surprise to Dannie when she finished the day by herself because Mikey never returned

By the time Dannie and Rebecca wrapped up their day in Hunter 2 there was a light but steady rain. John was in his cart waiting behind the booth to act as Rebecca's chauffeur to the office and after Dannie covered the sound equipment and stowed as much as she could in her backpack, she followed.

It was only three-thirty when the two women started toward their cars with Jake trotting happily between them. They agreed Rebecca would come down to Dannie's room about six. Dannie pulled out of the parking lot waving at Rebecca, dry in her car, but on her phone.

Though Rebecca had said she didn't want to eat, Dannie stopped at the Chinese take-out she had patronized the other night and bought herself some hot food, including a large order of Won-Ton soup. Surely the soup would appeal to Bec on this cold, rainy night.

Arriving at the motel, she stowed the food in the room's miniscule microwave, removed Jake's coat and rubbed him all over with a towel, and then took a chance by turning on the hot water handle in the shower. It was blissfully hot!

She took her shower, dried her hair and dressed in fleece and flannel for a night in. It was still only five so she opened her laptop and composed a long email to Jeff, finishing just moments before Rebecca knocked.

Dannie laughed to discover that Rebecca was just as ensconced in fleece and flannel as she was; it was just neatly hidden under a nearly floor length down coat.

Rebecca took her position on one side of the king-size bed leaning up against the headboard, which was actually just a barely finished piece of wood screwed into the wall. Jake climbed up and plopped next to her and Dannie brought a bottle of water for Bec and a beer for herself.

"I'm sorry this had to be late," said Rebecca. "If you hadn't had to wait for me you could have attended J-Bo's Thirsty Thursday," she winked.

"Yeah, quite a sacrifice," she said her voice dripping with sarcasm. "But no worries. After no hot water this morning it gave me time for a shower. Who knows if there will be hot water in the morning," said Dannie.

"There won't. Logan was on my gate yesterday and he said he's never had hot water in the morning any time he's stayed in this motel."

"Good to know. I'll have to put my electric kettle to work so I can wash my face," said Dannie, grimacing.

They continued to talk. Dannie told Rebecca about Jeff, about life after her father's death, Robbie, and the Silver Shores circus of the previous summer. Rebecca caught Dannie up on her life since her husband had died just two years ago, her health issues which were many though Rebecca downplayed their severity, and her daughter and granddaughter.

As Rebecca talked, Dannie studied her friend, noticing the pallor of her skin and the lines of fatigue around her eyes. She looked exhausted and Dannie said so.

"Bec, these long horse show days have to be hard on you...especially in the cold and damp like today. Maybe you should take it easy until the doctors get a bit more of a handle on things."

"Nonsense! I'm no more tired than you are sitting out in the weather. Besides I have next week off. I'll be visiting my daughter and her family for the week. I'll get plenty of rest."

"Oh, then you'll have Easter with your family," smiled Dannie.

"Well, no. They are going out of town for Easter dinner with her in-laws, so I'll just head down to Langston's show a day early."

"Surely you can go with them to Easter dinner?"

"No," said Rebecca, "my son-in-law and his family don't like me much."

Rebecca said this with forced bravado but Dannie's heart broke. "Well then, that's perfect!" she said.

"What?"

"That means you are free to come and have Easter dinner at my mom's after the show Sunday. You can join me and Robbie, meet Jeff, and Pat will be there too!" Bec's family lived only twenty-five minutes or so from Beth Hoffman so Bec would definitely be in the area.

"Oh, I couldn't intrude," Rebecca protested.

"Don't be silly," Dannie laughed, "Mom is already calling it 'Carney Easter' so you joining us puts us one step closer to making that a legit title."

Rebecca smiled and agreed to come to dinner, but Dannie could still sense her hesitation. She thought a change of subject was in order so Bec couldn't rethink her decision.

"A little birdie told me that Kent Mallory will be the show manager for the three weeks at Silver Shores this summer."

"Excuse me?" shrieked Rebecca. "The event planner? He's useless enough here what can he possible not screw up there?"

"Well, he has friends in all the right places and he's convinced them he's wonderful. Oh and...it would seem they want me to be his assistant, though I haven't heard that from Tootie or Mary Jane yet."

"I'm hired for Weeks 1 and 2," said Bec, "if nothing else it will be entertaining.

Dannie glanced at the microwave against the wall. She had almost forgotten the Chinese food. "Hey! Can I interest you in some dinner?"

Bec frowned. "No, thanks. If I eat now I'll colic."

Colic was a dreaded word to horse owners. Generally, it meant pain in the abdomen but in horses could range from mild to severe and possibly fatal. It could present itself as a blockage, a buildup of gas, or several other scenarios, but all horsemen feared a twisted intestine, also known as a torsion.

Dannie knew Rebecca's comment was lighthearted yet it would explain her pale, thin-as-a-rail appearance. "How about some soup?" she asked.

"No, I'm good with water. You go ahead, Dannie."

As Dannie heated one of the cartons, she broached a hard subject.

"Bec, this morning in the office...

"Are you going to talk about the three evil stepsisters?"

Dannie knew she was speaking of Barb, Muriel and Bea. "Well, yes. They're awful to..."

"Don't waste your time thinking about that," chided Rebecca. "They don't like me, most people don't like me. I'm an acquired taste," she laughed.

"That's not true!" Dannie returned to her place on the bed with the carton of food and a plastic fork.

"Of course it is. I'm abrasive and cranky and opinionated and people don't like that. More importantly, I don't care. Have you ever thought about it Dannie? I mean, women nowadays run around crying about how men treat them in the workplace. I grant you, some of them have a point and what has happened to them is wrong. But if you ask me, many of them are just whining. Why do I think that? Because the same women that cry about their poor workplace treatment, treat each other worse than most men have ever treated them. We women can be vicious to one another and are on a regular basis."

Dannie nodded. "I've seen that."

Rebecca continued. "That's why I'm happy as can be up in Montana. My dog and my cat love me and the only person I have to make happy is me. Now, it's late and I'm tired and I'm going back to my room. Loved catching up, Dannie. I'm glad we'll be spending some time at a few shows this year."

With that, Rebecca donned her down coat and disappeared out the door, leaving Dannie with her carton of Chinese food. Dannie spoke to Jake, who was looking hopefully at the carton in her hand.

"She has a point, Jakey. Women are horrible to each other. As for the idea she doesn't care, I don't buy it. I've seen the hurt in her eyes."

-5-

Friday morning Dannie walked directly to the gate at Hunter 2. She had allowed herself a few extra minutes as Mike was in charge today and would have already been to the office to pick up radio, clipboard and class sheets. As she neared the gate, she looked at the chair in front of the sound equipment and saw...no one. She scanned the area and warm-up arena but Mike was nowhere to be found. She put her pack on the table and then backtracked to the show office with Jake at her heels.

At this point, Mike should have already been at the gate for thirty minutes. There had been no barn pages made, no check-in lists started and the Hunter 2 day was planned to begin with equitation classes for pony riders. In equitation it was the rider that was judged on their skill and ability to ride the required course and do it in proper form. The pony kids were nothing if not enthusiastic and as Dannie headed back to the gate with her equipment she saw many of them darting around the table like hummingbirds, all trying to speak with the now present Mikey.

As she plopped the radio and clipboard in front of him she noticed he was looking quite annoyed and was making an effort not to engage any of the riders.

"Dannie! Dannie!" they cried as they all began to talk at once.

"Whoa! Good morning, ladies," she said holding up her hands to quiet them. "This is Mike," she said, "and today he is in charge of Hunter 2. If you have questions, he's the one to ask."

"Call me Mikey," he said sullenly.

Angelique Bancroft, a perfectly turned-out, precocious ten-year-old with large colorful bows at the end of both of her braided pigtails stepped forward. "Mikey, I have a small. When do the smalls go?"

Mikey looked blank. "You have a small what?"

With eye-rolling only a ten-year-old could muster she said, "Are you kidding?"

Dannie stepped in. "Angie, if you look out in the ring you'll notice the fences are pretty big. That means we'll start with larges, then mediums, so smalls about 8:45 I would think."

She answered a few more questions and gave a few riders spots on her list and they all headed back to the barns to get on their ponies.

"What the hell was that?" asked Mikey.

"That's the pony ring," replied Dannie.

"What the hell was that kid talking about? A small? Am I supposed to know what that is?"

Dannie knew her lack of empathy was showing. "If you were a parent, or just a spectator at the show, then no. But sitting at the back gate of the ring? Yes. Yes you should know that. Ponies are classified as small, medium or large based on their height, in hands, as measured at the withers. Each size competes over a course at a different height of fence. The distances between fences are different as well for each size pony. At this show, each size has their own division and the heights are adjusted between each group of classes."

"Why do I have to know all that?" Mikey said, petulantly kicking at the dirt with the toe of his shoe.

"Because you want to do a back gate and when you sit at the back gate, people ask you questions...lots of questions, and you are expected to know the answers or at least know where to find the answers."

"I don't want to do this, but the paycheck is too good to pass up." Mike raised his phone and gave it his full attention yet again.

Dannie was surprised. Just learning the gate job couldn't earn him much. "How big a check are you making this week?"

Mikey told her and she couldn't believe her ears. He was going to end the week making fifty dollars per day more than she was; an additional $250 for the five days of the show. He knew nothing, he wanted to know nothing and he was being paid more? She was going to have to talk with John about this at her first opportunity.

The morning went from bad to worse. Any thought Dannie had entertained about Mike Gregory learning anything from what she had said or done in the last two days had been ridiculous. To further complicate things, he ignored Dannie's suggestions and proved to have no patience and a hair trigger temper when dealing with ring crew, trainers, pony riders, and in what would prove to be his biggest mistake, the judge, Bea Thomas.

By eight-thirty he had told two trainers they were stupid, called a rider a 'whiney little baby', and marked two large pony riders as having completed their rounds when they had not. He had told the ring crew to adjust the jumps for the riders of the medium ponies and had taken results from Bea. He was preparing to announce those results when the trainers of the two disregarded riders rushed to the gate to make sure their students made it into the class.

Mikey stood, slack-jawed, with no idea what to do.

"First, call your crew and tell them to stop their change and to put the jumps back to the height for larges," Dannie said. "Then call Bea and tell her there are two more riders to go on each card for four total rounds and get on your barn page and tell the mediums to slow down their prep as they are still about twenty minutes away."

Mikey didn't move so Dannie took the radio from him, called Bea and made a barn page while waving over one of her crew guys. She picked up the mic that had a speaker directed at the warm-up area to tell the first couple in the order for the mediums to slow down their warm up. As she did so, she noticed Bea in her judge's booth talking on the radio and gesturing wildly with her free hand.

Mikey seemed to jolt from his unresponsive state and stepped forward reaching for the clipboard on the table.

Dannie snatched the clipboard and the yellow legal pad from his grasp and looking Mike in the eye said, "No. Just...no. You're done. Pay attention or don't. Learn something or don't. Just sit there or play games on your phone. I really don't care what you do but you will not be running this gate. In thirty short minutes you've made a nine-year-old cry, insulted two well-respected professionals, put a pony mother into "mother bear" mode, and done your best to confuse the judge. You've done more than enough for one day."

"But Kent and J-Bo want me to learn this job," Mike protested.

"Evidently. But you too have to want to learn the job and I have seen no evidence of that."

The radio crackled as Bea Thomas said, "Dannie? Would you give the radio to Mikey?"

She turned and handed the radio to Mike and then watched him stand and turn to face the judge's booth across the ring, the anticipated smile plastered on his face. "Yes, Bea," he simpered.

"Oh for Chris' sake, stop looking at me like some grinning hyena. I'm about thirty years too old to be charmed by the likes of that."

Dannie was aware of hearing the report of the radio in stereo, meaning another radio in the area was tuned to the Hunter 2 channel. She turned to see Kent Mallory approaching in his golf cart and found herself pleased he was hearing the same thing she was.

Bea continued, "Young man, I have worked many years in this industry and while I may not be well-liked, I know I am well-respected as a judge." Right on both counts, thought Dannie. "I don't like being hung out to dry by someone that can't seem to find his ass with both hands."

Mike responded, his tone high and bleating. "Well, I didn't see you paying attention to how many rounds had gone."

"My job is to pay attention to the riders in the ring as they are presented to me."

"Then I guess that's what you should..."

"MIKEY!" Kent barked to stop the conversation from going any further. "What's going on here?"

Mike spun, again with the million dollar smile, and walked the few steps to the cart to fist bump Kent. "Well, Dannie was late this morning and she didn't explain this pony thing to me, then this ancient judge wasn't..."

"Enough," said Kent, holding his hand up as a barrier to further comment. "Mike, get your things. I'm taking you over to the jumper ring to sit with Logan and learn about the jumper gate. I'll be back to speak with you in a bit, Dannie. I do want to mention that it would be much appreciated if you would periodically make announcements about tonight's Festive Friday exhibitor party and also about tomorrow afternoon's barbeque and Sunday's Jumper Special. All proceeds from the jumper class will go to the charity Muriel and I run, Steeds 4 Soldiers. We will also gladly accept donations during the event.

"You have a charity?" Dannie said, somewhat skeptically.

"Yes. Announce what I've asked please. I need to get Mikey to the jumper ring." And with that, he quickly sped off.

Dannie busied herself getting the last four equitation rounds in the ring so the crew could truly set the course at the medium height. She had to admit a real sense of relief that the gate area was once again her own, yet she wondered if there was some truth to what Mike said. Had she neglected to be as helpful as she could? Had she thrown him into running the ring this morning to jump start the learning process or to assure his failure?

No, she didn't want him to fail, but he never even tried to meet her halfway. He didn't want to do this job and the sooner management figured that out the sooner they could find someone that did.

The tone on her cell phone that alerted her to an incoming text chimed twice in rapid succession. The first, from Patrick at the jumper ring said, "It might have been simpler just to shoot me." The second, from Logan, said, "What did I ever do to you?" followed by a smiley face emoji.

Dannie laughed and as the final round exited the arena she used her radio to call Bea for results. She read the results taking note of John Bowman's incessant Caribbean rhythms in the background and started organizing for the medium and small pony riders. A glance at her watch told her she was already forty-five minutes behind the time schedule thanks to Mike and she was at this moment losing more time to the course change and the water truck and drag in the arena.

She reached down to give Jake a few pats trying not to worry about the time when her radio crackled with a call from Bea.

"You know, Dannie, where I come from, women don't do your job."

Dannie waited for the "punch line" and none was forthcoming. She crinkled her face and thought to herself 'why in the hell is she telling me this?' She almost asked why, but decided she didn't care and said instead, "That's too bad, how sad for you."

"I just wanted you to know that I've learned something today," Bea continued.

"Oh?"

"Yes, some women that do your job are nearly as good as the men."

"Actually Bea I believe you're either good at this job or you aren't and gender doesn't really enter into it...but that's just me."

Bea Thomas had no answer to that, so Dannie sent her first rider in the Medium Pony Equitation class into the arena.

The remainder of the day went well. Dannie actually was able to make up the time deficit in her schedule and finished twenty minutes ahead of the prescribed time when all was said and done. There was only one more instance of tears and that was caused by Bea herself when she pronounced all four riders in a 17 and under medal class work-off to be airheads that couldn't follow directions and then suggested they take up tennis. It was the first time Dannie could remember all four riders leaving the arena crying simultaneously.

As she and Jake entered the office there was already a spirited discussion raging between Bea and Kent, and standing by, looking as if he'd rather be anywhere else, John.

"Don't give me that crap," barked Bea, "it's not because he's a newbie, it's because he's an idiot. Did this boy come to you asking to learn the gate job?"

"Well, no, but he's in college so you'd guess he was smart and he has the look," Kent answered.

"THE LOOK?? This isn't a garden party. I don't care if he's purple and has two heads. He needs to not get in the way of me doing my job."

"Well, I don't think Dannie was helping the situation." Dannie wondered if he had seen her enter the office. Kent continued, "Tomorrow when you're at the jumper ring, Bea, I think..."

"Oh no, I don't want to see the golden boy at a ring I'm judging again. Wherever you put him, just make sure it's not near me!" Bea ended the discussion by snatching her briefcase from Kent's desk and sweeping out the door.

Kent watched her go and in doing so made eye contact with Dannie. "Oh, Dannie, a word please." He indicated he wished to go outside the office and he motioned for John to follow. The three went to the picnic table located outside the office door and Kent got right to the point.

"Dannie, I don't ever want what happened today to happen again."

Dannie felt a bout of sarcasm coming on and while ill-advised, she did nothing to stop it. "Is this twenty questions,

Kent? What thing that happened; leaving riders off the card, making five separate riders cry, making the crew reset a course? Gosh, there are just so many to choose from."

Kent looked at her blackly and took a step forward, stabbing his index finger in her direction. "I don't ever want to have a judge call me on the radio and ask me where I learned to manage a horse show."

Dannie couldn't believe the opening that gave her but even she knew better than to go there. Jake had stepped in front of Dannie at Kent's advance and he now stood motionless, staring at Kent and waiting for one false move. "Kent, Bea didn't call you because of me," Dannie said calmly.

Logan Peters was approaching the group, signaling the end of the jumper ring for the day. He was just within earshot as Dannie continued, "Mike Gregory wants a big paycheck but he doesn't want to do anything for it. He sure as shit doesn't want to learn anything new."

"Not if you won't teach him," said Kent, who had retreated a step when he saw Jake's steely gaze.

"Hold on, Kent," said Logan. "Dannie's right, the boy's a tool. I learned most of what I know about doing the job when I sat at her gate on crew and all I had to do was watch. Mike doesn't care."

Kent, clearly annoyed, abruptly changed the subject. "Oh, and Dannie, I didn't hear any announcements today about Steeds 4 Soldiers and the Jumper Special."

"That's true," she nodded. "I would like to be a bit more detailed; do you have any paperwork, pamphlets, something I could use to "flesh out" the announcement a bit?"

"Yeah", agreed Logan, "that would be great."

"Maybe in my car, um, I'll have to look. I have work to do now." Kent turned and hurried back inside the show office.

Dannie turned to John, "I'm sorry, John, I'm not trying to cause..."

"Don' fret 'bout it. Dat Mikey kid's ah losa," he winked. "Yuh ah coming to de party tonight?"

"No," Dannie said scratching the black dog's head, "Jake and I are turning in early."

"I'll be there, J-Bo" said Logan.

"Gud! Wi will miss yuh, Dannie!" He gave the pair a wave as he too went back to the show office.

True to her word, Dannie headed back to the Inn and Out Motel with no plans for the evening. She had leftover Chinese waiting for her in the incredibly small refrigerator in the room as Bec had eaten nothing the night before. That was, of course, if the refrigerator had actually continued to function the past twenty-four hours and the food hadn't spoiled. The appearance of the appliance did not encourage confidence.

Arriving in the parking lot, Dannie allowed Jake to nose around and stretch his legs for a moment as she retrieved her backpack and straightened up the coats, hats, and other accessories that she left in the car.

Pat arrived just a few moments later and the friends spoke briefly, agreeing to have dinner the following night. That was a rare treat for Dannie; she usually could only manage once a show with Pat. He was universally loved and respected and as such, in high demand as a dinner partner. But what most people didn't know was that Pat was much like Dannie, and at the end of a long day he didn't relish more socializing. He was a master at agreeing to just enough, but not overcommitting.

Mostly, he was a very private man that enjoyed his solitude. Dannie was sure the reason they got along so well is that neither put undue pressure on the other in their relationship, they took it as it came and had a wonderful understanding of what made each of them tick.

Dannie let herself in the room, fed Jake, and immediately took a shower before the hot water, or lack of it, became an issue. Refreshed and comfortable, she placed two of the cardboard containers in the microwave and placed a call to her mom. She was anxious to hear Robbie's voice, to hear about the world from a five-year-old's perspective.

"Oh, honey," said Beth Hoffman, "he's at a sleepover with my neighbor's grandchildren. I'm sorry."

"That's OK," Dannie said, not meaning it. "I'm glad he's having fun."

She and her mother chatted for a few minutes and Dannie informed Beth that she had decided to head her way as soon as she was done on Sunday rather than wait until Monday morning. "I'll be more than happy to get out of here."

She retrieved her food from the microwave after her call was complete, and sat on the bed with the box and a plastic fork, a bottle of water on the nightstand. She tapped her phone's screen again, this time to call Jeff.

"Barnes."

"Hey there," said Dannie softly.

"D! What are you doing?"

"Livin' the life. Sitting in a dive motel room eating day old Chinese food out of the box. You? Seriously, I miss you so much; it seems so long to a week from Sunday at moms."

"I miss you too, D." Suddenly, in the background on Jeff's end was a cacophony of cat-calling, loud "kissing" noises and a falsetto "Ooohhh, I luuuvvvvvv you, Barnes."

"Knock that shit off!" barked Jeff, then, to Dannie, "Sorry, babe. We're at Sullivan's watching hoops. Season's almost over, you know."

"Oh," she said quietly. "I'm sorry, I won't bother you."

"No, I want to talk with you." More cat-calling and general harassment in the background. "On second thought, maybe another time would be better."

"Yeah sure, another time. Bye." Dannie disconnected without giving Jeff the chance for another word. She plopped the paper carton of food on the nightstand and threw the fork in the top; suddenly she had no appetite.

She leaned back against the quasi-headboard and felt foolish. Ending the call with Jeff that way had been a juvenile move. What did she expect? That Jeff, and Robbie for that matter, should just sit and wait for her call? That they were somehow wrong for enjoying time with friends? No, she was acting like a spoiled brat just because she was somewhere she didn't wish to be.

She wanted to call and apologize, but this wasn't the time. She sent Jeff a quick apologetic text and told him she'd call when she left Jamaican Farms and was on her way north.

She quickly laid out clothes for the next morning, brushed her teeth, and mercifully called it a day.

Kent Mallory wasted no time making a nuisance of himself Saturday morning. He was on Dannie from the moment she arrived, demanding she announce again and again about both the Jumper Special and the wish for donations to Kent's charity as well as the end of show barbeque scheduled for that evening.

Dannie's texts to Logan and the Hunter 1 gate, Bill Roberts, confirmed she was not alone; Kent was riding everyone hard.

Pat was judging Hunter 1 today and Mikey Gregory had 'followed' him there as Bea wouldn't deal with him in the jumper ring and Dannie and he would not deal with each other at Hunter 2.

Rebecca passed Dannie on the way to the judge's booth and Dannie noted how drawn and tired she looked. When she saw Dannie however, she put on a big smile and gave a cheery wave and a few moments later, Dannie sent the first horse of the day in the ring.

Just before lunch. Kent and Muriel arrived in a golf cart together.

"How are those announcements coming for Steeds 4 Soldiers?" asked Kent.

"OK, did you have any luck finding a pamphlet or anything?" Dannie asked.

"Haven't had time to look," he said. "You know, with your financial situation, have you considered a donation?"

"What does that mean, my 'financial situation'?"

Muriel opened her mouth but Kent jumped in, talking first. "Nothing, it doesn't mean anything. Just thought you might like to contribute to a good cause."

Kent's radio crackled and after listening briefly he said, "They need me at Hunter 1," and with that, the golf cart sped away.

Dannie watched them go and wondered what on earth brought Kent to mention her finances. Since her father's death the previous summer and her subsequent inheritance, she was dedicated to protecting her privacy and financial details. She discussed it with no one but her mother and Jeff. What could Kent possibly know?

With a crew on top of every course change, Dannie's organizational skills and trainers and riders working hard, Hunter 2 finished forty-five minutes ahead of schedule Saturday.

Dannie had been pushing the exhibitor barbeque scheduled later that evening but admittedly had barely mentioned Kent and Muriel's charity. If neither of them could bring her some sort of text or information about it, it was their problem.

Rebecca and Dannie walked to the horse show office together and Dannie took note of the slow pace set by Rebecca. The pair entered the office to be immediately confronted by Barb Snowden who was looking at Rebecca in particular, as a spider looks at a particularly succulent fly.

"Say ladies, Muriel and I have been talking," she said, jerking her head over her shoulder to Muriel, sitting at Kent's desk. "Aren't you both going to be in Fryetag the week after Easter for Langston's Coast with the Most Show?"

Dannie and Rebecca nodded. "Why?" asked Dannie.

Well, Muriel and I are participating in the Fryetag Women's March Monday, the day after Easter. Wouldn't you like to join us?"

Dannie spoke first. "You'll both be in Fryetag?"

"Yes, Langston has hired Muriel and me to produce his parties each night," answered Barb.

Oh goody, thought Dannie, though she kept it to herself. "Thanks for the invite, but I won't be joining you," she said.

"Why not? Too good to support the struggles and rights of your fellow women?" sneered Muriel.

Dannie didn't take the bait. "No, I'll be seeing my son and my fiancé on Easter and I don't plan to leave for Fryetag until mid-Monday. You ladies can pump a fist for me," she said sarcastically.

"And what about you, Rebecca? Didn't you participate in the Women's March in Carolina in 1984?" Barb questioned.

Bec hesitated and then said, "Well, yes, I did, it was quite..."

Both Muriel and Barb burst out laughing. "Why am I not surprised," said Barb, "there was no march in 1984. I knew you'd lie."

Rebecca looked uncomfortable, tried to cover it, but then quickly handed her paperwork to Chelle and excused herself from the office.

Dannie felt sick and turned to go, but then just as quickly turned back around, zeroing in on Barb and Muriel.

"What the eff is your problem? Why would you do that? I wouldn't march to the parking lot with you."

"Oh, she's known to say she was everywhere and did everything. Setting her up is like shooting fish in a barrel," Muriel said.

Dannie felt her fists clenching. "She's not well. And did it ever occur to you that she is just lonely and wants to belong? She recently lost her husband, her daughter barely speaks to her...she just wants friends and instead of being a friend you make an effort to embarrass and humiliate her. No, while I believe there will be some women at that march in Fryetag that have a purpose and a mission and something of value to say, you two are sure as shit not those women. Frankly, I'm ashamed we share a gender. C'mon, Jake!"

Dannie handed her paperwork to Chelle and snatched her backpack off the table. She caught a glimpse of Chelle's 'thumbs up', displayed so only Dannie could see, before she made her way out of the office.

Dannie and Patrick met for a quick dinner at a small Italian place near the Inn and Out. Thoughts left Dannie in a rush; how mean the shrews were to Rebecca, Mikey, how much she missed Robbie and Jeff, and Pat did one of the things he did so well. He listened.

When most of it was out of her system, he said simply, "Dannie, this is why you are making the right decision leaving this life. I'll miss you so when you stop doing shows, but you are meant for other things. You're a good mother, soon you'll be a wife, and of course you want to spend time with them. And I know you, you may not know where you are headed right now, but it will be crystal clear when you get there and when you do, I'll be right there and be the first one to say, "You did it!"

Dannie's eyes filled with tears and she stood and gave Pat a hug. "What was it Dorothy said to the Scarecrow in The Wizard of Oz? Oh yes, 'I think I'll miss you most of all'."

Pat laughed and playfully pushed her back toward her seat but Dannie could see he was fighting a tear as well. "Let's wrap this up," he said, "I think I can only tolerate one more night in the good ol' Inn and Out. I want to be on the road tomorrow night."

They returned to the motel and Dannie spent the remainder of the evening organizing and packing her things; stacking them next to the door for early transport to the SUV in the morning.

Patrick was back as the Hunter 2 judge for Sunday and he and Dannie knocked out the schedule; one class after the other. By two o'clock the Jumper Special had begun in Logan's ring and as Dannie and Pat worked on their final class, Logan kept them entertained with his texts. First:

> 'Kent came by with our checks and when Mikey got his he
> said he had to go home...he's outta here.'

Then:

> 'Muriel is literally walking around with a coffee can
> wrapped in construction paper asking for donations.
> Hilarious!'

And finally:

> 'Posing for win picture. Muriel drops can, horse bolts,
> knocks off Muriel's hat, Kent waves arms to stop him,
> has to jump to the side and falls in a pile of horse crap.
> You can't make this stuff up'

Dannie and Pat were still laughing when they finished their final class about fifteen minutes later and Dannie was truly excited that by the time she wrapped up in the office and got her check she should be able to be on the road by four PM. She even had time to throw the ball for Jake out in the parking lot for a few minutes before they left.

Dannie approached the office and she was aware of Bob Marley wailing away over the loud speakers as she stopped at the picnic table to say goodbye to John Bowman.

John sorted through a stack of envelopes in his hand and pulled out the one with Dannie's name on it; her paycheck. She had been intending to take up the matter of Mike Gregory's pay with him but all she wanted to do was get on the road so she kept silent.

John handed the envelope to her and said, "Dannie, yuh really gwine dweet? Yuh don?"

"Yep, my last year. Thanks for the opportunities, John."

"Tank yuh, Dannie. Gud luck." He offered his hand and a genuine smile.

As she reached the parking lot, Pat drove past in his small sedan and said through his open window, "See you in a couple of days!"

Dannie waved and smiled, and then after a ten minute session of fetch with Jake, she and her dog got in the car and put Jamaican Farms in the rear view mirror.

-6-

Dannie awoke Monday morning in the beautifully decorated guest bedroom in Beth Hoffman's house. The room was light and airy; the walls the lightest of blue with hints of soft mauve and cream throughout the room in the bedding, the window treatments and the furniture. Beth had placed a beautiful bouquet of flowers from her English-style cottage garden on a corner of the dresser in anticipation of Dannie's arrival.

Feeling quite spoiled, Dannie gazed out the window at the rain dripping from the roof's edge and reveled in the fact that with a day off today the rain mattered not at all. She pulled the cozy flannel sheet up to her chin and considered drifting back to sleep but she had planned a day with Robbie and that was beckoning her far more than additional sleep could.

Dannie got up, put on her slippers, splashed some water on her face in the adjoining bathroom, and then joined her mother and Robbie in the kitchen. As she relished a cup of coffee poured by Beth, the three talked about the plans for the next two days before Dannie returned to work; this week for the Gala Horse Shows Spring Egg-stravaganza and show manager, Jane Thornton.

Today mother and son were visiting the local Children's Museum. It was filled with lots of interactive exhibits inside for busy, inquisitive boys and if the rain let up, plenty of outdoor exhibits too. Robbie had started school last fall and with Judith's bequest, Dannie was able to place him in a lovely private school in Silver Shores. One of the selling points to Dannie was that they encouraged parent involvement and learning outside of school. Last week, while Dannie was at Jamaican Farms, many of the day trips taken by Robbie and Beth could be used as learning tools so missing that week of school was applauded rather than frowned upon.

Tonight Beth, Dannie and Robbie would have an early dinner and then it was movie night, complete with popcorn and hot chocolate. Tomorrow it was a trip to a local warehouse turned into a place where kids could climb, jump, slide, and explore.

It would be a busy two days, but Dannie knew it would be Wednesday and therefore back to work, before she knew it.

As expected, Wednesday morning came in a flash. At six forty-five, Dannie was piloting her SUV into the staff parking lot at the Valley Hills Equestrian Center.

Much like Jamaican Farms, Valley Hills housed a small boarding operation for local horse owners but generated its main income from renting the facility to individuals and organizations wishing to produce horse shows. At Valley Hills any type of show was fair game; they hosted hunter/jumper, western, 4-H, intercollegiate, breed shows and everything in between.

This week Dannie had contracted to work for Jane Thornton and her company, Gala Horse Shows, and she was so looking forward to it. Everything about this week was different than the one before.

Jane was one of Dannie's favorite managers; while creating great shows for exhibitors was a given for her, she treated the staff better than almost any other manager currently producing events. All her staff was assured of nice accommodations and each and every one received a per diem; not just the judges as happened at many other shows. There was no caste system here and that cut down on resentment among staff members. Contractors at the Gala Horse Shows operated on a very level playing field and in Dannie's eyes it proved her long held theory; treat people with kindness and respect and they will return it in kind. Gala Horse Shows staff worked hard to make things hum.

It also lent credence to one of Dannie's other long-held opinions; the best managers were those that had worn many different "hats" at a show and understood what went in to each job. Jane was that person, in short, she got it. And if you were chosen to work at a Gala show, it was certain Jane considered you competent enough to get out of your way and let you do your job. She had no time for the Mike Gregorys of the show world.

The final testament to Jane's personality and her abilities as a manager was her loyalty. Loyalty was a word bandied about frequently by various managers but more often than not what they meant was they expected loyalty from their contractors. They wanted unwavering dedication to their own cause without understanding that a living couldn't be made by working for only one manager. To Dannie, possibly the most fascinating aspect to the 'loyalty rules' was the unwritten statute that once one manager was at war with another, contractors were expected to honor that conflict and make a choice.

For the mine field that was earning a living as an independent contractor, the loyalty often was a one-way street. Any member of the horse show staff could expect to be dropped like a hot rock at the whim of many, but not so in the case of Jane Thornton. She lived by a doctrine of fairness and if you worked hard and did the job you were expected to do, Gala Horse Shows did well by you.

Jane was not only a good manager but a genuinely nice person. The previous summer, when word of Dannie's firing at the hands of Jumpin' Jimmy Bittler spread through the show world like wildfire, one of the first phone calls of support that Dannie received was from Jane. She had offered Dannie as much work as she wanted and though Dannie explained she was trying to 'hang up her clipboard', she assured her she would be happy to help Jane whenever she was in need.

To that end, when Jane asked Dannie to work this show, she had also asked her to start training someone to do the back gate job. Jane told Dannie she completely trusted her judgement and to choose someone she thought would be a good fit for the position.

As Dannie approached the front of the Gala Horse Shows office she smiled as she caught sight of that someone; Summer Stanton. Summer was twenty and had some college under her belt. Dannie met her when she rode as a junior; a term describing a rider aged seventeen or under, with Dannie's ex-husband, Brian, as her trainer. Summer was a lovely rider that had a real feel for her horse and she and Dannie had hit it off right away.

Unfortunately, in the spring of her freshman year at college, Summer's father passed away unexpectedly and eight months later, her mother was diagnosed with a potentially terminal illness. So far, the fight was in her favor but the outcome was very uncertain. With those two events, Summer's riding career came to a screeching halt and currently any additional funds available to the family were going directly to her mother's care.

Six weeks from now, Summer would finish her sophomore year but then was looking at some time away. There wasn't enough money for her to re-enroll for the fall semester. Dannie had thought of her immediately when Jane made her request and was excited to spend the week showing Summer the job.

Catching sight of Dannie as she neared the front of the office, Summer broke into a huge smile and threw her arms around her friend.

"Dannie, I'm so glad to see you. Thank you, thank you, thank you for this opportunity! I have some supplies I figured I'd need," Summer said, holding up a large tote bag, "but I'm sure there will be a lot I haven't even thought of."

Dannie laughed out loud and a cloud of doubt crossed Summer's face, "Did I say something wrong?"

"Oh God no, I was just thinking that in my first 30 seconds here this is already so much better than my entire last week. Come with me, let me introduce you to Chelle and Jen, my friends in the office, and to the manager, Jane."

In the next few hours, Dannie's choice of Summer as apprentice for the starter job was confirmed. The girl was already head and shoulders above Mike Gregory because of her experience as a rider; she understood horse shows, classes, rules and schedules. But she was also enthusiastic, confident, got along easily with the trainers and other staff and she was smart. Dannie hoped she did find the job to her liking because she knew with a little practical experience Summer would be great.

This week's Spring Egg-stravaganza was a four-ring show; two hunter rings and two jumper rings. All of Jane's shows were well-attended and this was no exception as there were just over five hundred horses entered.

Dannie and Summer were assigned to Hunter 1, and as usual, the first two days of the show were dedicated to open classes; those that were typically entered by the professionals in the industry but also open to non-professional riders. Those professionals, the trainers, used these classes to promote their up-and-coming horses and to school client's horses for classes later in the week.

Hunter 1 ran the first three classes of the day with jumps set at 3'3", concurrently, meaning any rider entered in all three could ride all their rounds on a particular horse rather than wait for each class to conclude. For trainers that had a lot to ride, this was a courtesy to them as well as their grooms as there was a lot less getting on and off and much greater efficiency.

Summer took the results from the judge after nearly 90 rounds had finished. She announced them and Dannie noted she had a good, clear speaking voice. She had a casual style, which Dannie preferred, and she was not shy. The water truck and drag lumbered into the arena to groom the footing for the next group of classes as Summer sat back in her chair, pursed her lips and blew a huge burst of air from her lungs.

"Whew!" she said, "that was intense!"

"Actually, not at all, you're just nervous," Dannie smiled. "You did great!"

"I feel like I have so many questions."

"Ask away, that's what I'm here for."

"I think I painted myself in a corner. I was trying to move people around and help everyone but then they were mad because they thought I bumped them from their spot in the order of go, and then..."

Dannie held up a hand and said, "Not to worry. It's easily fixed. Have I told you about my 'Toby technique'?

Summer had no time to hear what Dannie had to say because a golf cart pulled up to the gate and a young girl jumped out and threw her arms around Dannie.

"Dannie, I've missed you!"

Dannie broke in to a huge smile and said, "You know, Summer, if I didn't know better I'd think this was my friend, Raine Forrest. But I just saw Raine last summer and this girl is much too tall and grown up to be Raine."

"No, it's me!" Raine laughed, still clinging tightly to Dannie.

Dannie hugged her back and looked over the top of her head to smile at her chauffeur in the golf cart. He was none other than Terrence "Blimpy" Forrest, co-founder of the wildly popular Chicken Feed Chicken fast food empire and Raine's father.

"Good to see you, Blimpy," Dannie said and introduced father and daughter to Summer. "Where's Sunshine?"

"She's back at the barn "helping" Manuel get Sultan ready," he said using his fingers to form air quotes around the word 'helping' and adding a sly wink. "She's anxious to see you."

"Dannie, where's Jake?" asked Raine.

"Robbie and I are visiting my mom this week and Jake stayed behind today to keep them company." Changing the subject she said, "I know you didn't come just to say hi, I bet you want to get Brandon on the list. Just let Summer know what you want to do."

Though this open hunter division was well entered with eight horses at the Egg-stravaganza, for the last year or two it had more often than not come down to a head-to-head competition between CFC Sultan, Sunshine Forrest's drop-dead gorgeous, chestnut stallion and Valenti, the bay stallion ridden and trained by her ex-husband, Brian Rossi. Both animals were blessed genetically and had talent to spare; Dannie enjoyed the opportunity to watch both compete. She knew the outcome was of particular interest to both owners and trainers, but no matter which horse won on any given day, the horse community as a whole was the beneficiary of having these two outstanding animals nearby.

Dannie looked toward her schooling area and saw Brandon Bochner, Sultan's rider, beginning his warm-up. Brian was approaching the schooling area on Valenti. She also glimpsed Sunshine walking in the direction of the Hunter 1 gate.

"Are you OK alone for a few minutes?" Dannie asked Summer. I won't be far, but I wanted to speak with Sunshine Forrest for a few minutes."

"I'm good," smiled Summer. "My first horse is at the gate."

"Don't hesitate to yell if you need me," Dannie said and walked toward Sunshine, motioning for her to go to a shady spot near the corner of the ring.

Sunshine and Dannie exchanged a hug after which Sunshine continued to hold Dannie, now at arm's length.

"I declare, Miss Danica, being a bride-to-be looks good on you. Let's see that ring."

Dannie dutifully showed her ring to Sunshine who oohhhh'd and aahhhhh'd before hugging her once more.

Sunshine Forrest, wife of Blimpy and mother of Raine, was an undisputed beauty whose every molecule spoke of wealth. She, like her husband, was kind, generous, and thoughtful and treated everyone as if they were her best friend. Of her very few faults, the fact that she was known to be somewhat naïve and too trusting was her Achilles heel. In fact, it was those qualities that ran her life right off the rails for a time at last summer's Silver Shores shows. That, and her driving ambition to make her way in the horse world as she and Blimpy had done in the fast food industry.

It was also these qualities combined with the events at Silver Shore that caused Dannie and Sunshine's lives to be inextricably linked, though as friends the two would seem a very odd couple to many.

"Is your facility finished?" asked Dannie.

Sunshine and Blimpy had been heading construction of a facility adjacent to their home in the south part of the state which they had named Forrest Equestrian Park. It was to be home to the family's trainers, Brandon Bochner and Timothy Jacobs, house a state of the art breeding facility where Sultan would stand at stud, and a show facility where Sunshine hoped to convince some prestigious shows to relocate.

"It's all finished!" Sunshine gushed. "It's beautiful and by fall...Dannie, you met Kent Mallory last week, didn't you?"

"Yes," she said flatly.

"Oh, don't you like him?"

"I don't really know him, but, why do you ask?"

"Well," began Sunshine, "he's bringing his dates to our facility."

"HIS dates? Where did he get dates?" asked Dannie, dubiously.

"When Darlette Simon's dates went up for grabs after her death his was the first application in line and he got three of them," said Sunshine. "Isn't that great?"

"I don't think so, Sunshine. I'm sorry, he's an event planner."

"Well, a horse show's an event, isn't it?"

"No," Dannie said," it's a horse show. And he has proven he knows nothing about horse shows."

As if on cue, a golf cart rolled up and stopped next to the two friends. In it sat Kent and Muriel Mallory...and Mike Gregory.

Kent oozed from the driver's seat to bestow dramatic air kisses on Sunshine's cheeks. He placed an arm around her shoulders and turned, drawing her with him, to face the warm-up arena where the Forrest's horse and several others were preparing for the class.

"Sunshine," he said grandly, waving his arm in the direction of a beautiful bay, "I declare, that horse of yours has no equal; what an animal he is."

"Kent! That's not Sultan. Sunshine's horse, the chestnut, is over there," Dannie said acerbically, pointing to the opposite side of the arena. "He's, you know, the red one not the brown one."

Dannie couldn't help herself. She knew she should just keep quiet and she also knew Sunshine would simply have been gracious and ignored the gaffe; but for Dannie, nothing was worse than grandstanding. She hated know-it-alls that knew nothing and it was one of her worst character flaws that she was compelled to point it out whenever she bore witness to it. The least Kent could do, she thought, was to verify the facts required to kiss the appropriate ass.

From the golf cart, Muriel, sounding amazingly similar to a ten-year-old on the playground, bleated, "That's the one he meant, and anyway, why aren't you over there doing your gate?"

"Gosh, I can't remember the last time anyone so eloquently put me in my place. The answer to your question is that Summer, my trainee, is doing an outstanding job and I don't need to micromanage her," Dannie said. She thought of continuing, but Sunshine frowned and gave a small shake of her head. Taking the cue, Dannie said, "If you'll all excuse me, Sultan and Valenti are showing soon and I'm going to watch from the gate."

Dannie returned to the gate to sit next to Summer whose only comment on the exchange between Dannie and the Mallorys was a rolling of her eyes.

The open division ended as many could have predicted; the two stallions earned the top two spots in the class with Sultan taking both firsts and Valenti, two seconds. Tomorrow was a new day and there were two more jumping classes; known as over fence classes, and the flat class which judged a horses manners and movement at the walk, trot and canter, still to be contested. The two horses were so evenly matched that anything could happen.

Having closed down the gate, Dannie and Summer walked back to the show office to turn in radio and clipboard.

"Well, day one is in the books," said Dannie. "How do you think it went?"

Summer smiled. "Pretty good, I think. I feel like I have a good grip on the basics but it seems like there's still so much to learn."

Dannie laughed. "There is always more to learn and often as time goes by you figure out a better way to do something. I won't be surprised if you get tired of hearing 'the-gate-according-to-Dannie' this week but I'll share anyway and you can take from it what works for you."

"Like what?"

"Well, like the 'Toby technique' I explained an hour or so ago."

"Yeah, that's amazing," agreed Summer.

"And my take on trainers," Dannie said. "I say with love...sometimes dealing with trainers is like herding cats, but with a few notable exceptions all the trainers around here are really good to work with and they work very hard. They have a tough job. But when I sit at the gate, I think of it as ten percent organization and ninety percent psychology. Learn your trainers. Some are on top of it and super organized. Some want to give a thirty minute clinic every time they hit the warm-up ring. Some are great with the animals but are, in all other respects, a hot mess. Not a judgement, but as it relates to you getting your job done you need to recognize that fact. There's a trainer that will never check in with you, just show up at the gate and expect to walk in the arena even if you have ten trips lined up and waiting. I have learned that when I hear his voice in a warm-up arena anywhere near me I write him down for a block of six or seven trips and then I'm covered. Things like that..."

"Brilliant," said Summer. "You just keep that info coming."

"So, on another subject," said Dannie, "Chelle, Jen and I periodically have a 'girl's night' during the shows. They're coming over tonight and we'd love to have you join us."

"That's so nice of you, but I promised Mom I'd come home and tell her all about today. She had a round of chemo this morning and I want to keep her company."

"Of course, next time," said Dannie. "See you in the morning."

-7-

Dannie reached Beth's house just two hours before Chelle and Jen were due to arrive. She was greeted by an overjoyed Jake. Beth and Robbie had left not ten minutes before for an early dinner followed by a children's theater production, but in Jake's book that was ten minutes too long to be alone.

She returned the black dog's greeting with equal enthusiasm, promised he would accompany her to the show tomorrow, and then headed to her room. It was traditional that these girl's nights involved a bit of alcohol, some snacks, and the most comfortable attire possible. To that end, Dannie planned to shower and dress in a favorite pair of yoga pants, a tank top and a big, toasty cardigan before getting some food and drink ready.

Showered and dressed, she headed down the hall toward the kitchen. It occurred to her how much she felt at home here. It was, after all, the house she grew up in, though in the seventeen years since Joe and Beth's divorce the house had definitely taken on a much more feminine appearance than it possessed in her childhood.

Beth lived in a Tudor-style house at the end of a cul-de-sac. The house itself had plenty of room and was set on a good-sized piece of property. The inside had seen many upgrades in the last nearly two decades and Beth lovingly tended her English cottage garden outside. It was a beautiful and welcoming home.

Reaching the kitchen she proceeded right to the refrigerator to start preparing some snacks for the evening ahead. She opened the door to three attractively prepared trays of appetizers covered with plastic wrap and ready to serve. Beth had also chilled a couple of bottles of white wine and made sure her built-in wine cooler had several bottles of red. Dannie smiled to herself. She was so thankful to have her mom; she was always so thoughtful and helpful and Dannie was filled with gratitude.

Realizing she had almost forty-five minutes before Chelle and Jen arrived she decided to call Jeff. She walked out the kitchen's sliding glass door to Beth's back patio and pool area, plopping down in a lounge chair with a huge soft cushion. She auto-dialed Jeff's number on her cell and waited a couple of rings until he answered.

"Barnes."

"Hey there. Is this a good time?"

"Sure, I have a couple of minutes."

That stung a little. No greeting, no 'I miss you', but she pushed herself to not read more into the exchange than was there.

Jeff continued, "So, what's up?"

She began to tell him about this week's show; seeing Sunshine, Summer, the Mallorys, but in no time she could hear the tap of his fingers on a keyboard and could tell he was distracted.

"...and then a hot air balloon crashed right into the middle of the arena," she said, ending her sentence.

"Yeah? That's great, babe."

"Listen," said Dannie, "it's clear this isn't the best time. I'll call later...or tomorrow."

"You don't have to be mad; I can't help it if I'm working." Jeff's voice plainly indicated the guilt he felt at realizing Dannie was aware of his lack of attention.

"I'm not mad; all you had to do was say you were busy. I just miss you and wanted to talk to you," Dannie said quietly.

Jeff's voice softened. "I miss you too, D. It's just, well, with you and Robbie gone the house is really quiet so I volunteered to cover some other shifts and then we were really slammed this week."

"It's OK, I get it. You are still coming for Easter, right?"

"I'll be there, D." There was some conversation in the background and Jeff said, "Gotta go," and the call disconnected.

Dannie sat motionless and stared at the phone. She felt empty. Since she'd left the beach house a week ago Tuesday her conversations with Jeff, when she actually managed to reach him, had left her unsettled. She wanted to look in his eyes, she wanted him to hold her and talk and laugh with her, she wanted to feel the love they had for each other and instead all she felt was...nothing.

With each show, she hated the traveling more and more. When she had been married to Brian they were on the road together but after their separation she had struggled with leaving Robbie behind last year, and now, well, she felt she could cry if she indulged herself. But she would not indulge herself. After all, the show world was full of people that left family, friends and homes behind and the world kept turning.

She glanced at the time and went in to prepare to host her friends.

Jen and Chelle arrived almost exactly at the time they had predicted. The three friends appreciated the rareness of this. When you worked in the show office you could never be quite sure when you would be done on a given day. You had to remain open until all rings were complete and you never knew what other tasks may crop up.

Jake greeted the guests at the door with frantic tail wags and an upturned nose in search of a treat but finally made way for them to go to Dannie's room and change into their comfortable attire.

The decision was made to sit by the pool. It was a peaceful evening, not yet too cold, and as soon as they settled in their chairs they all began talking at once; words spilling from them like water from an open flood gate. It had been some time since their last girl's night and they didn't want to waste a moment.

"Boy is Muriel Mallory mad at you!" said Chelle to Dannie.

"She told you that?" asked Dannie.

Jen chimed in. "Oh hell no, most people don't even notice we are sitting there...for ten to twelve hours," she laughed. "Muriel was bending Jane's ear about how rude you are to both her and Kent and how you shouldn't be doing the job you do."

"She'll get her wish before long but she has to live with me through Silver Shores this summer, doesn't she?" said Dannie. "What was Jane's answer to her?"

"Oh you know Jane," said Chelle, "she backed you up. Said you do a great job and suggested Muriel not go to Hunter 1 if she doesn't like the treatment there."

Dannie smiled and gave a thumbs-up. "Love her."

"Actually the Mallory's are pretty unhappy all around. They were here to hawk their charity and collect donations. They thought Sunday's Grand Prix was a benefit for them but Jane set them straight," said Chelle. "They are allowed to have some of the people in their program present the colors during the National Anthem and she'll have Gary Desmond or Patrick, whoever is announcing, do a short spiel on the charity but that's it."

"No collecting money in coffee cans like last week?" Dannie laughed.

"Jane said they could set up a table if people wanted to come to them but no soliciting donations. She also said if she receives a single complaint they're done," said Jen.

Dannie said, "That reminds me, why in hell did they bring Mike Gregory?"

"Oh, he was their ace-in-the-hole. They planned to have him use his charm and boyish good looks to beguile all the women with large checkbooks into writing big fat checks to Steeds 4 Soldiers," said Jen.

"Oh please!" Dannie couldn't hide her amazement.

"I should think you would root for him to be successful at that," said Chelle. "Did you know Kent talked Langston Rubicon into letting Mikey have his own gate next week?"

"Alone?" shrieked Dannie, and the three friends dissolved into fits of laughter at the thought.

There was still plenty of food on the trays, but Dannie noticed the bottle of white wine was nearly empty and excused herself to the kitchen to retrieve another.

As she opened the bottle at the sink, she watched Chelle and Jen having an animated conversation; laughing and gesturing to punctuate their words.

Dannie had been friends with Michelle Carpenter and Jennifer Brooks from the first time she worked a gate. They liked each other instantly and over time, developed a deep respect for the way they each took pride in their jobs.

Chelle was nearly ten years older than Dannie and the shows were her life and her family. She was divorced and had never had children. She was head and shoulders above other show secretaries so was in great demand among managers each year. Chelle had short brown hair and an olive complexion and as a friend, she was fiercely loyal.

In contrast, Jen was tall and thin with light, wispy hair and a fair complexion. She was close to Dannie's age and had yet to meet Mr. Right. She had developed some resentment toward Dannie last summer at Silver Shores and Dannie wasn't sure it had completely dissipated, but Jen was clearly making an effort to mend fences and Dannie was happy to meet in the middle. It was not a friendship she wished to lose.

Dannie walked back outside to Jen and Chelle still talking about Mikey Gregory. When she set the newly opened bottle on the small umbrella table Chelle said, "Speaking of trainees, how's this week's experiment?"

"Summer? She's awesome," said Dannie. "She caught on quickly today and she's so smart, she'll be on her own in no time at all. She's really receptive to my suggestions."

"Oh, I see," laughed Chelle, "the key is to stroke your ego." Before Dannie could protest she added, "And what suggestions would those be?"

"Well, like the 'Toby technique'," said Dannie.

"Huh? What the hell is the 'Toby technique'," asked Jen, "and how is it we are just hearing about this?"

"OK, so a common mistake when you're new on the gate is getting your trainers bunched up on your list," Dannie said, warming to her explanation, "and everyone gets mad and thinks you bumped them or forgot them and they have to warm-up again and, well, it's a big cluster. So, I decided to write a name every seven or eight spots on my order that didn't exist. Since

I've never known a rider named Toby that's the name I picked. So, when I read down the order so they could all gauge how long until they went in the ring I would read "Toby". If no one needed an adjustment I would just bypass it, if I needed a space to slide someone in, I'd say, 'Oh, Toby just told me he won't make his spot...you could go in four trips'. Then no one thinks they were bumped from their spot and everyone is happy."

"I'll admit it. That's kind of brilliant," said Chelle.

"But what if someone notices you skipped over Toby?" asked Jen.

"First thing you learn when you do a gate, you literally talk all day and no one listens. They only hear their own name or their trainer's name so 'Toby' is just white noise. It has never failed me."

"That's why you make the big bucks," laughed Chelle. "Speaking of which, I didn't get your pay sheet."

"Didn't do one. Summer is doing such a great job I pretty much handed it all to her today. I'll be there for any problems but she's doing the job. I asked Jane to give her my check on Sunday."

The friends talked about last week's show at Jamaican Farms, the Inn and Out Motel, and their upcoming week at the Coast with the Most show in Fryetag. Dannie could see Chelle and Jen were starting to think about heading to the motel but was surprised when Chelle said, "How's that hunky detective you live with?"

Dannie could tell by the look on Chelle's face that her reaction was unexpected.

"Uh-oh, have I said something wrong?"

Dannie's answer poured out of her in a rush. She told them about the last week and a half, the stilted phone calls, and her uneasy feelings. "But before you got here, I told myself I was being silly. After all, we all leave our homes and the people we love all the time and the world keeps turning," she finished.

"Who are you kidding?" asked Chelle. "Sure the world keeps turning, but you know this life is hard on everyone in it. The carney life has left a trail of divorce, broken hearts, addicts, alcoholics and depression in its wake. People that don't live this life don't understand it and resent the time taken from them. It takes a rock-solid relationship to withstand it. The good news is, I'm sure you guys have it and by the time next week is done it will be a non-issue. Hang in there, Dannie, and trust him…he's a good guy."

Dannie willed herself not to cry and instead suggested they take the party inside.

"No, no, time for us to go. It's a lovely motel this week, actually a pleasure to be there," Jen said.

Dannie turned down an offer for help cleaning up and hugged both friends making a promise they would do it again next week in Fryetag. She was washing the dishes and putting away the food when Beth and Robbie returned and she was delighted to watch Robbie's pantomime of the play before they all went happily to bed.

As Dannie and Jake exited the SUV the following morning in the Valley Hills staff parking lot, Summer's voice could be heard floating on the light breeze from the barn page speakers. When Dannie reached the gate, Summer was up and running with a list for trainers to check in for their rides, her binder for the calculations to award today's division championships, and she had even made sure that there was an extra latte for Dannie when she purchased her own morning coffee.

"Look at you go!" Dannie laughed with genuine pleasure and thanked Summer for the coffee. "I'm impressed. Good for you, you even have Toby checked in several times! Any questions for me so far?"

"Actually yes...one." Summer pulled a single sheet of paper from under her clipboard and held it out to Dannie. "That woman who was here yesterday, I think she said her name was Muriel; she brought this to me as soon as I got here and said I should announce it throughout the day. Should I do that?"

Dannie skimmed the paper. It was a crudely written plea for donations during the show to Steeds 4 Soldiers and it ended suggesting that interested parties find Kent, Muriel or Mike Gregory to arrange a donation.

"I happen to know, though I won't tell you how I know, that Jane specifically told them they couldn't solicit donations but instead could set up a table and people could come to them. Personally, I would be inclined to ignore the request as I think they're pushing the envelope but in all honesty, me thinking for myself gets me in trouble all the time." She winked at Summer. "The correct move is to call Jane, ask her to come to the gate when it's convenient for her, show her the paper and ask what she would like you to do. Frankly, it's a CYA move."

"CYA?" said Summer quizzically.

"Oh, you are so sheltered," laughed Dannie, "it means 'cover your ass'."

Summer's cheeks colored and she looked a bit sheepish still she did as Dannie suggested and gave Jane a call on the radio. Two riders came to place their names on the list for the first class and Summer turned her attention to them as Dannie's cell trilled. She looked at the caller ID in the hope it would be Jeff, but it was Rebecca Kirtlan.

"Hi Bec! Having fun with your granddaughter this week?"

"Loads of fun," Rebecca replied. "I know you're working so I'll get right to the point. I'm going to have to turn you down for Easter dinner."

"Why?"

"My daughter and her family have decided to leave for her in-laws this afternoon instead of Saturday, so I'm just going to head to Fryetag and get a hotel until the show next week."

Dannie could hear the hurt and sadness in Rebecca's voice. She knew Bec had been looking forward to every moment with her granddaughter.

"Nonsense!" Dannie said. "You drive right over to my Mom's house. We have a guest bedroom with your name on it. We can visit in the evenings and you can come with her when she brings Robbie to the Easter egg hunt at the show Sunday morning. It'll be fun."

"Oh, I don't think so, I mean..."

"Stop it right now. If you don't show up there in the next hour or so I'll have her come and abduct you."

"Well, OK, if you're sure."

"Totally sure. I'll see you tonight"

Dannie hung up and immediately called Beth to fill her in. "I'm sorry, Mom, I know I should have checked with you first but I couldn't wait. I was afraid she'd go and I just couldn't think of her sitting alone in a hotel room for the next five days. What's wrong with those people, how could they be so unfeeling?"

"You were right to invite her," said Beth, "I'm happy to have her, and Robbie and I will love the company."

Dannie filled Beth in on Bec's health issues to which Beth replied, "There's no pressure, we'll just take it as it comes."

Her mom was one in a million, Dannie thought.

She put her phone back in her pocket and looked up into the smiling face of Wyatt Waddell.

"Miss Dannie, I do declare, you are a sight for sore eyes."

"Flattery will get you everywhere, W. Are you with us today?" Dannie asked.

"Us? Have you made that black dog your apprentice?"

"No," Dannie laughed, "But let me introduce you to my actual apprentice. This is Summer Stanton. Summer, this is Wyatt Waddell, known to all that love him as 'W'. He's our judge today."

"Pleasure to meet you, Mr. Waddell. Go easy on me," Summer said.

"She's doing great," Dannie volunteered. "She's actually running the gate; I'm just here for oversight and to run backup for major catastrophes."

W shook Summer's hand. "Call me W, Summer. I'll go get set up." Then leaning in, adopting a somewhat conspiratorial tone he said, "By the way, you're learning from the best. Ta for now." And with a wave he was off.

"I pay him to say that," Dannie said dismissively.

"Everyone tells me you're the best," protested Summer.

"Most of them would tell you that about whatever starter you were sitting with, I think. Judges like starters that look out for them and provide the information needed for them to do their job well and there are plenty of those throughout the country. Just remember what I told you...most of this job is about managing people without letting them know they're being managed. And as far as the judges, show them by your actions that you will help them to do the best job they can and they will respond in kind."

"W seems really nice," Summer said.

"He's amazing; a great judge, keeps perfect records which makes your job easier, never forgets a name or a face and is, in a word, hilarious." Dannie checked her phone. "Hey, it's five minutes before eight; let's get this show on the road!"

It was a beautiful spring day and the morning flew by. Jane did indeed arrive to address the Mallory's flier with Summer and the answer was as Dannie predicted; no announcements were to be made regarding Steeds 4 Soldiers.

At around eleven, Summer had about twenty-five rounds of hunters left to show in her 3'3" division. She and Dannie agreed their energy was lagging and Dannie consented to take the short walk to the coffee concession and get them each a cup. While waiting in line, she received a text from Beth. Rebecca had arrived and at the moment the two women were having a cup of tea out by the pool and watching Robbie excavate a yet to be planted dirt area with his toy trucks.

Returning to the Hunter 1 gate area and walking carefully so as not to spill any of the fragrant, steaming coffee Dannie saw Sunshine having an amiable conversation with Summer.

Placing one cup in front of Summer, Dannie greeted her stunning friend.

"Oh honey," said Sunshine, "I'm glad you're back. Do you have a moment to talk with me?"

"Since Summer is killin' it this morning I have plenty of time," Dannie said, smiling.

"Come sit with me in my golf cart."

Dannie followed Sunshine to her cart which she had parked next to a small grove of young eucalyptus trees. Taking her place in the passenger seat, Dannie said, "What's up?"

"I've been thinking about what you said about Kent Mallory yesterday."

Expecting her to continue, Dannie said nothing but there was no more to come from Sunshine.

"And?" Dannie prompted.

"Well, it bothered me...what you said about him knowing nothing,"

"It should bother you."

"But, how do you know? You said you barely knew him."

"That's true," Dannie nodded, "I did. But I did work with him all last week and he is no more a manager than his current sidekick, Mike "The Smiler" Gregory. He knows nothing of the rules, scheduling, or set-up. John Bowman sets up his own facility, Barb Snowden, his assistant, does all the pre-show paperwork, hires staff, makes hotel reservations, you know, that kind of thing. My friend, Chelle, makes sure the schedule is right. All I can see that Kent Mallory really did was drive around in a golf cart barking useless orders and trying to look like hot shit."

Sunshine looked dubious. "But if he'll bring his dates to Forrest Equestrian we can have some shows later this year."

"Yes, but they are HIS dates. He can bring them, and he can leave with them. Kent Mallory wouldn't be the first manager to demand lots of high-priced infrastructure improvements to a facility only to leave a short period of time later and go do it all again somewhere else. Look, this decision is for you and Blimpy, it's not for me to say. The only thing I will say is be careful and try to get dates of your own."

Sunshine continued and seemed to be trying to convince herself as much as Dannie. "But a show this year at Forrest Equestrian Park could put us on the map."

"Also true, but the question is, which map? One thing I've learned from my time in the horse world is that the showing public is not a forgiving bunch. They'll give you a try, but if you don't get it right the first time it's doubly hard to get them back. You want to hit a home run your first time out and with Kent's total lack of experience and knowledge I'd be concerned," said Dannie.

"Well, if not Kent, who could I get to manage?" asked Sunshine.

"I'd talk to Jane," Dannie said. "She's honest as the day is long, would never leave you high and dry and runs her company like a business; contracts, complete records, and a buck-stops-here kind of attitude. You wouldn't think that's unique but it kind of is." Dannie sat quiet for a moment. "Sunshine, I've said too much. You and Blimpy need to decide what is right for you."

"I only asked you because you're my friend and I value your opinion," said Sunshine.

"I know, but the two of you didn't rise to the top of corporate America with Chicken Feed Chicken because you couldn't read the industry or make a decision. You'll be fine."

The remainder of Thursday, in fact, the show through Saturday had gone beautifully. Summer had surpassed Dannie's expectations as to how quickly and easily she caught on to the starter's job. Summer had two more weeks in her spring break and she had agreed to attend next week's Coast with the Most show for one more week of training, though Dannie thought it probably wasn't necessary. She would be glad for the company; the two women had an easy relationship and Dannie was excited to be a part of helping give another woman a start at the job. She had already offered her a place, Dannie's former place, on the gate for the three Silver Shores shows this summer.

Sunshine and Raine had been busy showing in their respective divisions and whether by choice or because they had been ordered, Kent and Muriel Mallory had stayed away from Hunter 1.

Away from the show, Dannie was most pleased she had insisted that Rebecca Kirtlan spend the end of the week with them. Rebecca had arrived looking somewhat better and more rested than when Dannie had seen her last at the Jamaican Farms show, but by Saturday night the change was profound.

Beth, Robbie, Rebecca and Dannie had a virtual egg-dying 'factory' going in Beth's kitchen. All four were pulling out their most artistic ideas for making the perfect brightly colored eggs and Bec was in the thick of it; laughing, joking, teasing Robbie. She and Beth had enjoyed a wonderful couple of days and become instant and fast friends. Bec had already told Dannie which parts of the Easter meal she would be helping with after they watched the egg hunt at the show.

Rebecca was still eating less than a bird and seemed to tire easily, but it was so good to see her relaxed and happy. Beth had worked her magic for sure, thought Dannie. Her mother had a talent for making the most uncomfortable people feel welcome and at home in no time and it would seem Bec was no exception.

The women had convinced Robbie that with all the Easter Bunny had to do, he most likely would visit Beth's while they all were at the show so there would be no five AM egg hunt thought Dannie gratefully. After tucking Robbie in to bed, she quickly fell asleep herself.

Easter morning dawned as all Easters should; a brilliant blue sky, warm sunshine and a breeze just strong enough to ruffle the new spring leaves on the trees.

Hunter 1 had started at eight, but the main jumper ring only had two classes, albeit important ones, after the Easter Egg Hunt which was scheduled for nine-thirty.

Summer was doing beautifully with the Children's and Adult Amateur Hunter Classics which were run in a Round 1 and Round 2 format with the scores averaged to determine the winner. Dannie was keeping a watchful eye on her scorekeeping but there had been no problems so far. The decision had been made to drag and water the ring before any second rounds showed in the Classic and Summer was taking a breather while the equipment worked.

Dannie, facing the ring, was checking Summer's math at her request when Summer turned to face her. "Does it look OK?"

"Perfect," said Dannie. "We're lucky W is back today, he's great keeping his own scores but the more checks and balances the better."

Suddenly, Summer said, "Holy crap! Who is that Prince Charming and why have I never seen him before?

Dannie turned, interested to see what Summer would call a Prince Charming. She dropped her notebook in the dirt, emitted a very uncharacteristic squeak and jumped up so fast she knocked her chair over spooking a horse standing near the gate. Running the twenty or so feet to the man in question, Dannie threw her arms around his shoulders and buried her face in his neck.

-8-

Jeff Barnes hugged Dannie back, and then laughed as he tried to disentangle her arms from around his neck. She didn't seem inclined to let go.

"D, c'mon!" He tried to sound stern but it wasn't working. "Dannie, I have someone I want you to meet."

"What are you doing here? I thought you weren't coming until tonight."

"Shall I leave?"

"No, but, how did you know where to go?"

"We all came together; the Rob-ster, your mom, Rebecca and Miles."

"Miles?" Only then did Dannie become aware of another man standing next to Jeff.

A nice looking man, maybe in his early thirties, held out his hand, "Hi Dannie. I've heard a lot about you; in fact, you were just about all this guy talked about on the way up here."

Dannie shook the offered hand, observing its owner to be about six feet tall with dark hair and brown eyes. He was dressed so as to be at home on any golf course and wearing a baseball cap with some sort of military insignia.

"D, this is Miles Wolcott," said Jeff. He joined the department about a month ago when he moved to the Silver Shores area."

"A pleasure to meet you, Miles. Where did you move from?"

"The east coast. I grew up there but finally had enough of the cold," said Miles.

Dannie laughed. "Did anyone tell you it can be pretty cold in Silver Shores?"

"Does it snow?"

"No."

"Then I'm good," Miles said with a smile.

Jeff said, "Miles was invited to Easter dinner with a buddy of his somewhere around here so he's taking my truck from the show and he'll pick Robbie and I up at your mom's tomorrow morning. I told him coming to the show with me was a great opportunity to see lots of good looking women in tight pants."

"Lovely," teased Dannie, "Jeff takes the high road."

Both men laughed then Jeff said, "Are you coming to watch the egg hunt? I know a young man that is so excited he is almost turning inside-out."

"Oh, I don't know..." Dannie glanced at Summer. "We're working on the classic and..."

Summer waved a dismissive hand. "Go ahead. I have your number if I need you."

Dannie paused just long enough to introduce Jeff and Summer properly and then headed to the egg hunt with the two men.

As Dannie approached the jumper ring she caught sight of her mom, Rebecca, and Robbie. Robbie saw her at almost the same moment.

"Mommmmmmmyyyyy!" he squealed running to her arms. "Look, Mrs. Kirtlan got me a basket to hunt with," he said as he held a basket of green, purple and yellow as high as his little arms could manage.

"Just the thing for the job," Dannie said.

She diverted her gaze to the ring. Jane and her staff had outdone themselves. Being that it was a jumper arena, all the jumps were already brightly colored and shone in the morning sun. The fences; what the jumps were sometimes called, were customarily in a neutral, earthy palette for a hunter arena, but the wilder the better was the rule for jumpers.

In addition to the jumps, Jane's staff had added cutouts of rabbits, chicks and lambs peering from behind jump standards or walls. Standing near the ingate was someone dressed as the Easter Bunny. He was not recognizable but Dannie suspected it was her fellow starter, Logan Peters. Everywhere you looked there were pastel flags, pinwheels, and kids; lots of kids. Anyone was welcome so the children of anyone from staff to grooms to exhibitors were anxiously awaiting their chance to share the plunder.

Patrick was up in the judge's booth. He would be announcing today and running the timing equipment while Gary Desmond marked the judge's card in the Grand Prix that was just about thirty minutes away. Pat didn't disappoint as he struck just the right note of welcome and celebration before starting the egg hunt.

The Easter Bunny opened the gate and children of all ages, shapes and sizes streamed onto the field. They laughed, called to each other happily and squealed at each new delight. Robbie was in the thick of it filling his basket with treasures found under jump rails, inside decorative flower pots, and perched on the arena fence posts.

As he rounded one particularly tall vertical jump intent on a blue egg he spied at the base, he witnessed an older boy plow directly into a beautiful Hispanic girl dressed in her Easter best, knocking her down in the dirt.

Dannie saw this at the same time and started toward the arena but Jeff grabbed her arm and shook his head. "Just wait," he said.

The little girl burst into tears when she fell and the small number of eggs in her basket spilled into the dirt. The boy that toppled her grabbed the fallen eggs and ran off.

Dannie wasn't sure, but believed the girl was Valeria, the three-year-old daughter of Michaela Reynolds groom, Santiago, and his wife. She felt horrible for the little girl, but what she observed next changed everything.

Robbie stopped, placing his basket on the ground and helped Valeria to her feet. He then helped brush the dirt off the back of her Easter dress and took her hand to continue the hunt. At this point much of what was available had been claimed, but Robbie had his eye on something in a flower pot and he pointed Valeria to the spot. While she was reaching into the pot, Robbie, standing behind her, took several of his eggs and placed them in Valeria's basket. He did the same thing two more times and then, still holding her hand, guided Valeria out of the arena and to her waiting parents.

Dannie and Jeff had come over to meet them as well and Valeria's father greeted Dannie as he had so many times at her gate.

"Miss Dannie, this is your son?"

"Yes," she said.

The tall man leaned over toward Robbie. "What is your name?"

"Robert," he said solemnly.

"Well, Roberto, my name is Santiago and this is my daughter, Valeria. May I shake your hand for the kindness you have shown to her?" Santiago extended his hand saying, "Gracias, Roberto."

"De nada, Santiago," said Robbie soberly. "I had to do it, I just really don't like mean people, even if they are kids."

Dannie hugged Robbie tightly as Santiago said, "I must go back to work. Miss Dannie I will see you in about an hour for the Pony Classic."

Walking back to where Miles, Rebecca and Beth were standing Dannie said, "I am so proud of you, buddy. But I want to know, how did you know how to say "You're welcome" to Santiago in his language?"

"Mommy, I know lots of things you don't know about."

Looking at Dannie over Robbie's head, Jeff mouthed the word, "Gotcha!"

Just as they reached the gathering of their family and friends, Patrick invited everyone to stand for the Star Spangled Banner. As a group of men dressed in various military and police garb walked to the center of the field to present the colors, Pat introduced them as men that were or had been involved in the Mallory's organization, Steeds for Soldiers. He described the charity as a 501(c)3 that aimed to aid veterans and first responders suffering from PTSD through therapy with horses.

As the men reached the center of the field the anthem began and both Jeff and Miles removed their hats. Dannie glanced at the insignia on Miles' hat and wondered about his service.

At the conclusion of the anthem, the men exited the arena near Dannie's little group and Miles approached one man, seemingly eager to speak with him. Dannie lost interest; she was far more intent on spending every moment she could with Jeff.

"Are you going to stay with me this afternoon?" she asked.

"No, I'm heading back to your mom's after Miles takes the truck." Seeing her obvious disappointment, Jeff explained further. "Your mom has a few things she wants me to do; fix two broken sprinkler heads for one and I thought I could help by keeping Robbie from being underfoot and making him my assistant while she and Rebecca make the dinner."

"Makes sense, you'd think she could wait until you were officially her son-in-law before she started giving you jobs. You're sweet to help," she said, kissing him on the cheek.

Miles returned to stand with Jeff and Dannie, looking perplexed. "That was really weird," he said, shaking his head and watching the man he had gone to talk with now retreating from the bustle of the arena. "What do you know about this Steeds 4 Soldiers?" he asked Dannie.

"Nothing really." She told Miles about last week and Kent's insistence she make fundraising announcements while providing no information or flyer about the charity. She also told him about Jane's decision regarding his hoped-for promotional activities this week at the Egg-stravaganza. "Why do you ask?" she said.

"Well, from 2008 to 2009 I was part of the US Army 1st Infantry Division deployed to Afghanistan." He pointed to his hat. "You may have heard it called The Big Red One." The insignia she had wondered about was a pentagon, pointing down, in army green with a large red numeral one squarely in the middle.

"Oh sure," said Dannie, "I'm sorry. My military knowledge is sorely lacking."

"The guy I went to talk with was wearing the insignia of the 82nd Airborne on his jacket sleeve. For a time we periodically crossed paths with those guys over there and so I wanted to ask him if he was there when I was. I patted his shoulder with the patch and said 'Death From Above, huh?' That's the 82nd's motto."

Dannie nodded; grateful she didn't have to ask.

Miles continued. "When I said that, not only did he have no idea what I was talking about, he said, 'Death From Above? Wow, chill man, it's just a bunch of horses and kids.' Then I asked him what his MOS was."

At this, both Dannie and Jeff returned blank looks.

Miles smiled. "It's a code. Military Occupational Specialty code. It's a series of numbers used to identify a soldier's job. Every soldier knows his MOS, but not this guy. He gave me an open-mouthed stare then mumbled something about 'having to go' and high-tailed it away from me."

Dannie, already feeling guilt about leaving Summer for so long and not terribly engaged with what Miles was trying to say excused herself to return to work.

"Can't wait until you get back to the house," said Jeff, giving her a kiss.

Approaching Hunter 1, Dannie observed Jane's golf cart pulling away. She reached the gate to find Summer absolutely glowing and sitting with a woman that looked very familiar to Dannie.

"Dannie, Jane paid me for the week!"

"Yeah, she's good about that. There is a group of managers that make you come and beg for your check but not Jane. She's always delivered them personally with a heartfelt thank you."

"But I thought I was just learning this week," said Summer.

"And learn you did, but you also did a very good job of running this gate with very little help from me and you deserve to get paid for that. Everyone should expect to be paid for a job well done."

"Jane asked me if I was working with you anymore and I told her about next week and about Silver Shores. She asked me to come back and work for her for two weeks in August and one in October." Summer couldn't contain her excitement.

"Congratulations!" Dannie said, "You must have made a great impression."

"It's because of you, Dannie," said Summer.

"I didn't say anything to her."

"Maybe not, but your bringing me here to teach me was the same thing. I can't thank you enough; these jobs will make such a difference."

"You're most welcome. You'll do a great job and make me proud, I'm sure of it."

Summer glanced at the woman sitting next to her. "Oh, I'm so sorry. Dannie you remember my mother, don't you?"

Dannie tried not to scrutinize Summer's mother but she could hardly believe her eyes. She knew her to be somewhere between forty and fifty, yet her skin was pale; nearly transparent it seemed, and she had aged immeasurably since the days she used to sit on the deck at Rossi Farms and watch Summer's lessons.

"Of course," said Dannie, "it's so nice to see you again, Mrs. Stanton. How are you feeling?"

"Please, call me Caroline. Surely we've known each other long enough for that. To answer your question, in a life that is currently measured in good days and bad days, today is a good day. I had a round of chemo earlier in the week and it gives me fits for a while, but today is such a beautiful day and it's Easter after all. I wanted to see Summer work… I miss our horse show days. Chemo monkeys with my immune system but the doctors don't worry if I'm out in the fresh air and take care not to get too tired."

"You didn't walk all the way here from the parking lot, did you?" asked Dannie, worried.

"No, Mr. Forrest was here with his golf cart when Mom called and he went and picked her up. Gave me a number to text when she was ready to go back too," said Summer.

W called Summer on the radio to ask her to check the jumping course posted on the board for the Pony Classic exhibitors. She stepped away from the table to do so and it was then that Caroline Stanton took Dannie's hand though it was such a light touch it felt as if a butterfly had landed on the back of her fingers.

"Thank you so much for giving Summer this opportunity."

Dannie smiled, "That's kind, but I'm just showing her the ropes. She's making her own opportunities and she's done a terrific job this week."

"I'm fighting as hard as I can, Dannie," Caroline continued, "but I'm scared. Oh, not for me but if something happens to me so soon after Summer lost her Dad. It breaks my heart she has to step away from school. She has been so happy this week."

Summer returned to the table and the discussion between Caroline and Dannie ended. The crew was adjusting to the height for large ponies in the Classic so that meant just an hour or so left for Hunter 1 but for Dannie, the revelations of the day weren't quite complete.

Glancing down the road toward the portable barns, Dannie saw her soon-to-be ex-husband, Brian Rossi, walking toward Hunter 1 with one of his promising pony riders. She heard him ask the girl to warm-up her pony at the walk, trot and canter and then say he would join her momentarily in the warm-up arena to school her over a few jumps. Brian motioned for Dannie to join him a little to the side of all the bustle at the in gate.

"Hey," he said, "um, I'll get right to the point. I got the final divorce papers in the mail at the beginning of the week. I wanted you to know I'll sign them and send them back in tomorrow's mail."

Dannie was stunned. It was, of course, what she wanted but she was unprepared for the overwhelming sadness she felt. She was a naïve young woman when she and Brian were married. She'd had no concept of the baggage he brought with him to their relationship, nor his complete inability to be a faithful husband or any kind of father at all.

When they first split up Dannie had wanted to hate him. She was hurt and the prospect of single motherhood terrified her plus Brian's super-controlling, social-climbing parents had thrown themselves into a custody battle for Robbie she was panicked they would win. But over time Dannie had come to realize that Brian was just not emotionally capable of coping with a great deal of what life threw at him. He disguised his failings and insecurities with alcohol, women, and an attitude of complete lack of personal responsibility and it became clear that the only time he was completely and totally at peace with himself was when he was with the horses.

Dannie's change in financial circumstances last summer had rendered the custody battle a moot point as Brian's parents had come to understand that she was now in a position to wage the fight dollar for dollar and they had rapidly lost interest.

Her biggest sadness was that her son had an emotionally absent father and she had failed. Every relationship took two and this one had failed miserably but it was no longer time to look back.

"Thank you, Brian, I appreciate that," she said, referring to the signature on the papers.

"I'm sorry, Dannie, for much more than I could ever say. Will you be at the Silver Shores show this summer?"

She nodded.

"Good, I'll see you there." With that, he turned and walked to the warm-up arena to prepare his rider for the Classic.

"To Carney Easter!" Beth said as she held her glass aloft and looked around her large dining table. "Thank you all for joining me and filling this house with love and friendship."

The guests around the table returned the toast and the sentiment. Beth had just put dessert, a decadent coconut cake, on the table and Rebecca was right behind with clean plates and utensils for the confection.

Dannie looked around the table with her heart nearly bursting for the love of everyone there; Jeff, Robbie, and her mom, of course, but also Rebecca and Patrick. These moments were so rare in a life on the road. Though that life was coming to an end for Dannie, Bec and Pat were still in the thick of it and she knew how much they had enjoyed these few hours of normalcy.

Everyone had relished an Easter dinner fit for royalty, spending the meal sharing horse show stories and memories of Easters past from all in attendance. Robbie had revealed his joy at helping Jeff; first to fix Beth's sprinklers and then as he helped clean both Rebecca and Beth's cars inside and out. In turn, everyone at the table congratulated Robbie on his thoughtfulness and quick thinking in dealing with Valeria that morning.

True to her prediction, Bec had eaten almost nothing but she was a lively participant in the conversation and Dannie was encouraged to see that the couple of days spent here had put faint color in her cheeks and a smile on her face.

At the conclusion of the meal, Dannie and Pat volunteered to wash dishes. Dannie was forearm-deep in the sink of soapy water and Pat was in charge of the dish towel when he brought up the Mallorys.

"What exactly did you do to enrage the Mallorys?" he asked.

"Which time are you referring to? Pretty sure there have been several," Dannie said with a laugh.

"Well, Muriel was just to the side of the judge's booth during the Grand Prix today snarling and gnashing her teeth about how you brought someone to grill their soldiers that presented the colors."

"Well, as you know, I 'brought' no one. Jeff brought a friend from the PD in Silver Shores that evidently wanted to talk to one of the guys he thought he might have met overseas, but I never met Jeff's friend before this morning. He was coming to Easter dinner at a friend's near here. I doubt he even knew there would be former soldiers at the show."

Pat said, "As far as I can tell, the facts have never stopped Muriel. She was quite vocal about not only your arranging the interrogation but making sure Jane didn't allow them to fundraise too."

"Of course, because Jane Thornton has proven herself to be nothing more than my puppet." Dannie raised a handful of suds and blew it playfully at Pat. "I don't want to talk about the Mallorys. Hopefully at this moment, Muriel is gleefully preparing her sign and her vagina costume for the march she and Barb are participating in tomorrow."

"Danica, for some people, them's fightin' words."

"OK, so it wouldn't be the first time that my compulsion to share my unfiltered opinion has created more problems for me than not, but I stand by the vagina costume remark no matter what. As far as the march, I believe there are many with the desire and conviction to try and effect change. I also believe Muriel and Barb are not among them. Now let's finish these dishes, I want to spend some time with Jeff before we both fall asleep."

Fifteen minutes later, Dannie and Jeff were sharing the garden swing in Beth's beautiful backyard. Pat had said his 'thank yous' and returned to the hotel and Beth was taking advantage of her final night with Robbie by tucking him in and reading a story.

Jeff, holding Dannie's left hand and idly twisting the ring on her finger sighed happily. "Great day today," he proclaimed.

"Mmm," murmured Dannie as she laid her head on his shoulder. "Thanks for being everyone's knight in shining armor."

"I don't think so..."

"Absolutely. You made Robbie feel important by letting him help you and teaching him new things, you checked over Bec's car for her. Even though you said it was to keep Robbie occupied I know it was to make sure everything was safe for her drive to Fryetag tomorrow. You let Mom order you around." She smiled at that one. "And for me, you were mostly a knight in shining armor for me."

"Oh? I barely saw you today."

"But you were *here*. I could see you and hear your voice and touch you and let go of all the doubts that were running rampant through me."

"You have no need to doubt me, D," said Jeff softly.

"The distance makes me doubt us. Not because I should, but there's too much alone time, long, tiring days; let's face it, the best parts of a relationship don't happen over a phone line."

"I admit it's been harder than I'd have guessed. Knowing you'll be home a week from today, well, I can manage that but I hope you're not planning more of these jaunts around the state without me."

Before Dannie could answer, she and Jeff heard the sliding door and Rebecca's voice. "Could I interrupt for a moment?"

Jeff stood and said, "No interruption at all, Rebecca. Join us."

"Oh no. I'm going in to make sure I have everything packed and ready to go for the trip to Fryetag tomorrow. But I wanted to thank you both; Jeff, my car looks wonderful. You and Robbie did a great job and I am so appreciative you gave it the 'once over' for me."

"It was my pleasure, glad to help."

"Dannie, thanks so much for insisting I come here. You know I was resistant but it's been a wonderful couple of days; you all made me feel like family and I've had so much fun."

"So have we, Bec. We'll see you in the morning," Dannie said.

"You bet. Good night."

Miles would be arriving to pick up Jeff and Robbie at around nine tomorrow and Dannie and Rebecca planned to leave for Fryetag in their respective vehicles about ten. Though it was just a little less than twelve hours away, Dannie was already beginning to feel the anxiousness of separation.

At her feet, Jake groaned and stretched in his contentment. Not only had he spent a good part of the week as companion to Beth and Robbie, he'd had plenty of swims in the pool and today had provided a pure cornucopia of delights for the Lab. Bites of ham, prime rib, potato and even coconut cake had left him stuffed and happy.

Again placing her head on Jeff's shoulder, Dannie said, "I have a question for you."

"Shoot."

"Today when Valeria fell in the dirt, why did you stop me from going to help?"

"I wanted to see what the Rob-ster would do."

"But what if he didn't do anything?"

"Well, we essentially had two scenarios. If he didn't help Valeria it was a teaching moment so he would know for the future what is expected from a gentleman. But the right thing happened and he did help so it was everyone's opportunity to reinforce that behavior by telling him how great it was...which they did."

"You're a good man, Jeff Barnes, and I love you so much," said Dannie squeezing his hand.

"I love you more," he said kissing the top of her head.

"I don't suppose you'd like to show me how much," teased Dannie.

"Um, certainly not. In your old bedroom in your mother's house with her just two doors down the hall? The very thought is giving me flashbacks."

Dannie was laughing now. "I'm sorry; did that happen to you in high school?"

"You can't fool me lady. You can't interrogate me without reading me my rights and I happen to know that I have the right to remain silent. I intend to invoke that right."

"Chicken!" she taunted.

They sat in quiet contentment for a few minutes before Jeff said, "So, these Mallory people."

"Oh not you too," Dannie said. "Pat wanted to talk about them earlier."

"Miles was quite worked up over the soldier he spoke to. He bent my ear about it for quite a while and I would guess I'll hear more on the drive home tomorrow. I think he wants to do some investigating on his own time."

"Investigate what?" Dannie said.

"He thinks the guy was an imposter which is a huge deal to the guys that actually served."

"I understand that," said Dannie. "Not sure why it matters, but I'll be at the show with both the Mallorys next week so if I can help let me know."

"Thanks, D. Think we should go to bed?" Jeff said

"I thought you'd never ask," Dannie said with a conspiratorial wink and a kiss.

-9-

As expected, Monday morning arrived much too early for Dannie and Jeff and they were both craving more time with each other. But both Jeff and Miles started their shifts at four and Jeff had to get Robbie to his favorite babysitter before going to work.

Dannie dressed while Jeff showered and shaved and then the two walked to Beth's kitchen with a brief pause to leave Jeff's small duffel at the front door where Robbie's things were waiting. Rebecca, Beth and Robbie were already seated around the big island that doubled as a breakfast table. There was hot coffee, juice, fresh fruit, muffins and cereal for the soon-to-be travelers yet all but Robbie picked at the food. No one really wanted to go and their lack of appetite was evidence of that.

Miles arrived about quarter to nine and agreed to a quick cup of coffee for the road. While pouring the hot liquid into his travel mug he said, "Dannie, you'll be home next week, right?"

"Yes, that's right," she said.

"I really would like to pick your brain about this charity. Would that be OK?"

"Honestly, Miles, I don't know how much help I can be but I'm willing to answer whatever questions I can. Is it that important?"

"Don't know, really. I just really got a weird vibe yesterday," Miles said.

"And there you have it," laughed Jeff. "A cop's best investigative tool, the weird vibe."

Beth filled Jeff's travel mug as well as the two men readied to leave and then the group formed a kind of impromptu parade as they trooped out the front door to stand in the driveway near Jeff's truck.

Jeff secured Robbie's safety seat in the back of the extra cab while Miles loaded the duffels and the food that Beth had packed for the road. Goodbyes were said between Beth, Miles, Jeff and Rebecca and Robbie gave his Nana a big hug. Dannie put her arms around Jeff and he returned the gesture, both loathe to let go.

"Oh, gross," said Robbie, turning his back on the couple and climbing into his car seat.

"Yeah, Barnes...gross," chuckled Miles.

Jeff made a face at the two, gave Dannie a kiss and in no time the three were headed out the driveway and on the way back to Silver Shores.

Just over an hour later having helped Beth clean up the breakfast leftovers, Rebecca and Dannie left the driveway in a mini-convoy on the way to the Coast with the Most Horse Show in Fryetag.

Beth had seen to it that each of them had a small brown bag with a sandwich made from the leftover Easter ham, a sliced apple and several small, foil-wrapped, solid chocolate eggs. As Dannie approached the freeway on ramp she glanced at the bag and was reminded once again how much she appreciated her mom. She reached across the seat and stuck her right hand in the bag thinking a chocolate egg might hit the spot. She felt a large oddly-shaped object and pulled it free of the bag discovering that Beth had even thought of Jake. It was a large bone; knowing Beth it was grain-free, wrapped with a huge slice of ham.

"Jakey," Dannie said, glancing at the big dog in her rear view mirror, "here's a present from Nana."

Jake jumped to his feet and eagerly yet gently claimed the bone, hunkering down to guarantee not a morsel would remain.

Dannie had agreed to follow Rebecca. It occurred to her that while most everything in Rebecca's personality screamed 'full speed ahead' evidently driving did not make that list. They were in the slow lane of I-5, at exactly the speed limit. Dannie guessed Rebecca was making good use of her cruise control and so she followed suit as cars in the other three lanes whizzed by at least ten to fifteen miles per hour faster.

Smiling to herself, Dannie didn't really care. After all, their destination was Fryetag, considered by some the armpit of the valley. Fryetag was close to everything; ocean, mountains, the lure of Southern California, but had almost nothing to offer of itself.

Her smile grew wider as Jake, having polished off his treat, stood and placed his chin on Dannie's shoulder pushing down firmly as only a Lab can do. She reached up to pet the big, soft head and viewed his expression of bliss in her rear view mirror. Jake had experienced a great week what with horse show, swimming in Beth's pool, playing with Robbie and trolling for Easter dinner treats, but there was no doubt that Dannie was his person and he was happiest as just the two of them motored down the freeway to their next adventure.

The screen on her center console notified her of an incoming call and she touched the button on her steering wheel to answer.

"Are you following me?" laughed Rebecca.

"As a matter of fact, yes," Dannie laughed along with her.

"Listen, I've been thinking. I know you wanted to do dinner tonight but I think I'm just going to lay low in the hotel room once we've checked in. I'll probably just eat your mother's care package."

Dannie doubted she would eat at all, but Bec was a big girl and the decision was hers. "OK, I'm sorry to hear that but I get it. Are we still on for a little shopping tomorrow?"

"You bet!" said Rebecca. "By the way, before I go to let you drive in peace I wanted to tell you how much I like your Jeff. He impressed me; the way he interacted and involved Robbie, and what he did for your Mom, for my car. It wasn't like most guys that seem to be trying to score points, it just seemed that's the kind of guy he is. Anyway, I know you don't need my approval but I just wanted to tell you."

"Don't you apologize, Bec. I'm happy to hear that my friends like him. I'm pretty partial to him myself."

"Oh yeah, and it doesn't hurt that he's gorgeous!" Rebecca cackled gleefully. "See you at the hotel, kid. Bye!"

No sooner had the call disconnected than the phone rang again. This time the ID showed the caller to be Tootie Bittler. Tootie was the Grande dame of the Silver Shores community and the first wife of the late Jumpin' Jimmy Bittler. She'd had enough of both sense and her own family money to leave Jimmy behind many years prior to his death. Tootie had always harbored sentimental feelings for Jimmy however, possibly because of their daughter, Shelaigh, now twenty three, or for the unfulfilled promise their lives held those many years ago. She had recognized the futility of their relationship, fueled by his vulgar personality and his utter failure to be a faithful husband and had ended their marriage, but she had stayed involved in the Silver Shores Horse Shows. Tootie was a social force; involved in many charities, she knew the power the shows possessed to further her fundraising goals. At Jimmy's death, it was revealed that he had bequeathed his dates for the shows in equal parts to Tootie, and in a twist only the horse world could understand, his widow, Mary Jane Bittler.

Mary Jane, one woman of many with whom Jimmy had cheated on Tootie, but the one he ultimately married. Now the two women, vastly different in personality, had become a team focused on carrying on the tradition of the Silver Shores Horse Shows. There was but one problem; neither woman had any idea how to produce such an event.

Dannie again depressed the button on the side of her steering wheel to answer the call. "Tootie, how nice to hear from you."

"Danica, how are you? I hope you had a wonderful Easter with your little boy and your family."

Dannie said she had before inquiring about Tootie's holiday as well. Then, the niceties out of the way said, "To what do I owe the pleasure of your call today, Tootie?"

"Well, I was hoping you, Mary Jane and I could get together for lunch at my home. Are you free tomorrow?"

"Oh, I'm sorry...no. I'm on my way to Fryetag as we speak."

"Oh, of course," said Tootie. "Langston's show is this week, isn't it? Well, how about next week? Wednesday?"

"Sure, I'm free next Wednesday."

"One o'clock?"

"I'll be there. I'm happy we'll get to catch up. I'm getting a little nervous. After all, the first week of the shows is a little less than three months away and it seems we still have a lot to do; prize lists, go over staffing, hotel and travel arrangements for officials, sponsors, if any..." Dannie's voice trailed off.

"Yes, we can go over all that next week. One more thing; this week I believe you'll be working with Kent Mallory," said Tootie.

"Yes, I worked with him two weeks ago at John Bowman's show too," replied Dannie.

"Good! Isn't he just a darling man?" Tootie gushed.

Dannie didn't have a clue what to say so she said nothing.

"Danica, did I lose you?"

"No, Tootie, I'm here."

"I was asking what you thought of Kent Mallory. Don't you just love him?"

"I don't, said Dannie. "Granted, I don't know him well, but my initial impression is not a good one. I hear that you and Mary Jane have chosen him to manage the shows this summer."

"We thought it was just a perfect fit. But I surmise that you don't agree."

"He knows nothing about horse shows, Tootie."

"That's why we have you. We hoped you'd be Kent's assistant. But listen, I don't want to keep you. We can talk about this more at lunch next week. Drive carefully, Danica."

Dannie promised she would and ended the call. Her heart sank. If she was truthful with herself, heading the Silver Shores shows was a challenge she had been looking forward to and it was clear that was not to be. She hoped she hadn't cost herself a job at the show altogether with her brutal honesty about Kent Mallory. Tootie and Mary Jane had been good to her over the years and she wanted to help them but she just couldn't pretend to like the weasel.

She glanced again at the brown paper bag from Beth sitting on her passenger seat. With nearly another hour before she reached Fryetag, Dannie decided it was time for lunch particularly as she had eaten almost nothing for breakfast. She reached to open the sandwich bag containing Beth's handiwork and extracted one half. She took a bite and sighed, wondering what ridiculousness the upcoming week would bring.

True to her calculations, a little less than an hour later Dannie followed Rebecca into the parking lot of the Fryetag Roadhouse. The name of the establishment brought to mind a much different imagining than reality provided. While one might envision an ivy-covered stone building with quaint, leaded, stained glass windows, in actuality the Roadhouse was right off the busy freeway in the heart of Fryetag's business district. It was a two-story affair, probably built in the sixties if the blue paint and orange trim was any indication.

Surrounding the motel were tire shops, used car lots, a liquor store and an adult novelty and bookstore. Lining the street in front of the Roadhouse were all manner of eighteen wheelers, most with sleeper cabs, and Bec and Dannie had to steer through an obstacle course of provocatively dressed women strolling back and forth in the parking lot.

Rebecca piloted her rental car into a spot next to the sign indicating "office" with a faded blue arrow. As Dannie pulled in to her right, Bec was already in her full-speed-ahead mode and striding toward the office.

Dannie jumped out of her car and said, "Bec, wait!" When there was no response, she increased the volume, "BEC!"

Rebecca paused in mid-stride and turned to face Dannie who motioned for her to come closer.

"What's up?" said Rebecca.

Dannie waved her arms in the direction of the motel. “This is a disaster.” Then, gesturing toward the parking lot, “Hookers? No, just.....no!”

Bec laughed. “Everyone deserves to be able to make a living.”

“I don’t wish to stop them from making a living,” Dannie said, “I just don’t wish to be here while they’re doing it.”

“Well, then, what do you suggest?” asked Bec.

“Hold on,” said Dannie as she began tapping away on her smartphone. “I have this great app that “Sticks” Hansen told me about. You know Sticks, right?”

“Of course, southern gentleman first and judge second,” Bec smiled.

“Anyway, this app uses your GPS to figure out where you are and then gives you everything you may need to know for that area; restaurants, coffee bars, laundry, grocery stores, and motels. I don’t want to stay here; it doesn’t feel safe...or even pleasant. I propose we find another nearby decent, with an emphasis on decent, motel and see if they have room for us.”

“Won’t they charge Langston anyway? Not sure I can afford the lodging myself.”

“I have a plan. Trust me?”

“I’m with you, kid,” said Bec.

Dannie set to work. Using her app she found a motel only about five miles from their present location but far more desirable. She booked two rooms and then called Chelle. She explained the situation and asked if she and Jen would like her to reserve rooms for them as well. There was a brief discussion and in the end the two friends declined.

“I can’t imagine it’s that bad,” said Chelle. “Jen and I will stay with Langston’s reservations.”

Finally she called Summer who was totally agreeable to joining Bec and Dannie at the new motel.

Next, Dannie entered the motel office, canceled the rooms for Bec and herself, paid the manager for the one day as they had arrived after the time set for refunds, and obtained a signed agreement from the manager that Langston owed them nothing for rooms he had reserved for both Dannie and Rebecca.

Exiting the office, Bec laid a hand on Dannie's arm. "Wait, you didn't cancel Summer's room."

"There's no room for Summer," Dannie said derisively.

"I thought you said she was coming for more experience."

"Oh, she is. But you know Langston, he holds every nickel so tightly the buffalo bellows. He would simply act as if he forgot and then try to make her share with someone." Noticing Bec's skepticism she continued, "Watch."

Dannie stuck her head back in the doorway and called out to the motel manager, "I forgot I need to cancel Summer Stanton's room as well."

The manager studied his list, finally answering, "I have no room reserved under that name."

"Silly me!" Dannie said and pulled back from the doorway.

Bec was laughing uproariously. "Amazing!"

In just over an hour, Dannie and Bec were checked in to their rooms at the Come and Stay Inn; second floor for Bec and the usual ground floor for Dannie and Jake.

The motel was by no means fancy, but that had never been a requirement. It was clean, quiet, away from the freeway and any craziness as far as Dannie could tell. There was a school right across the street with a big open grass area for Jake to play some ball and the desk clerk had said breakfast was served in the lobby starting at six AM.

Bec had already unloaded her car and was in for the night. Dannie took Jake for the anticipated play time and then hopped in the car to go just down the road to a bakery and café where she purchased a take-out salad and a chocolate chip cookie.

Her only obligations tomorrow were to go shopping with Bec around ten AM and then to appear on the show grounds for Langton Rubicon's mandatory staff meeting before dinner with Pat. Feeling relaxed she ate, organized, showered, and fell asleep to Law & Order reruns on the television.

She awoke to the rhythmic thumping of a large otter tail coupled with soft, yet insistent pushes on her cheek from a cold, wet nose.

"You have to go out?" Dannie asked Jake. "OK, buddy, just a sec."

She got up and pulled on a pair of navy sweatpants, a navy hooded sweatshirt with the Silver Shores logo emblazoned on the front, and slid her feet into a pair of flip-flops. She thought about a hat, but decided to just utilize the hood on her sweatshirt. Before heading outside, she grabbed the small pack that contained the plastic bags attesting to her responsible dog ownership and snapped the leash to the metal ring on Jake's collar.

Ten minutes later, business handled and ten or twelve tosses of Jake's favorite tennis ball completed, they returned to the room where Dannie freshened the dog's water and fed him breakfast. She left the room again, this time to wander to the breakfast offered in the motel lobby.

Entering through the glass door she immediately spotted Bec. At just six-fifteen she was already impeccably dressed with perfect hair and make-up. Dannie looked down at her own ensemble and burst out laughing. "Don't come any closer! I'll just look more like a bag lady the nearer you are."

"I just was awake very early so I decided to get up and get on with it," said Bec. Dannie hoped she had eaten some breakfast but saw no remnants of plate or utensils, just a cup of tea in front of her friend. Bec continued, "Are we still on for this morning? Ten?"

"You bet. I'm going to grab a bite to take back to the room then I'll hop in the shower. I promise, I'll look presentable by ten," she winked.

She glanced at the food offered; for a no-frills motel the breakfast presented was quite decent. She made her selection of a small cup of juice, vanilla yogurt and granola and a banana and headed back to the door. Just then her phone rang so she plopped everything on a table and answered.

It was Chelle. "Oh, Dannie, I'm sorry to call so early. Did I wake you?"

"Certainly not. What's up?"

The words tumbled out of Chelle. "You were so right. The Fryetag Roadhouse is abominable. Jen and I agree we can't stay there. We are on our way to the show grounds but we checked out before we left. Are you happy with where you are now?"

"Very."

"Any chance they have two more rooms?"

"Well, I'm standing in the office so I'll check."

Dannie walked to the desk and ascertained there were indeed two available rooms. "Thank you, please hold them with the credit card I gave you yesterday and my friends will check in late this afternoon," she said.

"Oh, thank God! Wait until I tell you about last night," Chelle said. "Oh, and one more thing, have you seen the Silver Shores prize list?"

"It's printed?"

"No, draft copy."

"Get me a copy, Chelle. I'll see you this afternoon."

Dannie returned to the room and took her breakfast to the small table provided. Jake had already settled in for his after-breakfast nap. As she ate, her mind wandered and she came to thoughts of the monotony of a life on the road…at least her kind of life.

At least once or twice a show, an exhibitor or parent expressed their admiration and envy for the exciting life Dannie and other show staff must experience; traveling to beautiful locations, the restaurants, shopping, and beautiful horses.

The horses were the grain of truth in those opinions. She loved them all whether show quality or pasture ornaments, big or small, old or young. She was always happy to be in their company. As for the rest of it, it was a job like any other job.

Those marveling at the beautiful locations had only frequented venues like Silver Shores, not Fryetag. Restaurants, at least notable ones, were for those that had time for a fine dining experience. It was far more likely that after a very hot, or windy, or cold, or busy day, dinner would consist of what could be purchased pre-made at a nearby grocery store, fast food joint, or pizza or Chinese take-out and brought back to consume in a hotel room while staring at the television or laptop screen.

Finally, there was lodging to consider. Dannie was well aware that to be responsible for twenty or more hotel rooms for five or six nights each was an enormous liability and staff were at work all day, they really only needed a place to shower and sleep. But when it came to that place she didn't feel it was too much to ask to expect one that was reasonably secure, didn't present evidence of bedbugs, roaches or rodents, and seemed moderately clean. It didn't happen nearly as often as one would think.

It seemed managers were either like Langston or they were like Jane Thornton; there was no middle ground. Jane respected the people that worked hard for her shows and showed them as much with her attention to the details that made their lives a little better while they worked for Gala. Conversely, Langston, whose singular focus was always Langston, respected few and received little respect in return.

It was a lonely existence, this carney life. It consisted of far too many hours in a small, cramped motel room, bad food, long hours and little rest. If you were in a relationship you fought like hell to keep it going amidst the doubts created by distance and time away. If you were trying to establish a relationship you were on shaky ground trying to explain to a partner how much they meant to you as you packed yet again for another four weeks away. You worked when you were sick; you missed holidays, birthdays, graduations, weddings and funerals.

So, Dannie asked herself, why do we keep coming back? Though the money was the answer for some, for more like Dannie, it was the love of the horse. She had longed to be in their presence since the day many years ago that she first stroked the soft muzzle of the old pasture horse down the road from her parent's home.

She looked into the old gelding's eyes and saw wisdom, strength, and tolerance. Long before she ever learned to ride or had a horse of her own, she would stop by the pasture fence on her way home from school and tell that horse her worries, her fears and her secrets. He always listened and he never betrayed her. She had found a comfort and acceptance through the years from that old horse and many after him that had never left her.

As for working your way from town to town, show to show, Dannie knew if you were smart you found ways to stave off the isolation and the sometimes crushing loneliness. Jake, her constant companion, was a primary reason she had been able to keep pressing forward these last years. Friends like Pat, Chelle, and Bec were kindred spirits and they all understood each other's struggles with life on the road without a word being spoken.

She would be lying to herself if she said she was not thrilled that the end was nearly in sight. She wanted to keep horses in her life somehow but she was not yet sure how that would be accomplished. All she knew was that she would be the happiest girl in the world when she drove into her driveway in Silver Shores Sunday night.

Dannie took a deep breath, and shaking off a case of the blues threatening to take hold went to shower and prepare to meet her day head on.

-10-

Dannie and Bec's shopping was somewhat of a non-event which both had known it would be. They had a couple of things to pick up; shampoo and a nail file for Dannie and toothpaste and hand lotion for Bec, but it was really just a way to kill a few hours in each other's company. It was an agreeable arrangement for both and wandering the large mall they'd found not far from their motel they even discovered a dinosaur of sorts in an age of online shopping.

They stumbled upon a little Mom and Pop bookstore which they were delighted to roam through. The owners loved each and every book in their store and were happy to have two customers that treasured books as much as they did. Both women left pleased with their selections. Bec had chosen several books for Robbie that her daughter had prized when she was young and Dannie's bag contained a classic she had never read but always wished to.

After a few hours, the friends drove back to the motel where Bec used the time to rest and Dannie organized for the show the following day.

Dannie arrived at the show grounds almost forty-five minutes before the appointed three PM start time for the staff meeting. She had hoped to hear from Chelle and Jen about their abrupt change of heart regarding the Fryetag Roadhouse. The exhibitors, however, had other ideas and a steady stream checking in to the Coast with the Most Horse Show meant the conversation would have to wait. Only Jake managed to steal a moment of Jen's time as he jumped up placing his large paws on the counter waiting for a treat from the basket they kept there; a desire which she obliged.

Wandering out the office door Dannie saw fellow starter, Logan Peters. "Where's this meeting supposed to be?" she called to him.

He didn't answer but instead turned and pointed to a set of bleachers about twenty yards away.

"Thanks, Logan," Dannie said, and started to head in that direction.

She had only advanced ten feet or so when she heard someone call her name. She turned and saw Summer.

"Hey, you made it," Dannie said with a smile. "How's your mom?

"Pretty good the last few days, thanks for asking."

"So, are you ready for this meeting?" Dannie asked.

"What exactly is it all about? Does every show do this?" questioned Summer.

"Thankfully, no. I only experience them when someone in management wants to make sure everyone understands who is in charge. Last one I went to was last year before the summer series at Silver Shores. I find them to be, overall, a waste of time and annoying as can be since no one intends to pay you for your time to attend. But form your own opinion, I'm probably just cranky today," Dannie smiled.

Jake plopped on Dannie's feet as Summer and Dannie took a seat to the side of the crowd on one of the lower bleacher rows and were joined moments later by Logan. The third starter, Mike "The Smiler" Gregory was seated on the opposite side of the stands.

Dannie waved at the judging panel for the week; Bec, Pat, and Wyatt Waddell. Normally, judges wouldn't be likely to do two shows in the same geographical area on two consecutive weeks but as the attendees were generally at a very different level of riding and showing than the Egg-stravaganza participants no one would have a problem with it.

Those gathered on the bleachers became aware of a commotion coming from the direction of the show office. Dannie looked to see show manager, Langston Rubicon, Esq., approaching with Barb Snowden and Kent and Muriel Mallory scurrying at his heels. As the group reached the bleachers, Langston and Kent continued to the cement pad in front while Muriel and Barb, arms full of some sort of paperwork, stopped at the corner near Dannie, Summer and Logan.

"Welcome everyone to the Coast with the Most Horse Show!" said Langston grandly.

Muriel and Barb immediately began handing stacks of the paperwork to Dannie and Logan saying, "Take one and pass them around."

Dannie did as instructed and when the stack had been sent on its way she glanced down to see about ten or twelve pieces of paper held together with a clear front report cover similar to what she had used to house her papers while in college. Through the shiny, flimsy plastic she could see the title; 'Coast with the Most Staff Handbook'.

"Oh crap," she muttered under her breath.

The bustle continued throughout the bleachers as the handbooks continued to find owners. Dannie took the opportunity to study Langston.

Langston Rubicon, Esq. was, sadly for him, far less magnificent than his name implied. For starters, Langston had no connection to the law nor did he possess a law degree which was the typical manner with which one earned the title of 'Esquire'. He was self-titled, and true to form for Langston the most important word in that and every description was 'self'.

Langston was what Dannie's grandmother used to call a 'tall drink of water'. He was several inches over six feet tall and incredibly thin with sandy hair and blue eyes. Though not a redhead, he possessed the complexion that many do; pale, translucent skin overlaid with blotchy redness. Langston was always neat and clean and he dressed in a GQ-meets-big –box-discount-store manner. He attempted style on a pauper's budget though he was no pauper. Finally, he fancied himself superior to nearly everyone he came in contact with and often the disdain he felt when interacting with others was quite evident.

Dannie believed that Langston once rode, but she wasn't sure of it. If he had it had been a long time ago.

She actually liked him when there was not a horse show involved. When he wasn't trying to prove his greater intellect he could be charming and funny and he was quite intelligent. But in charge of a horse show he was a feudal lord ruling over the serfs beneath him; and everyone in the bleachers were serfs and they were all beneath him.

Langston scanned the group and satisfied that everyone held a handbook began the meeting. "Once again, welcome everyone to my show. For those who don't know me, I am Langston Rubicon, Esquire."

Langston paused. Maybe he was expecting applause, Dannie thought, but none was forthcoming.

Holding his copy of the handbook aloft, he continued. "I have gone to great trouble to produce a staff handbook for the week that will be a valuable reference for each of you. It details everything from radio and ring assignments to expected behavior and chain of command in the event of an injury or another emergency."

"Another emergency, does he mean like a plague of locusts?" Dannie whispered to Logan and Summer. She had already lost interest and flipped through the handbook to determine where she would be working this week. She was assigned to the Jumper ring and found herself looking forward to the riders and trainers that didn't obsessively apply shiny oil to the horse's hooves or wrap and unwrap equine legs like some sort of religion. She understood the practice, but it made her job of getting horses and riders in and out of the arena in an efficient manner much more difficult to achieve.

Langston's voice jolted her back to the moment. "As I said, great trouble was taken to create these handbooks and as such it is my intent they be used for many years. To that end, no paychecks will be issued until your handbook is returned in good condition; no doodling, no dog-eared or missing pages. I think that is clear to everyone, is it not? Now, I'd like to introduce my right-hand man this week, Kent Mallory."

Langston clapped Kent on the shoulder a couple of times and in response Kent puffed up like a pompous pigeon.

"As I said, chain of command is very important here and any problems will be reported to Kent who will report them to me."

"Who's on first," muttered Logan under his breath.

"Kent Mallory has a plethora of talents and I know you will agree that he is a welcome and valuable asset to the show. And please take note; we will be featuring Kent and Muriel's charity, Steeds 4 Soldiers, throughout the week."

The verbosity continued as Muriel and Barb were introduced and proceeded to expound in great detail their plans for the nightly parties and the system of passing out first place prizes.

"And here I just thought you found the person holding the blue ribbon and gave the prize to them. Too simple for this lot, I guess," Dannie murmured.

"Did you have something to share, Dannie?" Muriel paused to ask.

"No, nothing to share."

Muriel and Barb took another couple of minutes to wrap up their address and Langston stepped forward once more.

"Before we conclude, I want to remind everyone about my yearly sportsmanship award. You will find the specifics in the prize list and I want all staff members to keep an eye out for a display of sportsmanship that must be noted. I have put the starter at the Main Hunter ring, Mikey Gregory, in charge and you may all make suggestions to him. His will be the final decision."

Dannie, Logan and Summer were floored. Had Langston just said he chose the person that knows nothing about horse shows or anyone attending to be in charge of selecting a sportsmanship award recipient?

Langston continued, "Everyone is dismissed now except my starters. Mikey, Logan, Dannie and Summer, is it? I want a few more words with you."

Those excused created a near stampede in their haste to leave the area before Langston changed his mind. Jake jumped to his feet in alarm as the many footfalls crashed down the metal slats and Dannie soothed him with a pat.

Langston waved Mike Gregory over to sit with the other three and started in earnest. "I wanted to speak to the four of you so we could talk about the proper way to run a back gate."

Dannie did her best to stifle a response but it was no use. A half cough, half snort escaped her lips.

"Is there a problem, Dannie?" Langston said, clearly not wanting an answer.

"Well, yeah," she said. "Are you the one that plans to tell us how to do this?"

"Of course."

"OK, then yes, my problem is that you have never in your life worked a back gate at a horse show." She could feel her arrogance showing but there was no turning back. "I can add you to the long list of people that think they know everything about this job. There are many things I don't know, but if I want to know about brain surgery I ask a neurosurgeon, not a history teacher. You, Langston, are the history teacher, at least when it comes to this subject."

"And you are the brain surgeon?" he said with disdain.

"Metaphorically speaking, yes. I learn all the time from people that have done this job longer than I have, or better than I have, or both. However, I haven't picked up too many tips from folks who have never done it. Logan and I work well together; he knows his stuff. I have the utmost confidence in Summer. You may find it beneficial to spend some time with Mike as he is very new to the job."

Langston's face had become even more red and blotchy and he spit out his words as if they were burning the inside of his mouth. "It doesn't surprise me that you have no idea how fortunate you are that I even hired you for this job. If I had my way only men would work the gates. They take direction and they command respect and the women that ride prefer dealing with a man at the gate."

Dannie fought the urge to yell back and instead willed herself to be calm. She lowered her voice and measured her words. "Oh, Langston, I don't even know where to begin. You're making most of this up as you go. The women and men that ride don't prefer a gender, they prefer a starter that is organized, pleasant, communicates with them and gets them in the ring when they say they will. The professionals want you to help them do their job well by getting them in and out and on to their next client. The amateurs and juniors, for whom this is recreation, want a friendly face and an encouraging word. None of them want us to 'command' anything; respect is a two-way street. If the day ends with trainers, exhibitors, and judges happy and everything has been contested within the rules on a level playing field, a starter has done his or her job. If you have no understanding of the basics, you have no business holding a how-to session."

"So you have all the answers," Langston fumed. "I guess that just makes me an idiot. Can you give me one reason why I shouldn't just fire you on the spot for speaking to me this way?"

"You can't fire someone you never hired. If you recall, Summer is hired for this show. I told you I would come and train her but she was to be hired and paid for her work. I am confident in her abilities already and though I will certainly stay and fulfill my promise to you, if you feel I should leave, you will be in good hands if she is your starter."

Dannie shot an encouraging look at Summer and noticed a hint of panic in her eyes at the suggestion Dannie might leave but she needn't have worried.

"I guess that was the agreement," Langston conceded, "but you won't have all that money very long if you keep making these arrangements. And for the record, Dannie, I am not happy with this attitude of yours."

"I want the same thing you want, Langston. I want your show to be successful. People having fun and coming back year after year creates work for people like us," she said indicating the little group. "Don't micromanage. Hire people who are good at what they do then get out of the way and let them do it."

"All that money has made you quite pompous, hasn't it?"

"What are you talking about, Langston?"

"Kent told me all about your, windfall, shall I call it?" Langston said. "If you want my show to go well you should have thought about sponsoring part of it."

Dannie sat in silence for a moment, unsure which of the many remarks swirling in her brain she should give voice to; anger at Kent and Langston for discussing her personal business, Langston's never-ending belief that everything should benefit him in some way, or his position that any woman hired by him wasn't contributing but instead should just feel fortunate he did her the favor of allowing her to be at the show. In the end, she said none of those things.

"Langston, it is no surprise to either of us that we have never quite seen eye-to-eye. It is evident that this year will be no different but I think we should be able to make it through the next five days, don't you? Now I have an appointment that I will be late for if I don't leave now. I'll see everyone tomorrow morning."

Dannie picked up Jake's leash and began to gather her things.

"Well, the three of us can proceed then," Langston said looking at Logan, Summer and Mike.

Logan sprang to his feet. "I'm with Dannie, I'm out of here."

Dannie, her back to Langston, flashed Logan a smile. Summer, after just a brief hesitation, came to her feet as well and joined Logan, Dannie and Jake as they headed to their parked cars.

Dannie glanced back once to see Langston and Mike Gregory looking blankly at each other and thought how much they deserved one another.

Dannie slid into the booth at the restaurant where Pat was already seated and barely dispensed with the formality of a 'hello' before she began talking a mile a minute. She told him about the exchange with Langston; his condescending opinions, his arrogance, his jabs about her inheritance, but she primarily talked about herself.

"I acted like an ass. I let him get to me and in the end I brought myself down to his level. I should have just shut up."

"Then why didn't you?" Pat asked, sipping his iced tea.

"He just makes me so mad. I hate that he thinks he's getting away with it."

"Away with what?"

"Treating everyone like dirt on the bottom of his shoe, acting like the supreme ruler, frankly, believing he has a clue about anything related to the showing world."

Pat placed his tea back on the coaster the server had provided. "Dannie. I say this to you with the utmost love and respect. You take this too much to heart. You have known Langston for some years. Do you actually believe he cares that you have his number, so to speak?"

"I want him to know I know."

"That's my point, Dannie. He doesn't care what you know. He sees you once, maybe twice, in a year. You are a small annoyance. Most of the time he is a self-congratulatory braggart who is full of his own importance. He likes it that way and he won't change."

Dannie directed a look of utter frustration at Pat.

"Honey," Pat continued, "I understand who you are. I love who you are. But this just makes you unhappy, it doesn't change anything. The horse world is full of Jimmy Bittlers and Langston Rubicons and Kent Mallorys. I'm not telling you not to care, not to fight for the underdog or for people to do the right thing, that's a part of you. But if it doesn't always go your way, and it won't, probably best not to tilt at windmills."

"Windmills? You're saying I'm making it up?"

"No, probably an expression not to be applied too literally. What I mean is that you'll find yourself in fights that just waste your time. The result won't change."

Dannie sipped her water, deep in thought, before she replied. "I know you're right but I don't know how successful I will be. I'll try not to react so badly."

"That's all you can do. You know, most of the jerks we come across are fairly transparent. Most people know who and what they are. But it's like I told you during Bowman's show, you've made the right decision to get out of this. Right now you're just a moth beating yourself to death at the light."

"I've missed you," Dannie said.

"Missed me? We just had dinner at your mother's two nights ago."

"It's not the same. We can't talk like we can at our 'dinners for two'."

The server arrived to take their order and the rest of the evening was spent happily catching up on life's mundane details. Dannie filled Pat in on the exodus from the Fryetag Roadhouse, Pat brought Dannie up to speed on his continued attempts to start some sort of relationship with Mary Jane Bittler, Jumpin' Jimmy's widow.

Pat had been carrying a torch for Mary Jane for many years, but had always kept his distance out of respect to her marriage with Jimmy. It wouldn't have mattered for many, but it did to Pat; that's the kind of guy he was. But now that Jimmy was gone Pat's attitude had changed and he was trying to find the happiness he longed for. Dannie had her fingers crossed that her friend would have his chance with Mary Jane.

With dinner complete, the pair was waiting only for their server to return with the check and a small container for Jake's leftovers.

"I almost forgot," Pat said, producing a sheaf of papers. "Chelle asked me to give this to you."

"Thanks," said Dannie, recognizing it as the draft of the Silver Shores prize list and tucking it in her bag for later scrutiny.

"You know, I envy your peaceful Come and Stay Inn," Pat said somewhat wistfully.

"It's great for sure," said Dannie, "but what brought that to mind?"

"When I returned to the Roadhouse after the meeting, it wasn't long before Barb and Muriel were holding court in the parking lot."

"The parking lot?"

"I guess they thought it was the best way to make contact with any show staff coming or going," said Pat.

"Contact about what?" Dannie asked.

"Well, I have to say I wasn't out there, I was listening to most of it through my open window. They touched on their combined top 5, I think. Starting with; the smart crew guy will be aware that Kent will be hiring for many shows in the near future including those at Sunshine and Blimpy's Forrest Equestrian Park, to Dannie Rossi's attitude is giving starters a bad name and everyone should distance themselves. Then Barb cornered a couple trainers to tell them all about John Bowman's plans for new party ideas..."

"Nothing about fixing the schedule though," winked Dannie.

"No," smiled Pat. "Then they finished with the one-two punch; encouraging everyone to report any incompetency or mistakes on Rebecca's part to show management, and asking everyone if they didn't find it odd that you had so much money yet you didn't make a move to sponsor anything at the shows to improve the industry."

Dannie glossed right over the comments about her and instead went right to the attack on Bec. "What a pair of malicious, spiteful hags they are to go after Bec, as if either of them would recognize competency if it slapped them in the face. What in the hell is in it for them to disparage her?"

"No idea. They are obviously miserable, bitter and resentful to many things and many people and I think they have found symbiosis with each other. "

"Idiots," Dannie hissed.

The server brought the small Styrofoam box to the table and as he scraped his leftovers into it Pat said, "I was quite surprised to see Muriel enter a room at the hotel after concluding her parking lot revival meeting."

Dannie laughed at the characterization. "Why surprised? Everyone needs a place to stay."

"She and Kent have an RV. Granted it's an RV held together with duct tape and baling twine, but an RV nonetheless."

"Well, it's probably nice to have a home away from home to take on the road."

"Not a home away from home," countered Pat, "it's their home, period. They live in it. They don't have a house, or property, or anything but that RV."

"Seriously? As much as the Mallorys aren't my best buds, everyone deserves to live the way they wish. I don't fault them for living in an RV. But it does beg the question 'where do they house the horses for their therapeutic program for soldiers if they have nothing'," said Dannie.

"I'm with you. Where is their home base to run this program and if they're on the road for weeks on end how is the whole thing administered?"

When she returned to the room Dannie placed the leftovers from dinner in Jake's bowl, then thought about her conversation with Pat at the restaurant as she organized for tomorrow and prepared for bed.

She couldn't determine what she was missing in the spectacle that was Kent and Muriel Mallory but she knew there was something.

As for the vengeful duo of Barb and Muriel and their campaign against Rebecca, she could see no reason for it other than the two perceived weakness and were determined to prey on it. Dannie was equally determined to see her friend wasn't hurt and was still fuming about Muriel and Barb as she finally fell asleep.

-11-

Dannie and Summer had settled in to the routine of the back gate on the first morning of the Coast with the Most Horse Show. It was around ten AM and they had been up and running since eight.

The two women had picked up right where they left off at the Egg-stravaganza; Summer in charge of the ring and Dannie there to assist if needed and answer questions. Dannie knew it was the best way to learn and Summer was doing a great job. Dannie wanted her to have as much experience as she possibly could by the time she arrived in a couple of months to do her own gate at Silver Shores.

They had already completed the first three of twelve total classes for the day in the jumper ring and at the moment had a lull in the action as they waited for the water truck and tractor to finish grooming the footing in the ring. Summer checked to make sure the top of her jumping order was warming up, made another barn page to let people on the grounds know what was going on in her ring, and then turned to Dannie.

"I just have to ask," she said as she glanced around to make sure no one else could hear, "why is this show called the Coast with the Most? I think Fryetag can only really boast about an aqueduct."

"Some years back the show was in the far north of the state and yes, it was on the coast. It was a pretty location but hard to access with trucks and trailers. I showed there once or twice as a kid. Anyway, it was a poorly maintained facility; lots of infrastructure problems with electricity, rocks and other things always cropping up in the arena footing, but the exhibitors probably would have continued to go because the town was such a pleasant destination spot. Unfortunately, though they used to support the show en masse, Langston couldn't stop berating trainers for not bringing enough clients, exhibitors for not entering enough classes, and people for not writing large enough checks to sponsor his classes and parties. Whatever they did, he made sure they knew it wasn't enough."

"Who wants to go to a show only to be browbeaten by the manager?" asked Summer.

"You're a smart girl," said Dannie, holding her hand up for a high five. "So, the end result is the show moved to this more central and accessible location, is no longer a 'destination' show, and changed its focus and schedule. Langston believed the name of the show had such recognition that he would keep it." She added a small shrug to the last remark.

Further discussion was halted as trainer Justin Hamilton appeared at Summer's elbow.

"Hey, Summer! The schedule is my enemy today and I think I'm backing myself in a corner. I need to figure out where to go. Could you call the guy at the Main Hunter ring...what's his name; Huey, Stuey?"

Summer couldn't hold back her laugh. "Mikey?"

"Yeah, that's him. Could you see where he is in his schedule?"

Summer placed her printed schedule so Justin could see it when Mike answered. She depressed the button on the side of her radio. "Mike, do you copy?"

Silence.

"Mike Gregory, do you copy?"

Nothing.

"Main Hunter, anyone over there?"

"Yeah."

"Mike, is that you?" Summer questioned.

"It's Mikey."

"OK, whatever. Justin Hamilton is wondering what class you're working on?"

"Who?"

"Never mind. What class are you on?"

Mike started talking before he depressed the button on his radio. "......Class 35."

Justin and Summer looked at each other, incredulous. So much so that Dannie leaned forward to peer at the schedule too. Class 35 was the first class of the day in Mike's ring. It only had nine riders and had been scheduled to start at eight and end at eight-thirty.

Summer spoke into the radio again. "I think I misheard. You said you're on Class 35?"

"No brainless, I said I just finished it."

Summer made a face and set her radio on the table. I'm going to have a serious problem with that guy." Turning to Justin, she said, "Do you need to get over there?"

"I'm in the fourth class. At this rate, evidently it will be right before dinner," he joked. "Can I get on one for you?"

Before she could answer, Langston and Kent arrived in a golf cart. "Summer," said Langston, "Why is it you are so far ahead in your schedule and Mikey Gregory is so far behind?"

Dannie held her breath, hoping Summer wouldn't be defensive but she needn't have worried.

"I am not ahead; I am right on my printed time schedule." She waved the rider standing at the gate into the ring to begin her next class. "I am scheduled to start this class at ten-fifteen," she paused and checked the clock on her phone, "and it's twelve after."

"Then how is it that Mikey has just finished his first class?" Kent asked.

"I have no idea," said Summer, "doesn't he know?"

Dannie feigned a coughing fit to avoid the gales of laughter that threated to erupt. Both Langston and Kent looked on disapprovingly as she took a huge drink from her water bottle and said, "Wow, the dust is really bad. Sorry."

Kent stared at Dannie a moment longer and then looked back to Summer. "We're going to have to make some adjustments. I'll get back to you."

"OK," she said cheerily as she picked up her pen and readied to write the score for the rider exiting the ring.

As Langston's golf cart sped away, Summer turned to Dannie with a mischievous smile.

"Good Lord," said Dannie, "that was priceless! Nothing makes me happier than to see Kent realize that his golden boy is anything but. I don't want to see the kid fail, but it's worth it to see that Kent's idea that all he needs is "the look" and Langston's idea that all he needs is to be a guy does not a starter make. I mean, Logan is a cute guy and he always looks good but the difference is he actually knows what he's doing."

Summer took note of the next rider's score called to her by Bec, their judge today, announced it and then said, "That was kind of fun, really."

"You handled yourself well," Dannie said. "Just keep doing your job and stay on top of things. There will always be someone that wants to rock you back on your heels and put you on the defensive. The blame game is alive and well at horse shows. You did exactly the right thing."

They had almost concluded the current class when Langston again arrived in his golf cart. He began to speak before the cart even stopped moving.

"Summer, grab your things. You're going over to the Main Hunter ring. Mikey says you have not been allowing the riders to come to him and that's why he's behind."

Justin Hamilton had ridden up moments before from the warm-up ring ready to go in his jumper class. "That's crap, Langston. The guy's an idiot. Summer tried to get me to go there first but he was too far away from my class."

Langston walked over to stand next to Justin's horse and continue the conversation. Dannie took the opportunity to whisper to Summer, "They are probably hoping you'll fail so Mike doesn't look so bad, but you've got this. Do the job you know how to do and don't let 'em see you sweat. I'll send you anyone I can and don't worry...you'll do great."

Summer lifted her backpack off the table and went to sit in Langston's golf cart. He returned and prepared to take Summer to the Main Hunter ring. As he sped away, Summer turned and fixed Dannie with a nervous gaze.

Dannie picked up her radio and said to Bec, "You're stuck with me for the rest of the day."

"Great, but what happened?"

"Long story. I'll tell you tonight."

Dannie was pleased with her plans for this evening. The usual girl's night of Chelle, Jen and Dannie was being expanded to include Bec and Summer; all the ladies at the Come and Stay Inn. It was predicted to be a pleasant evening and Dannie had elicited promises from everyone to meet by the pool somewhere around six.

She let go of thoughts of the evening and brought herself back to the moment. They were preparing for the first class of the day for riders 17 and under. According to Dannie's gate sheets there were fifteen horses and riders to see in the class, but Dannie wouldn't be surprised to see the number go up or down by a few. Often the first day of the show presented different situations than when the entries were made and riders either wanted to add or scratch out of the class at the last moment.

Ring crew foreman Petey Anderson, also known as P.T., gave her the thumbs up that the course was set and ready to go as he passed by her table.

"Thanks buddy," Dannie said, as she raised her microphone to announce the start of the class.

Her first horse and rider were waiting at the gate and Dannie called the exhibitor number to Bec and waved the pair into the arena to begin their round. She leaned down to check Jake's water bowl and give him an affectionate pat on the head, then returned to a sitting position to see Barb Snowden and Muriel Mallory approaching in a golf cart.

Picking up her microphone, she introduced horse and rider and gave a brief explanation of the manner in which the class was to be judged. Jumper classes had a different selection of ways to be scored and this was called 'power and speed' by the riders. A competitor jumped all the fences in the first round and if there were no faults proceeded immediately to the jump-off course. If faults were incurred in the first round, the 'power' phase, the rider would hear a whistle or tone and would not be permitted to proceed to the jump-off.

Having dispensed with the formalities, Dannie greeted the women. "Hello, ladies, what brings you to the Jumper ring?"

"Well, aren't we cheery?" Muriel sneered.

Deciding she would not rise to the bait, Dannie simply said, "I am, it's a beautiful day."

"We're here to check on ribbons and prizes and to take your lunch order," said Barb.

"Oh, thanks, but I brought my lunch," Dannie replied.

"What, too good for the food Langston provides?" Muriel said.

Muriel's hostility was over the top, Dannie thought, and she wondered what had brought on this latest barrage. Maybe Muriel somehow blamed her for Mike Gregory's current failure which would make no sense, unless you were Muriel.

"No, I always try to bring my own food. I sit in one place for hours on end, I don't like to compound the problem by eating high-fat, fried food. Nothing sinister in my decision. Look at it this way, one less meal you ladies have to deliver."

There were several riders, trainers, and parents milling around the back gate and several looked as if they wished to speak to Dannie so she turned her attention in their direction. One rider, Carley Petit, was standing patiently with her dad.

"Carley, did you need me?"

"Hi Dannie, I wanted to check in for this class."

Dannie consulted her class sheet. "I don't have you listed in the class, Carley."

"Oh, I added it, sorry." She dug in the pocket of her windbreaker and pulled out what everyone called an add slip. It was given to a rider when they added a class in the office and was supposed to be turned over to the back gate.

"That's OK. I had a few other adds so I have about fifteen total left to see, can you get it done by then?"

"I have to go get on but my horse is all ready to go. I can be ready in fifteen, well, fourteen rounds," Carley smiled.

"Done! See you then," Dannie said.

Muriel and Barb were wrapping up their adjustments of the ribbon table and Muriel, seeing a golden opportunity, turned to the people spread around the vicinity of Dannie's gate. She spoke, her words rife with insincerity.

"I just wanted to take the opportunity to welcome all of you to the Coast with the Most show. If we've not yet met, my name is Muriel Mallory. I am married to Kent Mallory, the show coordinator. On behalf of Langston Rubicon, Kent, and my co-worker, Barb Snowden, I want all of you to know that if you have any concerns; you know, like rings being off schedule or judges," she stole a glance at Bec in the jumper judge's booth, " making mistakes, we would be happy to hear from you."

Dannie noticed Langston returning in his golf cart, as well as the group that just received Muriel's small speech looking uncomfortably at each other and inching away from the area. It seemed suddenly, everyone had somewhere else to be.

"Dannie," Langston started, "I was...."

Dannie wasn't listening but instead was staring at Muriel. "What the eff is wrong with you?"

"What are you talking about?"

"Why would you suggest to exhibitors and everyone else that the judges could be making mistakes?"

"Well," she said, waving her hand in Bec's direction, "everyone knows that..."

"Stop it! Just stop. Don't you understand that by suggesting a judge, any judge, is incompetent, which by the way is not true in this case, that you have just suggested that Langston has no clue what he's doing and is not able to hire a competent judge? That they should be questioning what goes on at the show? It doesn't really help when you cast doubt on the staff."

"Muriel, is what Dannie says true?" Langston asked.

"All I did was tell some people at the gate that we wanted to hear from them if judges made mistakes, well, just anything they were concerned about. Dannie just thinks she's smarter than all of us."

"In this case, Muriel, I agree with her. It's one thing to let them know our doors are open to hear from them, entirely another to suggest to them that anyone on this staff is incompetent. I suggest you and Barb continue with what you were doing and leave the rest to me."

Muriel flounced to the cart where Barb was already in the driver's seat, dropped into the seat so hard the cart rocked, and stared straight ahead without another word as Barb drove away.

Langston stared after them for a moment before turning to Dannie. "I came back to tell you Summer is really good. I took her to the Main Hunter and she had it in hand in a matter of minutes."

"I'm sure she did."

"You don't like Mikey, do you?"

"Personally, I find him a bit vapid, but professionally, he has no business running a gate. He hasn't the knowledge or the interest."

"Well, Kent recommended him, so..."

"Kent hasn't the knowledge either. And I probably shouldn't have said that because I'm guessing you'll tell him I did," she said ruefully.

Langston made no reply. Bec called Dannie on the radio and while Dannie was talking with her he slipped away in his cart.

A few moments later, Dannie used her radio to call up to Bec in the booth. "What a bizarre day this has been; Langston coming and going like a bee to a hive, Muriel lecturing me for 'dissing' Langston because I brought my lunch. The day has felt disjointed, it hasn't flowed at all yet we keep getting our rounds through the ring."

"Thankfully, I'm a little isolated up here. Hang in there," answered Bec.

The two friends returned to work on getting the rest of the rounds through the ring. There were about three left to go when Carley appeared on her horse with her trainer and dad in tow.

"I'm ready, Dannie."

"Great, Carley, perfect timing. That bay horse at the gate goes next and then it's your turn."

"I have a favor to ask, Dannie. Would you use my phone to video my round? My Dad is all over the place," she laughed.

"How about this," countered Dannie. "Let me use my phone and I'll send it to you. I'm more comfortable with mine and then people won't get the idea that I'm here to video everyone. If that was the case I'd never get my work done."

"OK, thank you," Carley said.

As she received last minute instructions from her trainer, Dannie marveled at Carley's composure. She couldn't be more than twelve, yet she was comfortable with adults, polite, and well-spoken. Dannie observed that was the case for many horse show "kids"; it seemed the show atmosphere encouraged it.

The horse in front of Carley exited the ring and Dannie announced the time and score before introducing Carley. She had her phone at the ready and as Carley stepped through the gate Dannie pushed the button to begin recording.

Contrary to the plan she had made with her trainer and likely fueled by nerves, Carley headed right for the timers set about twelve feet before the first jump. Bec saw it too and quickly sounded the tone. If Carley passed through the timers before the tone sounded she would be eliminated so Bec was doing her a favor.

Just on the other side of the timers, Carley made a circle. It was often customary for a rider to make a small circle before beginning the course, but not after passing through the timers; that would cost her some penalty points.

Carley continued through the eight fences that comprised the first round and Bec immediately sounded the tone before Carley proceeded to the jump off.

"Four faults," Bec called over the radio.

Dannie stopped the video and announced Carley's score. Carley headed toward the gate looking somewhat confused but her trainer, Michaela, was waiting to talk about it. Carley's dad, on the other hand, had a much more vocal reaction.

"Four faults! She didn't knockdown one jump, is the judge blind?"

"Dad!" Carley motioned to him frantically, looking mortified.

"Carley, you heard what that lady said. I think..."

Michaela Reynolds, Carley's trainer, had walked to her father and taken him by the arm with a 'don't-mess-with-me' look on her face. She indicated that Carley should follow them on her horse and they walked some distance from the gate to have what appeared to be a heated discussion.

Dannie was somewhat distracted by the things she needed to do before her next class began and when she again turned the small group was gone.

The remainder of the day in the Jumper Ring was problem free and Dannie presented awards for her final class at about three PM. Rebecca headed down from the judge's booth and the two women made their way to the show office to turn in their paperwork.

They entered the office door to find Carley's father, plainly not cowed by Michaela's explanation, in full cry.

"I saw it with my own eyes. She didn't circle. That judge is an idiot."

He was so involved with his audience of Langston, Kent, Muriel, Chelle and Jen, he wasn't aware that Dannie and Bec had walked in behind him. Dannie saw Bec's shoulders droop at the last comment but knew Bec would say nothing. Not so for Dannie. She stepped into the line of sight of the angry father.

"I'm afraid you are mistaken about what you saw." He started to protest and Dannie held up a hand to silence him. "I have it right here on video," she said, waving her phone.

Langston held his hand out for the phone, took it from Dannie and walked to stand next to Carley's father. "Let's watch it together. Dannie, do I tap the arrow?"

She nodded and Langston started the video. He calmly watched how the events unfolded and then returned the phone to Dannie.

"Sir, I understand your disappointment, but the judge, Mrs. Kirtlan, made the correct call. That is a four fault round and your daughter should not have gone on to the jump off."

Carley's father extended his hand to Langston, who shook it. "Thank you for addressing this," he said. Likely more of the 'bro code' Dannie thought because an apology to Rebecca was sorely lacking.

Dannie and Bec didn't wait around to see what happened next but instead headed for the staff parking lot.

"Dannie, I think I'm going to opt out of ladies night"

"Oh no, Bec! It's only three-thirty. Go back to your room, put your feet up and rest and then join us, even if it's just for half an hour.

Bec agreed, albeit reluctantly, and the two left the show grounds with day one completed.

The evening was as beautiful as predicted and the five women had claimed a wrought iron umbrella table and five cushioned chairs next to the pool at the Come and Stay Inn. First beverages were barely poured when Dannie addressed herself to Chelle and Jen.

"OK, let's hear it! I am dying to know the details of your migration from the Roadhouse to here."

"Oh my God, I don't even know where to start," said Chelle. "But first," she said and raised her glass to Summer and Bec, "welcome to the two new, very refreshing additions to our ladies night."

Everyone took a moment to toast and then Bec said, "OK, spill it."

Chelle began again. "Let's start with the parking lot. People milling everywhere and nothing but eighteen wheel…."

"…ers and hookers," said Dannie finishing Chelle's sentence.

Jen chimed in. " And we arrived fairly late Monday evening so when we went in the office to check in we were told, 'Yes, Mr. Rubicon did include you on his list but all we have left are two ADA wheelchair accessible rooms'. Chelle and I didn't care, so we did the paperwork and took our keys."

"Biggest mistake ever," said Chelle. "Our rooms were next door to each other and about five minutes after I loaded my stuff in the room and bolted the door because of all the creepers walking around, the phone in the room rang. It was Jen."

"I told her I didn't think I could stay there. Everything was dark and just looked so dirty. To top it off there was some unnamed substance running down the wall near my bedside table. I just wanted to douse myself in disinfectant," said Jen.

"We talked it over and decided it was too late that night to make a change in a strange city, but agreed I would call you first thing the next morning. And believe me," Chelle continued, "I haven't even mentioned the bathrooms or the sting operation."

"Sting operation? Dannie gasped.

"Yes, evidently the Fryetag P.D. looks unfavorably upon solicitation so about two AM the place was awash in floodlights, a helicopter hovering overhead, people banging on doors and lots of johns and hookers being arrested, " said Jen.

Dannie was laughing so hard there were tears running down her face.

"And there's more?" Bec said, laughing too.

"Our bathrooms were very large rectangular tiled rooms. In the corner was a hand-held shower head attached to the wall and a drain in the floor," Chelle said.

"Well, they were ADA rooms," said Summer.

"OK, even an ADA room should have a shower curtain or something for privacy, right?" asked Jen. "I mean, that was it; shower head and drain in the floor in this big open room. I'm not positive, but I'm pretty sure I had a taste of what it's like to shower in prison."

"I dropped my toothbrush this morning and it was so gross in that bathroom I just threw it away and stopped on the way here this evening and bought a new one," said Chelle, laughing.

Everyone had brought something delicious, though pre-made, to the little impromptu potluck and the women munched, talked, drank, and laughed as they all shared stories of their crazy lives on the road and at the show.

"How did it go with Mike, Summer?" asked Dannie.

"I feel evil for saying this but he doesn't have a clue what to do. Did he really sit with you for a week?" she asked.

"He was there, but spent his time looking at his phone. I think half the time he was just looking at his reflection," Dannie said.

"It isn't that he messed it up as much as he did nothing. Once I got riders and trainers organized, we only finished fifteen minutes past our prescribed time. Of course, my arriving too bail him out didn't win me any points. He so wants to be taken seriously," Summer said framing air quotes around her last word. "But Dannie, remember how Justin thought his name was Huey or Stuey?"

The rest of the table laughed uproariously at that piece of information.

"Well," Summer continued, "it's epidemic." Everyone that came to the gate called him Marky, Joey, Maxie, everything you can imagine with a 'y' at the end except Mikey. I think one trainer even called him Sparky."

As the evening went on the women laughed until their stomachs hurt. Dannie was going to bring up the Mallorys and Steeds 4 Soldiers but she was having too much fun to bring down the group. It could wait for another time.

She glanced around the table at these women that were part of her tribe. Women that had not traveled the horse show circuit could never understand each other the way these women did. There wasn't any real unkindness in them, but the laughter and camaraderie was a stress reliever; a voice in a world that was far too lonely much of the time that said 'you're not alone'. Dannie wasn't the only one that fought to be respected and treated well in her job; it was a universal struggle for everyone seated at the table.

She considered Barb, Muriel and the Fryetag Women's March. The intent of the event hadn't changed the attitudes of the two old biddies and she wasn't sure what they thought they accomplished. It seemed to Dannie that the men that most needed to hear the message of the marches didn't, and would never care. Having never been much of a joiner, she felt much more confident fighting for herself in this world and she believed confidence in that would better equip her to fight for others. She looked again at the other four women at the table and knew, though they had ups and downs, these women had her back and she had theirs.

The little party broke up nearly thirty minutes later. As they walked to their respective rooms, Bec paused at the foot of the stairs leading to the second floor and turned to Dannie.

"Twice in one week you have insisted I be a part of something and I'm so glad you did. This was such fun and I had a wonderful time. Thanks for including me."

"It wouldn't have been the same without you, Bec," Dannie smiled.

Rebecca threw her arms around Dannie, hugging her tightly and the hug spoke volumes more than her words were able to. Without another word, Bec turned and climbed the stairs to her room.

-12-

Next morning as Dannie and Jake approached the steps leading to the horse show office the door at the top of the steps opened to reveal Bec, clipboard and radio in hand. She flashed her usual brilliant smile when she caught sight of the two, but Dannie noticed that behind the smile Bec was pale and drawn.

"Morning, Sunshine!" Bec said to Dannie as she reached down to greet Jake with a scratch behind the ear.

"Good morning," Dannie replied. "You're up and at 'em early today."

"Oh, couldn't sleep so I figured I might as well get up and hit it head on. I'm with Summer at the Main Hunter today."

Dannie turned a small giggle inward as she noted that yet another of the show staff had put Mike Gregory on the 'useless' list and was already thinking of it as Summer's gate.

"I'd better get in and grab my stuff too," Dannie said. "And Jake is waiting for his treat."

"Can't get in the way of that treat," said Bec. "We'll talk later. Have a good day, Dannie."

"You too."

Entering the office Dannie realized immediately that any hope of conversation with Chelle and Jen was fruitless; each had a customer and a line after that.

Dannie grabbed her clipboard and radio and was on her way out the door when she realized Jake was not with her. She turned to find him sitting patiently next to the customer closest to the treat jar. As the woman looked down at him, he produced a wag from just the tip of his tail accompanied by adoring eyes and what passed for a smile.

"Oh, what a handsome boy, do you want a treat?" she asked him.

He replied by scooting closer to her and thumping his tail loudly on the linoleum floor of the office.

"What a ham!" Chelle said rolling her eyes but Jake, already chewing on the offered treat, was oblivious to the name-calling.

The instant the treat was dispensed with Jake jumped up, spun and ran past Dannie and out the door, waiting for her at the foot of the stairs.

"You're such a bad dog," she laughed, not meaning a word of it.

She had barely reached her place at the Jumper gate when a golf cart holding Muriel and Barb rolled up to disgorge a cargo of ribbons and trophies. Barb walked to the small table adjacent to Dannie's to begin setting up while Muriel approached Dannie.

Thrusting a piece of paper in Dannie's direction, Muriel said, "Here is the information for announcements about Steeds 4 Soldiers. Langston wishes you to announce what's on the sheet several times per day. I suppose you have some sort of problem with that?"

"Not at all. This is just the sort of thing I was hoping for so I could be accurate with my announcements," said Dannie.

Muriel looked doubtful and Dannie conceded she was right; there was no part of her that wanted to do any PR for the Mallorys, but it was her job so she would do it.

As soon as Muriel and Barb left the area, Dannie sent a text to Chelle asking if she happened to have extra copies of the

Steeds 4 Soldiers flyer. Chelle responded that she had created the document in her computer to which Dannie replied with a request to print three extra copies. She added she would explain later and requested both Chelle and Jen mention it to no one.

Glancing across the ring she saw Pat, her judge for the day, making his way to the stairs that led to the judge's booth. Pat would be announcing today. The sound equipment in the booth was superior to Dannie's at the gate. Bec didn't like to announce so Dannie had done it yesterday, but she was glad to hand the reins to Pat for today. She gave him a cheery wave, which he returned, then picked up her radio to make a barn page.

While she was on the radio, Langston arrived at the gate, with irritation oozing from every molecule. He stood impatiently while Dannie finished her announcement and began speaking before she managed to return the radio to the table.

"Trying to manage my business, are you?"

"Pardon me?" said Dannie, baffled.

"I've heard you took it upon yourself to move members of my staff to another hotel without consulting me?"

"Why would I consult you? It doesn't affect you one way or the other."

"Well, that remains to be seen," he snapped. "Let's just start with why you would do such a thing?"

"The hotel you selected is a dive and from my observation didn't appear to be safe. It's nowhere I wanted to stay and I gave my friends, single women traveling alone, the chance to go somewhere we would feel safer," said Dannie.

"So I can add you to the list of people that have their hand on my wallet," Langston sneered.

"How do you figure that?"

"What about the rooms I am committed to paying for? Did you think about that?"

"I personally paid for the first night for Bec's room and for mine. I canceled the remaining days for the two rooms and have a signed declaration from the manager saying you are in no way responsible for one penny on those two rooms. Chelle and Jen stayed at the Roadhouse for one night and I'm sure you will be charged for that, but they checked out and canceled their remaining nights as well. You never did reserve a room for Summer so you have no responsibility there."

Langston continued, clearly not convinced. "So now you are all at a hotel that costs more per room per night and I'm just supposed to fork that over because you decided you are too good for the Roadhouse and I should pay?"

"Bec, Chelle, Jen, and Summer will include reimbursement on their pay sheets for exactly what you are paying the Roadhouse. I have secured my own room and you have no responsibility for that. The remaining balance of their rooms is taken care of, but not by you. So you see, you will pay, to the penny, exactly what you would pay if they had remained at the Roadhouse."

"And you are paying the extra out of the goodness of your heart? Fat chance. What do you get out of it and why would you?"

"Let's be clear here, Langston. I have no idea why all of a sudden everyone is so interested in how I spend my money, but it is none of your business. Period. I didn't want to stay there so I left, and I gave my friends the same opportunity. It didn't change your circumstances at all and as for the hand-on-your-wallet comment all I can say is you are much more impressed with the desirability of its contents than I am. Now, if you'll excuse me, I have work to do."

For a moment Langston stood open-mouthed then he spun on his heel and retreated to his golf cart, speeding away in a cloud of dust.

Dannie's phone rang with the caller identified as Pat. She answered, and looked to the booth to make eye contact while they talked.

"What on earth?" Pat began. I couldn't hear what you were saying but that was certainly heated. Didn't want to ask on the radio...too many prying ears."

"It's a long story and we need to get going, but I'll come up to the booth and fill you in during the first water and drag. Deal?"

"Deal," replied Pat.

With that Dannie got down to the business of sending horses in the ring and wondered what would happen next.

True to her word, Dannie climbed the stairs to the booth and filled Pat in on her morning when given the opportunity by the work of the water truck and tractor.

"I don't get it, one day he is praising my selection and training of Summer, the next he's going ballistic over nothing," Dannie said.

"That's the way despots work," laughed Pat. "They are never happy you have done the right thing, only that you have done what they can be happy about or take credit for. And going over their head never makes them happy. On another note, did you know that you will be announcing the stake class Sunday afternoon?"

"Me? How did that happen?"

"W will be marking the card and I will be running the timers. We both told Langston we insisted on you being the announcer."

"Who will run the gate?" Dannie asked.

"Summer or Logan, whoever is finished; just not Mikey. We insisted on that too."

Dannie laughed and gave Pat a quick hug. "Looking forward to it," she said. "Now I'd better get back to the gate, we're on the down side of the day now."

It turned out her comment was a bit premature. The class scheduled to begin after the tractor work was the 1.0 meter Jumpers. The fences were about three feet tall; certainly not high by jumper standards and the class was often used by intermediate riders or trainers that were giving experience to young horses.

On this day the class had twenty-five riders competing and was nearly half done when Michaela Reynolds' assistant trainer, Meaghan Parks, came to the gate on a young horse, Hell Bent, which was currently in training with their barn.

HB, as they called him, was having difficulty keeping his mind on his job and was giving his owner no end of problems. Neither Michaela nor Meaghan was worried, HB was even-tempered and had talent. On the other hand at his young age he had the attention span of a toddler so the two women were working on him to create a better ride for the owner.

Michaela had schooled Meaghan in the warm-up arena and she would stand by at the gate and watch the round from the ground. It was always helpful to riders to have an experienced eye observing. To the untrained eye it was only a horse jumping poles and galloping between the jumps, but to those in the know there was so much going on in a two-minute round and every round was a learning tool for both horse and rider.

Meaghan trotted into the ring on HB as Pat announced the pair and then sounded the tone to indicate they could begin their round.

From the moment Meaghan asked HB to canter, his youth was in evidence. He moved forward quite willingly, but his canter was rangy and disjointed. Meaghan tried to pull him together in a more compact frame and he shook his head and became somewhat light on his feet. It wasn't so much a buck as an exaggerated up and down motion.

"Someone feels good today," Michaela said to Dannie. "Big oaf, at least he's having fun."

Dannie smiled and nodded in agreement.

Meaghan jumped the first four jumps in the course with little evidence of trouble, though Dannie knew she was working hard to keep the big guy's mind on his job. The fifth jump in the course was at the far end of the ring, almost exactly diagonal from the gate and HB approached it quietly and more focused than he had any of the first four.

But in the blink of an eye, it all went wrong. On the landing side of the jump, HB threw his head in the air, let out a squeal and pulled his enormous hindquarters underneath him in an attempt to dart forward. Meaghan was ready for him; they were after all, normal actions for an exuberant young horse. She held fast to the reins and as she began to turn for her next jump Dannie saw her smile at the horse's antics.

HB, however, was having none of it. If he couldn't run forward he would spook and leap sideways. He did just that and Meaghan was caught unaware just enough that she lost her center of gravity and slipped off the side of the horse, landing in a sitting position in the sandy footing, laughing.

With no rider, HB felt even more boisterous and he squealed again and kicked out as he passed the sitting Meaghan. There was a sickening thud that Dannie and Michaela heard clearly and Meaghan fell backwards, prone and no longer laughing.

At that moment, as in many moments of urgency or stress, time simultaneously slowed to a crawl and yet Dannie's senses were heightened to the point that without trying she was aware of everything, no matter how small, happening around her.

The second the thud was heard, Michaela took off across the ring at a dead run. She yelled, "Get the horse," to her groom without breaking stride.

At the same moment, Dannie heard an "Oh God" from the usually calm and controlled Pat.

Dannie herself had started after Michaela, but just as quickly stopped, grabbing some clean towels off her table that were meant to clean equipment but had not yet been used. As she started to run across the arena she raised her radio to her lips and said, "Drew...Andrew Polski, to the Jumper ring...now."

She willed herself to sound calm yet to also convey her sense of urgency to the show medic.

"On my way," came Drew's voice over the radio.

Covering the last thirty yards to Meaghan, Dannie felt anxiety at what she would find. The distance and the jumps in the arena had not allowed her a clear view, but it had appeared to her that Meaghan had been kicked in the face. As she reached Meaghan and a now kneeling Michaela, Dannie was relieved to see no injuries to her face, but relief turned to more anxiety almost immediately.

While conscious, Meaghan was eerily quiet and pale. Michaela had unbuttoned her hunt coat, the jacket riders donned for the show ring, with the intent of loosening the top buttons on her shirt. But as she opened the coat, both she and Dannie saw a crimson stain on Meaghan's chest that seemed to be increasing in size.

Dannie dropped to her knees placing one of the towels over the blood and began to apply pressure. "I swear, Meaghan, what you won't do for a little attention." Her attempt at sarcasm was as much to reassure Meaghan as to quell her own panic. The blood was already starting to soak through the towel.

Michaela was holding Meaghan's hand and Meaghan, as so many riders were likely to do, was worried only about her horse.

"He didn't mean it, Michaela," she said, "he was just playing. Is he alright?"

"HB's fine. Don't worry about him; just lay still until Andrew gets here." Michaela exchanged a worried look with Dannie.

Having already discarded the first towel off to the side, Dannie was applying pressure with the second when Andrew arrived. Andrew Polski served in the medic position at many of the shows where Dannie worked and he had the confidence of riders and staff alike.

Dannie removed the towel and moved to the side so Andrew could evaluate the situation and though he said nothing, he pointed toward Meaghan, indicating Dannie resume the pressure while he stepped to the side and used his radio to ask the office to call an ambulance. Whatever he saw he didn't like and he wasn't wasting any time.

Andrew continued his conversation on the radio, answering questions from the 9-1-1 dispatcher as conveyed by Chelle, while Michaela chatted about nothing with Meaghan to keep her calm.

Dannie was in danger of soaking through the third towel when the ambulance arrived, led by Langston and Kent in a golf cart.

After briefly speaking to Andrew, one of the paramedics approached Dannie, putting his hands on her shoulders. "I'll take over," he said kindly.

Dannie stood and moved back, watching the team work quickly to prepare Meaghan for transport. She felt a little numb. No one involved in this sport was unaware of how dangerous it could be yet they were all masters at putting that out of their minds; that is, until accidents like this happened.

Meaghan was already on the stretcher and two of the paramedics began wheeling her to the back of the ambulance. The third, carrying a gear bag, stopped for a moment next to Dannie. "You guys did a great job."

"Will she be OK?" asked Dannie.

"We'll get her to the ER so they can work their magic," he smiled and moved on to the rig.

"You didn't do a great job at all." Dannie turned to see Langston, staring contemptuously at her.

"What?"

"Did you even read the staff handbook?"

"WHAT?"

"Chain of command. You are to call the medic, then the office, then Kent, then me. You are to follow the procedure in the staff handbook."

Dannie was staring at her hands, incredulous. It was only then she noticed they were covered with blood, Meaghan's blood. She held them up in front of her, palms facing Langston.

"Sorry, I've been a little busy."

Langston turned slightly green and grabbed at the golf cart for support. He evidently didn't do well with the sight of blood. Good. Dannie wished he had fainted dead away. She couldn't get over the ridiculousness of his current issue.

She reached down and picked up the three discarded towels and began her walk back to the gate.

"Dannie!" barked Langston. "I'm not done with you."

"That's too bad because I'm done with you; I'm going to clean up." She continued walking without turning around to see his response.

That evening found Dannie sitting near the hotel pool again, Jake at her feet. They had the area to themselves for the moment. She had arrived from the show nearly two hours before and had already showered, washed her hair and walked across the street to the school yard to throw the ball for Jake.

Summer had stopped her as she was loading her car that afternoon and offered to bring dinner back to the hotel. Dannie's first reaction was to decline; her overwhelming desire was to lock herself in her room with Jake and avoid the world. She had reconsidered though when it occurred to her she really needed to talk with Summer one on one.

She heard the metal gate in the fence around the pool open and close and turned expecting to see Summer but it was instead, Chelle.

"Oh, hey!" said Dannie.

"Hi," Chelle replied. "What are you doing out here? I just caught sight of Jake as I was passing by."

"Summer's bringing dinner. Would you like to join us? I'm sure there'll be plenty."

"Oh thanks, but no. I'm looking forward to some solitude," said Chelle. "Rough day for you, huh?"

"A bit stressful, but it's Meaghan I'm worried about. Any news?" questioned Dannie.

"There was nothing up to the time Drew filled out his medic's report in the office. Langston was having a go at him because no one bothered to 'respect the chain of command' but Drew was having none of it. He told Langston that he should be happy that competent people responded to the situation and prevented a more serious state of affairs. He also reminded him that since Langston is on the same radio channel as Jen and I and Drew himself, all he needed to do was listen and he would know everything it was necessary for him to know."

"Love it," Dannie smiled. "Glad to hear that someone trounced Langston's 'superior' gene, even if only for a moment."

Chelle was standing, arms folded around a pastel-colored file folder. She glanced down and with a small start said, "Oh, I almost forgot, you didn't pick these up." She thrust the file folder in Dannie's direction.

Dannie took the folder and perused the contents; it was the three copies of the Steeds 4 Soldiers flier she had requested.

"Thanks Chelle. I did forget."

"Are they important?"

"I don't know really. Jeff introduced me to a colleague that's new to the Silver Shores PD; he came to the Egg-stravaganza last Sunday. He was in the military and was extremely interested in the charity, the soldiers presenting the colors, well, everything about it really. I'll probably learn more when I'm home next week, but I just thought the more bits and pieces I can collect, the more helpful something might be; hence the fliers," she said waving the folder.

"Mmmm," Chelle said. "Have you had a chance to take a look at the Silver Shores prize list draft?"

"Unfortunately, yes. It's a disaster. I worked on making notes a bit last night but it's a little overwhelming, it's so bad."

"I'm with you," said Chelle. "Let me know if I can help."

"Hello ladies!" Summer called from the gate.

Chelle and Dannie smiled and waved.

Reaching the table, Summer plopped a large paper bag at one edge and began removing the contents. "I found a great deli. I got some fruit salad, broccoli salad, chicken salad and marinated mushrooms," she said, raising her eyebrows to seek approval.

"Sounds great," Dannie said.

"I bought plenty, Chelle," said Summer. "Can I interest you in dinner?"

Chelle thanked Summer but declined and with a cheery wave headed off to her hotel room.

As she began serving herself from the various containers, Summer said, "I'm so glad you agreed to have dinner with me, but I've been worried all afternoon. Ever since you told me you wanted to speak with me, well, Dannie have I done something wrong?"

"Oh my, no. It's me, Summer. I feel as if I owe you an apology. I proposed you for this job because I thought you'd be great at it, and you are, and it furthered your goal of having the financial means to finish your education as well. But in order to continue to be good at the job you have to like it. And I wanted you to like it, yet for the nearly two weeks we have been together it seems all I have done is complain. Every time I turn around I'm in a disagreement with Muriel, Kent, Barb, Langston... I've done my best to make it look like the most miserable job in the world."

"Dannie, you forget I've known you for far longer than these last two weeks. I rode at Rossi Farms when you and Brian were together and I have appeared as a rider at your gate many times. No apology from you is necessary. You suggesting me for this has created such an opportunity and opened a door I thought was closed for good."

Dannie managed a half-smile. "I had a long talk with Pat the other night and he convinced me that I take these things too much to heart. Knowing I have just a few days left I am trying to see things differently but I felt my attitude has done you a disservice and I wanted to tell you so.

"Thanks," said Summer. "Don't worry about me though; I am one of your biggest fans. You haven't steered me wrong yet on anything you've told me about this job and like I said, I am so grateful for the opportunity. I also know how much you put in to doing the best job you can. What I'm trying to say is that overall, I respect you and the job you do and I appreciate everything you're trying to teach me. Don't ever apologize for things like that."

Dannie was touched by Summer's words but before she could say so, her phone trilled. She glanced down and said, "Oh, I have to answer this."

Dannie tapped the phone to begin the call. "Hi Drew, any news?"

She listened intently, absent-mindedly scratching one of Jake's ears with her free hand. It was a short, one-sided conversation and in less than a minute Dannie said, "Thanks so much, Andrew. See you tomorrow."

Dannie placed her phone on the table and said to Summer, "That was the medic, Andrew. I asked him to call if there was any news on Meaghan. Did you hear about that?"

"Oh, yes. Please don't tell me anything bad."

"All things considered it sounds good. Evidently when the horse kicked out and connected he hit her shoulder and something; a loose nail in his shoe maybe, tore the skin and nicked an artery, or vein, I'm sorry, I'm not very good at anatomy."

Summer shrugged. "Go on," she said.

"Well, as you heard it was a short conversation and not a lot of details but Andrew says the doctors have taken care of it and though she will be off for a bit, Meaghan will make a full recovery. I'm so relieved."

"Ditto," said Summer and she raised her diet soda can in a toast. "To Meaghan and a quick and complete recovery."

"Absolutely," Dannie said "clinking" her water bottle to complete the toast.

Changing the subject Dannie asked, "How's everything in the Main Hunter Ring?"

"Mostly good. Mike Gregory is an idiot, nothing's changed there. Trainers and riders have been really good about getting to the ring and I finished a bit ahead of schedule today. Barb and Muriel never brought lunch to Bec."

"What?" screeched Dannie.

"They took her order about ten along with the rest of us, brought everyone's lunch but hers by noon, apologized profusely and said they'd take care of it right away and never came back. Petey went and bought her something."

"It would seem all they need are brooms and big, pointy black hats to make the characterization complete, the old peahens," muttered Dannie.

"And I'm sure this will not be a surprise, but Mike is completely overwhelmed with the responsibility of this sportsmanship award that Langston saddled him with at the staff meeting. He's asked Logan and I to help, and Logan and I want you involved too."

Dannie laughed. "Yeah, not surprised. Of course I'll help you both."

Summer started packing up the food. "I guess we should be going in," she said.

Dannie nodded and reached down to scratch Jake under the chin. "What do you think, buddy? You ready?"

Jake jumped to his feet, immediately wagging his huge otter tail.

Summer laughed, "I just love Jake."

"Me too," Dannie smiled. "See you tomorrow?"

"Wouldn't miss it," said Summer.

Dannie began to walk toward the gate, and then turned. "Summer...thank you. Thank you so much." And before Summer could respond, Dannie and Jake had gone.

-13-

Sunday morning dawned bright and clear and warm. 'This is it', Dannie thought as she and Jake drove to the show grounds. By evening, she would have closed a chapter of her life; one that between riding, showing and working at the shows had been twenty years in the making. She knew she would still be involved through her association with Silver Shores but it was to be a completely different situation.

She felt tremendous excitement and a strong melancholy at the same time. Horses and showing weren't an interest, for Dannie they had been a way of life. She was giving up a life that though far from perfect was comfortable and known.

On the other hand, she had not forgotten the counsel of her dear Pat. The things that drove Dannie to distraction about this job were not going away, in fact if anything, they were escalating. Horse shows of today were often run by men and women that had left the welfare and love of the horse out of the equation. Those in charge were greedy, or self-important, or domineering, and sometimes all those rolled into one. There were exceptions of course, but not nearly enough for Dannie to keep trying.

She had to look forward to the new opportunities life was offering her. A life with Jeff and Robbie and the chance to prove that shows could still be presented as she believed they could. She had complained long enough, with Silver Shores she had a chance to put her theories into practice and produce the kind of show she knew was possible.

As she pulled into a spot in the staff parking lot, she resolved to enjoy her final day at the starter job come what may. She opened the lift gate for Jake and instead of jumping out immediately as he normally did he stuck his big, square nose toward her face and gave her an enthusiastic, sloppy kiss on the chin as if to say, "We've got this, Mom."

The first half of the day was not much different than every other Sunday at a horse show. The last classes of the many jumper divisions were being contested with show championships awarded and Dannie was kept quite busy. There was, however, one very noticeable difference.

Throughout the morning, trainers, riders, ring crew, even some parents came in a steady stream to Dannie's gate. They thanked her, lamented her departure, related a funny story or shared a memory of some common moment or experience.

No one was more taken aback than Dannie herself. She hadn't told anyone it was her final day and had, true to her nature, hoped to just fade away from the job. But it was such an outpouring she was sure some of her friends had been passing around news of her leaving.

She was so touched but though she thanked everyone that came to speak with her, beyond that, words failed her. She felt she could quite easily become emotional and she wished to avoid that.

She was just four horses from awarding ribbons in the final division before the ring crew set for the jumper stake. As she sent a horse in the ring, a movement caught her eye and she turned to find a woman pushing a wheelchair toward her. Meaghan Parks, the assistant trainer that had taken an ambulance ride to the hospital just a few days prior was the chair's occupant. When she caught Dannie's eye, she beamed.

"Hi there," said Meaghan, "I couldn't miss your last day."

Dannie rushed to hug her but when she bent to actually do it, hugged her as if she was made of glass. "Meaghan, I can't believe you're here! I'm so glad to see you, how are you?"

"I have a way to go but the doctors say I'll be fine."

Dannie clasped her hand and said, "I'm so glad, you've been in everyone's thoughts."

The woman standing behind the wheelchair thrust her hand out to Dannie. "I'm Denisa, Meaghan's mother."

Dannie shook the offered hand. "So pleased to meet you."

Denisa continued. "We know you are working and we don't intend to keep you but we came specifically to tell you something."

Meaghan jumped in. "I had to thank you, Dannie, for helping me."

"Oh, Meaghan, of course you're welcome but you would have done the same for me."

"You were so kind. I was so scared and you made me feel like everything was going to be OK. I...well; we all are going to miss you so much. It won't seem right without you on a gate," Meaghan said.

"I too wish to thank you," said Denisa. "Thank you for taking care of my daughter."

"We take care of each other. Well, most of us do," Dannie smiled. "And we are fortunate to have someone like our medic,

Drew, right here, but you're most welcome. Thank you for making a point to stop and say hello."

Over Denisa's shoulder Dannie saw fellow starter, Logan Peters heading her way. It would seem his ring, Hunter 2, had finished and he would be taking over Dannie's gate while she went up with Patrick and W to announce the jumper stake. Logan's backpack hung from one shoulder and he ambled toward her, joking with exhibitors as he came.

Dannie had known Logan since he was a young teenager just starting out on the ring crew. He'd spent many hours sitting at her gate and while on the crew asked many questions and showed an interest in learning to be a starter. He was smart and a natural for the job; people loved him and he'd done well.

"Hey, Miss Dannie! Reinforcements have arrived," Logan joked as he reached her table. "How long until the stake?"

"Two left in this class, then we set and walk," she answered, referring to the practice of riders taking time before the class to walk the path they intended to ride. They stepped off the distance between jumps and got a birds-eye view of any possible issues they might encounter while on course.

"Perfect," Logan said. "Go take a bathroom break or get some water or something if you want. I'll finish it up."

"Oh no," she said, "I'll..."

"Nonsense. Go on. Mr. Jake and I will visit until you get back."

Jake thumped his tail in agreement upon hearing his name and after a moment's hesitation Dannie headed to the office for a bottle of water.

She returned five minutes later to find the course designer and crew in the ring setting an entirely new course for the stake class. When they were done, the tractor and water truck would do their work and then riders would have the opportunity to walk the course. All in all, the class itself wouldn't start for nearly an hour.

"So, anything I need to know?" Logan asked.

"Well I think the way this is going to go is we will present the sportsmanship award first. Langston wants to do that in the ring so as I start the intro you can make sure you have recipient, trainer, and Langston ready to go. Then Kent tells me some of his soldiers from Steeds 4 Soldiers will be presenting the colors for the National Anthem and then we'll start the class."

"Seems simple enough," said Logan.

"You know this class is also a Lower Valley Jumper Bonus class," Dannie said. "Langston has been on my ass all day to promote the hell out of it. I feel like all I've talked about is jumper bonus, jumper bonus, jumper bonus," she said making a face.

The Lower Valley Hunter Jumper Association was an organization based in Fryetag and surrounding areas whose membership was comprised mostly of local riders, trainers, and owners. They gave special cash awards to their members fortunate enough to place well in the stake class and Langston was beside himself they'd selected the Coast with the Most Show to host the class.

"OK," Logan said, "I'll stoke the fire right along with you." He picked up the mic and began a detailed explanation of the Bonus class and how it worked.

Dannie thought she should probably make her way up to the judge's booth but she had one more thing she wanted to say to Logan. He was still speaking so she glanced behind her to see the soldiers practicing their drill for presenting the flag. They seemed to be wrapping up and a thought struck her but Logan was also done and she turned her attention to him first.

"Logan, before I go up...."

Logan took one look at her face and held up his hand. "Do not get all sappy on me, Dannie."

"No, I....."

"This is harder for me than I imagined," Logan said. "Ever since I started working shows, you were always there. Whether you were riding, helping your husband's barn, doing a gate, well, you were always so kind to me."

Dannie could feel tears beginning to burn her eyes and she waved her hand dismissively, hoping Logan wouldn't continue. But he did.

"No. Let me get this out. I learned a lot of what I know about this job from you. No one knows better than you that sometimes it feels like just us starters against the rest of the show trying to get them through the day in spite of themselves."

She nodded.

Logan continued. "I know you'll be at Silver Shores, but I couldn't let you go without telling you how much I have enjoyed working with you, what a great job I think you do and how much you'll be missed. I wish you the best and wherever your life takes you, give 'em hell, Dannie."

Logan stepped forward and hugged Dannie and two of the very tears she had been trying to avoid plopped on his shoulder.

She gently extricated herself from the hug and again waved her hand, for the moment unable to speak. She had no idea she would react this way but she had suddenly come to a startling revelation.

Throughout her childhood her dad had told her again and again, 'the important thing is a job well done. Pride is to be found in the compassion, the accuracy, the satisfaction and the detail of doing your best each and every day Dig ditches or build empires, if you do your best you will experience the same sense of self-worth'.

Suddenly, Dannie understood in a way she hadn't before. This job had taught her so much; she had improved her skills in dealing with people, she'd benefitted from daily 'lessons' in showing and horsemanship from the judges she worked with each day, learned to stand up for herself and discovered you create your own opportunities by always demonstrating a willingness and eagerness to learn what others could teach. Some days at the job had been tough, but no day had been wasted.

But this, the unexpected procession of people taking a moment out of their day to let her know how they felt, this was what her father had been speaking of. This was the feeling of a job well done. She realized she had never cared about the managers; trying to make them happy was like trying to rake leaves in a tornado. But to have the acknowledgement of the trainers, riders, and maybe most importantly her co-workers sent her away today knowing she had done her best.

The starter's job was a strange one. Most people outside the horse world couldn't even understand what it was. As happens with every job, in no time people wouldn't even remember she had done it. But at this moment, in her heart she knew she had given it her best and she hoped to take the lessons learned forward to the next challenges in her life.

Dannie used the back of her hand to wipe away the tears as she hugged Logan once more. "I can't tell you how much that means to me. Thanks, Logan. Now, I'd better get ready for the stake class. I'm not done yet!"

She reached down and picked up her backpack and Jake's leash and began heading toward the raised judge's booth. She smiled as she passed by the five soldiers that had been practicing their flag ceremony just moments before and was no more than a few steps beyond their little group when she stopped and turned.

Before she spoke to Logan it had occurred to her that she might be able to gather a bit of information for Miles. Kent and Muriel were nowhere to be seen so she was assured of no interference but she was confident that just asking a bunch of questions would get her nowhere.

She thought she recognized the very man Miles had spoken to last week, a man who at this moment was flashing a mega-watt smile in Dannie's direction.

"Hi," said the man. "You work here?"

Dannie couldn't help but notice he was movie star handsome. She shrugged her shoulders, giggled, and then speaking in a higher voice than normal said, "Yeah, I do a few things for the show. What are you doing here? I don't think I've ever seen soldiers at a horse show before." She giggled again.

The man walked the few steps to where Dannie was standing. "I'm Bobby. This your dog?"

Dannie shrugged again as Bobby reached down to pet Jake. "Yeah, this is Bruno and I'm Amber."

She had no idea why she had acted this way but it had clearly been the right choice, Bobby seemed to go for the simpering airhead type.

"Well, Amber, do you know anything about all this stuff?" he said as he waved his hand in the direction of the arena.

Dannie giggled again and shook her head. "Oh this is jumpers. I know that, but there's too much math stuff in jumpers for me."

"Math stuff?"

"Faults, penalties, time allowed...too hard," Dannie said adding a pouty lip for emphasis. "If you're a soldier though, I bet you're smart enough to understand it."

Bobby hesitated and then looked around him, for what, Dannie wasn't sure. "I'm not supposed to tell anyone this but I know you won't say anything."

Dannie shook her head in an exaggerated motion from side to side and then pantomimed zipping her lips and throwing away the key.

"I'm not a soldier. None of us are. I'm an actor," said Bobby.

Dannie fought any sort of reaction save what 'Amber' might do. "An actor? I think actors are really cool. Are you doing a movie or something?"

"No, I don't know why this guy has us doing this. He contacted my agent and got a bunch of clothes at the military surplus store and here we are. It's no feature film, but an acting gig is an acting gig."

"And I'm sure you're really good, Bobby. Well, I'd better take these papers to the people waiting for them. Hope to see you again."

Dannie climbed the stairs to the judges booth not sure what she had expected to hear but quite sure the reality was much more than she expected.

The moment Dannie entered the judge's booth Pat took her to task.

"Did my eyes deceive me? Did I just see you flirting with that soldier down there?"

"Actually yes, but I call it information gathering."

"News of this could get back to Jeff," Pat teased.

"Not likely. That guy down there thinks my name is Amber."

Pat and W laughed as Dannie pulled her hair into a ponytail and threaded it through the back of a baseball cap. Then she reached in her bag and pulled out a pair of oversized sunglasses.

"What are you doing, Miss Dannie? Are you taking up espionage?" asked W.

"Well, I'll never be mistaken for Mata Hari but blonde bimbo got me the desired results. Jeff's cop friend, Miles, wants more info on Kent and Muriel's charity so I gave it the old college try."

"Any luck?" asked Pat.

"Don't know, I'll let you know after I speak to Miles."

"Why the change of 'look'?" asked W.

"In case he looks up here I want to be under the radar for now. How about we get ready for my swan song," she said, smiling.

As previously planned, the first order of business that afternoon was the presentation of Langston's sportsmanship award. Dannie had told Pat and W the reasons she, Summer, and Logan had made their choice.

"Karen Butterfield has been riding and showing as long as I can remember. Her young son shows too. A year ago she was diagnosed with an extremely aggressive form of cancer and she's been fighting so hard. She had her eye on this show as her return to the show ring since she recently finished her treatments. She has the most saintly horse and her trainer has been keeping him fit and show-ready so she could do this. She shipped the horse and came to ride, but realized on warm-up day that she just didn't have the strength or stamina to show. She and her trainer were sitting in the food area shortly after she made the decision and they overheard a mom and daughter talking about going home. The daughter was clearly crushed and Karen asked the mom why they would go home before the show even started. She replied that her daughter's horse had come off the trailer lame and she wouldn't be able to ride. Karen immediately took them to meet her horse, Jasper, and offered him to the girl to show this week. They ended up Reserve Champions in the Children's Hunters."

"Just like a movie of the week," said W.

Dannie made a face. "I know you're joking, W. Karen Butterfield has been supporting and cheering on other riders forever. This last gesture just made her the perfect choice."

Dannie looked toward the back gate and received a thumbs up from Logan. She had prepared her remarks about the award, Langston, and most importantly, Karen Butterfield, and as Langston, Karen and her trainer began walking to the center of the arena Dannie eloquently made the case for this year's nominee.

In typical Langston fashion, once the trio reached the center of the arena he never stopped flapping his gums. Dannie knew he wasn't listening and could only hope that he would know it was time to present the beautiful bronze when the crowd cheered.

"I'm sure you'll agree this was any easy choice to make this year," Dannie said. "On behalf of the Coast with the Most horse show; show manager, Langston Rubicon, Esquire; and show coordinator Kent Mallory; we present the sportsmanship trophy to this year's recipient, Karen Butterfield."

Langston, still talking, received a nudge from Karen's trainer. He turned and handed the trophy to her and she, in turn, handed it to Karen.

After a moment's hesitation, Langston took the trophy from Karen and again handed it to her trainer then took her elbow to lead her forward for a picture.

The trainer turned to Karen, held the trophy out to her and gestured for her to come forward for the picture.

"What the hell is he doing?" asked Pat.

"Oh god, this is like the Keystone Cops present trophies," said Dannie. She picked up the mic and this time, off the cuff, began talking about Karen and memories of her through the years. She did her best to fill the awkward silence during the photos and the exit from the arena with Langston about three strides in front of the two ladies.

When they reached the gate Karen and her trainer continued back to the barns but Langston stayed with Logan. He was clearly agitated and waving his arms wildly. Dannie was curious, but she needed to continue.

She welcomed the spectators and thanked them for their attendance, introduced show officials, talked about the Lower Valley Jumper Bonus, explained how the class would be judged and finally, talked about Kent and Muriel's charity, asked for donations, and introduced the Steeds 4 Soldiers color guard.

She stumbled over one sentence in the prepared text about the charity. It indicated that the Steeds 4 Soldiers program was housed at Forrest Equestrian, Sunshine and Blimpy's facility. She was surprised Sunshine hadn't mentioned that to her.

The color guard lacked the expected military precision but still did a respectable job and once the national anthem was concluded the first horse in the order entered the ring.

Dannie announced the horse and rider, Pat sounded the tone for the round to start and they were underway. At that same moment, Langston burst through the door of the booth, frazzled, red-faced, and looking to unload on someone.

"What the hell was that?" he bellowed.

"Langston, lower your voice," Dannie begged.

"Why didn't you tell me?" he said, though not one decibel more quietly.

"We did tell you...this morning...Logan and I," said Dannie.

"Well, I, you didn't, I mean, I don't think." Langston sputtered and stammered because he knew Dannie was right. "It's supposed to go to a trainer," he said finally.

"You never said that," Dannie said.

"Of course I did. It goes to the trainer that brought the most horses to the show."

The first horse had finished and Dannie paused to announce the score for horse and rider and introduce the next competitors. Then she turned in her chair to look at Langston, standing behind her, right in the eye.

"Then why do you call it a sportsmanship award? You should call it the who-brings-the-most-money-to-my-show award," she said.

"Your opinion is of no consequence in this," Langston barked. "Pay attention to the job at hand and don't forget...Lower Valley Jumper Bonus!"

Dannie hoped with that he would leave, but instead he retreated to the corner of the booth, muttering to himself. In spite of Langston, she, Pat and W worked together as the professionals they were and the class progressed smoothly. The only deterrent to the enjoyment of the afternoon was that every five horses or so, Langston would pace behind the three friends murmuring 'Lower Valley Jumper Bonus'.

After thirty-two rounds of good competition and an exciting jump-off, the winner of the class was amateur rider, Kevin Turner. Langston had mercifully left the booth to be part of the awards presentation but Dannie was feeling the pressure of 'Lower Valley Jumper Bonus' ringing in her ears.

Logan sent in the top eight finishers in the class for the trophy and ribbons and Dannie picked up the mic and said, "Please join me in welcoming Kevin Turner, winner of this year's Lower Valley Jumper Boner Class."

There was a moment of complete silence and Dannie thought, "wait, what did I say?"

She didn't wonder long as both Pat and W howled with laughter. At the same moment, Langston spun from his position in the arena to glare at her up in the booth. The spectators cheered and hooted loudly and even Kevin stood in his stirrups to applaud her.

She was momentarily mortified and then her sense of humor took over. She rose from her seat and bowed to the masses below her which earned an even louder ovation. Sitting back down, she composed herself and presented awards with decorum. She invited the winners to a victory gallop and then said to her friends in the booth, "That's it. I'm done."

W, still chuckling about her gaffe, said, "I declare Miss Dannie if that isn't the way to go out." He stood and enveloped her in a big bear hug. "Don't be a stranger, girl. I'm so going to miss looking over to see you in that booth. There aren't many like you, for sure."

Teary again, Dannie pushed to free herself. "Stop, W, don't make me cry."

W ignored her, bestowed a kiss on her cheek and said, "Love you, kid." He picked up his briefcase and overcoat and with radio and clipboard in the other hand, headed out the door and down the stairs.

She began collecting her things too and turned to look at Pat, who looked as if he was also about to speak.

"NO! Not one word," Dannie said. "Don't you say a thing, leave me some dignity. I don't want to sob and disappoint you. I will see you in a few weeks at Silver Shores."

Pat wrapped his arms around her and hugged her tightly. He put his lips next to her ear and said, "Don't you know by now that nothing you could ever do could disappoint me." As W had, Pat kissed Dannie's cheek and left her alone in the booth to compose herself.

Dannie turned in her clipboard and radio at the office, letting Jake have one more treat before the drive home. She found Summer, and made sure she understood the procedure for picking up her paycheck from Langston.

"See that little table over there and the line of staff?" she asked Summer. "Get in line and he will write your check when it's your turn. Don't forget to hand him that ridiculous handbook."

"What? But I filled out my pay sheet three days ago."

"I know. He wants to see if you'll take less. The whole process reminds me of Oliver Twist asking Mr. Bumble for more gruel. Stand your ground and don't take less. I'll wait until you get paid."

While waiting, Dannie sat down at a table with Bec. She looked exhausted, pale, shrunken, but she brightened at the sight of Dannie.

"So you're done? No regrets?"

"I'm done," said Dannie. "Onward and upward, right? And I'll see you at Silver Shores before we know it. Do you have far to go tonight?"

"Staying here tonight and then to the airport in the morning. Can't wait to see my dog and kitty."

"I bet, it would be torture to leave Jake behind."

"Dannie, I want to thank you again for all your kindnesses," said Bec.

"Nonsense. We're friends. I'm not being kind; friends spend time with each other."

"Nevertheless, I'll never forget you."

"You won't have the chance. I'm going to haunt you at Silver Shores. I will expect you to have dinner at the house with Jeff and me at least a couple of times," Dannie smiled, though she felt some unease at this conversation.

"Love to," Bec said. She hugged Dannie and said, "Be happy, my friend."

"What?"

"You know, in your new not-a-starter life. Now it's time for me to head back to the hotel," said Bec and she did just that.

Dannie waited long enough to ensure Summer received her check and then she and Jake made their way to the SUV. She had loaded all her things this morning before she left the hotel and with Jake now loaded up and ready to go she pulled out of staff parking and headed off the show grounds. She was teary again and felt sad, but with every mile nearer to the interstate she started to feel lighter and happier. She called Jeff and told him she was on her way, and then she turned on the radio, increased the volume and sang at the top of her lungs the rest of the way home.

-14-

It was just after seven when Dannie turned into the u-shaped driveway of the beach house. She was home! Though it had only been three weeks it seemed much longer and she could hardly believe she was finally here. Even Jake was standing; pacing back and forth and whining as he looked out the window at the familiar surroundings.

She stopped the SUV and flung her door open, drawing a deep breath of cool ocean air…heaven. She walked to the back of the car and opened the lift gate for Jake who launched himself from the opening and ran with tail erect and ears flopping, disappearing around the side of the house. He would satisfy himself with rolling and cavorting in the sand. He never went far.

The front door opened as she was collecting some of her and Jake's belongings. Jeff walked toward the SUV with a huge smile of greeting. He met Dannie, kissed her on the cheek and took the bags from her hands. She turned to go retrieve more and Jeff stopped her.

"No. Leave it all and I will unload your car. Come inside."

"But….."

"D, come inside."

They reached the foyer and Jeff placed the bundles on the floor against the wall. He turned and took Dannie by the shoulders. "Now it's time for a proper 'hello'."

He kissed her so tenderly she could barely breathe for the happiness she felt at that moment, and then he wrapped his arms around her, chin resting on the top of her head and said,

"Tell me we won't be doing that again for the foreseeable future."

"That?"

"The three week absence. I'm not a fan." Jeff kissed the top of her head. "Now, go pour yourself a glass of wine and find a spot to relax on the back deck. I'll unload the remainder of the car and park it in the garage then I have steaks and vegetables to grill."

"I'll help, Jeff..."

"D, away with you," he smiled. "I'll be out in a minute."

She acquiesced. "OK, where's Robbie?"

"Oh, funny thing," Jeff said with a silly smile on his face, "today the Rob-ster and I were grocery shopping and we ran into Donte and his mom."

"Donte? From his class?"

"The very same. Well, I guess I was whining about how long you'd been gone and how much I'd missed you and next thing we knew, Donte's mom invited Robbie for a sleep over tonight."

"But it's a school night," Dannie protested.

"Oh, so it is. Well, mom will see that both boys are at school on time tomorrow morning. I guess that means we have the whole evening to ourselves." He smiled and gave her a conspiratorial wink then calmly walked out the front door to unload the SUV.

Dannie did as Jeff suggested and helped herself to a glass of her favorite red blend. Just before she stepped through the sliding door leading to the deck she took note of the quickly encroaching fog and donned a bulky cardigan.

She settled into an Adirondack chair putting her feet up on the hexagonal bench-type seating around the fire pit. Low flames were dancing invitingly and convincing the chill to stay at bay. Dannie took a slow sip from her wine glass and closed her eyes, deeply breathing in the salty air. This was bliss!

A sand-encrusted Jake bounded up the steps from the beach at almost the exact moment Jeff stepped through the glass slider with a large tray, barbeque tongs and a beer for himself. Jake plopped on a towel they kept for him outside and Jeff headed toward the grill along the deck railing.

"Hungry, D?"

"Until five minutes ago I didn't think so, but yes, I'm famished."

"Happy to be home?" Jeff asked.

"I don't have words to describe it. I feel so much lighter. I was worried it would be hard to put my carney life behind me but I'm already more relaxed."

She went on to tell him more about the last three weeks; the good and the bad. Jeff told her about his current cases, and about what Robbie had been doing. They talked of nothing really, just reveled in the luxury of inhabiting the same zip code.

While Jeff finished preparing the dinner Dannie grabbed a brush and rid Jake's coat of any remaining sand and a few minutes later, Jake led the way into the house where Dannie fed him as Jeff readied their plates.

Dinner was delicious and Jeff and Dannie spent the meal happily in each other's company. Dannie took a moment to remind herself such moments counted as one of the few benefits of a life on the road. She had learned to appreciate an evening like this; good food, great wine, being in the company of the one you love. Others called it "the little things" but Dannie knew it wasn't a little thing at all. It was everything.

Jeff cleared their dishes to the sink and pushed the 'start' button on the coffee maker. "Apple crisp?"

"Get out!" Dannie said. "You did not make apple crisp."

"OK, you got me; Mrs. Peretti had just made some at Ravioli Brothers when I stopped in. She was taking heat from her sons for the non-Italian baking so she gladly sold it to me." Ravioli Brothers was Jeff's favorite deli in Silver Shores.

Dessert equaled the deliciousness of the dinner and feeling full and happy, Dannie and Jeff drank their coffee in front of the fire in the great room.

"I took tomorrow off," said Jeff. "You're mine for the day."

"I'm yours every day."

Already holding her hand, he raised it to his lips and kissed it. "What does your week look like?"

"Well, I think I'm going to hit the ground running. Tuesday morning I have an appointment with Jerrold Ryan, you know, my financial advisor. Then Wednesday I've been invited to Tootie Bittler's home to lunch with her and Mary Jane. I'm guessing they want to talk about the summer shows," Dannie said.

"Anything Thursday?" asked Jeff.

"No, why?"

"We're having dinner guests, I mean, if you're on board with it we are."

"Sure," said Dannie. "Who?"

"Miles is chomping at the bit to talk with you about this Steeds 4 Soldiers group."

"I actually have some information for him. Don't know how helpful it will be, but...you said guests, like more than one. Who else?"

"Miles wants to bring the woman that runs the local equine therapy group for soldiers, first responders, and such."

"Oh, he's really serious about this, isn't he? Are they involved?"

"Involved? Oh no," said Jeff. "I think they are both just passionate about the work her group does."

"Well, sure. Invite them both and make sure they know we are casual," she said with a laugh.

Jake was snoring soundly on his bed by the fire as Jeff took Dannie's mug from her hands and placed it with his on the raised hearth.

"I'll deal with these dishes in the morning. Now it's time for some serious one on one time with my girl." He offered his hand to Dannie, who took it and rose to walk with him to their room where through the huge west-facing window the sun dipped below the horizon leaving a blazing riot of red, orange, yellow and pink streaks across the sky.

Monday didn't disappoint though again Dannie delighted in the normalcy of it all. She arose to a clean kitchen with all dishes done and put away, then she and Jeff had breakfast in town at a favorite café and bakery right on the water. They returned to the house and Dannie started the first of multiple loads of travel laundry before they headed out on a beach walk behind the house with Jake and his ever-present stick tagging along.

In the early afternoon, she and Jeff went together to pick up Robbie from school and from that moment until Dannie read him a bedtime story he was bubbly, excited and chattering a mile a minute. She could tell he had missed her.

As Dannie prepared to sleep she marveled at how lucky she was to have this little family full of love. It would be even better when the divorce from Brian was final and they could go ahead with their plans. She hadn't told Jeff about her talk with Brian. She was afraid to jinx everything and wouldn't say a word until the signed papers arrived. As she began to drift into sleep, she considered the possibility they may not arrive. No matter, she had everything she wanted right here inside the four walls of her home. She had perhaps the most relaxing sleep she'd experienced in many nights and it would be many more nights before she had another.

As predicted, Tuesday was the beginning of several full days for Dannie. After dropping Robbie at school, she headed for her appointment with Jerrold Ryan.

Ryan was her financial advisor and had been a great help to her in negotiating her sudden, sizeable inheritance. He had worked many years with her father, Joe, and when Dannie had first met him she thought if Joe had trusted him she could too. Jerrold Ryan had proved equal to the challenge.

Today's meeting was part of a quarterly review that Jerrold wholeheartedly believed in. He insisted on transparency both to and from his desk and liked to guarantee he and his clients were on the same page. Dannie had a few extra questions for him at this meeting.

Jerrold himself met her in the lobby of the complex and escorted her back to his own office. The furnishings were tasteful and comfortable and the large window looked out on the bay.

She accepted the offered cup of tea and settled into a butter-soft gray leather armchair.

"So good to see you, Danica," said Mr. Ryan. "I trust you have been well?"

"Oh yes, and you?"

"I can't complain," he said smiling. "Do you have any questions for me before we get down to the repetitive part of our review?"

"Actually, yes," said Dannie. "I...well; I don't know quite how to ask this. I'm a very private person, Mr. Ryan, and quite cautious when it comes to my finances. I just have never talked about money and never felt it was anyone's business but my own, even when I didn't have much. In the past few months several people, people that are certainly not in my confidence, have made comments leading me to believe they know more about my worth than I would wish them to. How could they possibly know? Is there some gap I need to close that I am unaware of?"

"A good question, but I suppose I don't have the answer you would want. You know the story. Your father started his company with a couple thousand dollars and a great idea. He worked incredibly hard, the company grew through that hard work and a bit of luck, in fact grew I think beyond his biggest dreams. It eventually became a publicly-traded small company and Joe was a majority shareholder and very successful. When he made the decision to retire he sold his shares, a substantial amount, and he was bound by the requirements of the SEC in doing so. Are you with me so far?"

Dannie nodded.

"I don't have to tell you your dad was a by-the-book kind of guy and this was no exception. We spent many hours filling out forms, dotting every "I" and crossing every "t" and jumping through every SEC hoop we had to. But back to your question; sales of this magnitude are reported and become public knowledge. The basis of these reporting regulations is transparency to the markets and to other shareholders. So, while it isn't front page news, the information is available if one wishes to find it."

Dannie frowned. "OK, but how do we get from that to someone knowing my worth?"

"Did they actually give you a figure of some sort?"

"No, they just said things like 'someone in my position'."

"Well an estimate of your inheritance could be inferred with some intermediate math skills and the publicly reported information, but it would be difficult for anyone to know what assets your father had or investments he made after his retirement. Do you feel threatened in some way?"

"Oh no, like I said I'm just very private and the people making reference to the funds are some I wish to know as little about me as possible."

"I understand completely, Danica, but I'm afraid you may have no choice."

She agreed, albeit grudgingly, then drank her second cup of tea while reviewing her current portfolio and discussing any potential changes.

Just before leaving, she told Jerrold about an idea that had been floating around in her head. She'd told Jeff about it yesterday and he was one hundred percent on board so she now gave Mr. Ryan the task of exploring the options and getting back to her which he promised to do soon.

Dannie turned into Tootie Bittler's sweeping circular driveway on Wednesday at five minutes before one. Her invitation had been for one on the dot. Perched on the top of a hill, Tootie's home was accessible only by the winding driveway.

She parked facing a beautiful fountain surrounded by a carpet of blooming, seasonal flowers.

At the front door she was greeted warmly by both Tootie and Mary Jane and invited by Tootie into the library. Dannie had never been here and so far, the house was impressive.

The three entered the library and Dannie was presented with her first surprise of the day.

"Dannie, you're here!" Sunshine Forrest rose from her chair and gave Dannie a huge hug.

Tootie spoke. "Sunshine has offered a very generous sponsorship for the summer shows and has indicated she would like to help in any way she can so Mary Jane and I thought you wouldn't mind if we invited her to join us for lunch."

"Mind? I'm delighted," said Dannie.

"Actually, the plan is for the four of us to have a light lunch and then at three we'll be joined for tea by Kent and Muriel Mallory," Tootie added.

"I see," Dannie said dubiously.

"Please excuse me while I go check on the lunch, I'll be right back," Tootie said. "Dannie, there are some beverage selections over there on the cart, please help yourself."

Dannie wandered over to the cart and selected a Waterford glass already filled with chilled water while Mary Jane and Sunshine conversed about the selection of books on the many shelves in the room. It gave Dannie a moment to look around her.

She chuckled to herself that Tootie, Mrs. Bittler Number One, and Mary Jane, Mrs. Bittler Number Two, had joined in a seemingly unlikely alliance to pull off the Silver Shores Summer Series.

In many ways they were night and day. Take the library here for example, thought Dannie. Tootie had done her library in pure hunt country fashion; polished wood, stone fireplace, leather, plaid, brass fixtures and silver trophies of days gone by.

Conversely, Mary Jane's library reflected her to a tee with antique white furniture, floral prints and wallpaper, crystal vases and picture frames.

Dannie liked each woman very much and hoped the collaboration on the show would work out for them both, for all of them really. After last year's fiasco she wanted to see the venerable old shows succeed.

Tootie returned from the kitchen and invited her guests to follow her to the dining room which Dannie found to be on par with the beauty found in the rest of the house. The centerpiece of the room was a flawless dining table and chairs that appeared to have been in the family for years though still in pristine condition. Today it was beautifully set for four and bespoke of Tootie Bittler's wealth in the same understated and comfortable manner as the rest of her home.

The room was awash in natural light from the floor to ceiling bay windows that looked out on a terraced coastal garden. Dannie admired the immaculate flagstone pathways winding amongst beds of ornamental grasses and sea lavender. Scattered throughout were large ceramic urns filled with yarrow and marigold and hanging baskets brimming over with fuchsias in shades of red, pink and purple. Beyond the garden from the edge of the mountain was a spectacular view of the Pacific Ocean.

The four friends took their seats and almost immediately a woman appeared with a tray of four delicate Meissen bowls filled with fragrant, steaming crab bisque.

"This is my friend first, and my cook second," Tootie said smiling. "This is Grace and as you all know I don't cook but she does and she is incredible."

Grace, placing a basket of crusty sourdough rolls on the table, blushed though Dannie could tell she was pleased at the compliment. Grace disappeared back toward the kitchen and Tootie spoke again.

"Alright ladies, let's get right to business. Please, start your meal but let's brainstorm while we eat. Danica, I hope you will start. We are aware you have some concerns."

"Oh, uh...well, yes, I do." Dannie felt like a bug under a microscope but decided to press on. "Let's start with the prize list."

"Oh yes!" Mary Jane exclaimed. "Can you believe it is already done and ready to go to print?"

"Actually it's not, far from it." Dannie noticed Mary Jane's sudden frown. "When Chelle told me there was a completed draft, I asked her to print me a copy. It was nowhere near ready to print. It was all wrong."

"In what way?" Sunshine asked.

"In every way. In a word, it was a disaster. Some required divisions were missing altogether, some were there but with the wrong specifications, some were missing prize money, or the prize money offered was incorrect," Dannie said.

"Oh dear," said Tootie, "It looked so nice. But I'm afraid none of us would know anything about the rest of it."

"Unfortunately, neither does Kent Mallory," Dannie said disparagingly.

Tootie sipped her iced tea. "Dannie, I must ask. I know you were unhappy we did not choose you as our manager. Does what you're telling us now have anything to do with that?"

"Absolutely not! If a show doesn't follow the rules and regulations of the sanctioning organizations there can be fines, large ones, and more punishments if they feel like it. Not to mention if the classes aren't held to specification they won't be eligible for year-end points and that will create a boatload of unhappy exhibitors. I'm trying to help…I thought you knew that." Dannie felt a great deal of frustration as she had the overwhelming feeling she had quite an uphill battle in store for her.

"We know you are," said Sunshine. "But Kent says the look is so important and this was so beautifully done."

"If I hear about 'the look' again I may scream," Dannie said. "It can still look nice, but that means nothing if it is not also correct and easy for the exhibitors to find the information they need."

"What can we do?" Mary Jane asked.

"I've taken the liberty of going through the copy I had and rewriting most of it. There is a company in town that can take my flash drive containing the original draft, with corrections, and have it ready for you to preview by Friday."

"Wonderful," said Tootie. She looked at the other two at the table and asked, "Are we agreed that Dannie should get us a corrected copy by Friday?"

Mary Jane and Sunshine nodded enthusiastically and it was decided.

Grace had returned to take off the soup bowls and having removed them to the kitchen came back with four beautifully presented Pear and Cranberry salads. Complementing the two main ingredients were red leaf lettuce, crumbles of bleu cheese, red onion, and toasted walnuts. Dannie managed a small smile as she thought, "It's perfect…of course it is."

Tootie continued. "Now, I alluded to it a moment ago, but let's get the elephant out of the room. Dannie, I'd like to hear your thoughts about Kent and the manager position."

"You don't make much small talk, do you Tootie?" Dannie laughed and the others joined in. "My concern is that Kent knows less than nothing about what it takes to run a horse show. We all know I had my problems last year with Jimmy and Darlette, but they both had a history in the business, had been competitors themselves, and they studied the industry. They had the respect of the exhibitors and you need that."

"But Dannie," said Tootie, "men command respect. We all know that. Kent will too."

"Oh, not you too. I think respect is earned, not commanded. He might be a great event planner, but when it comes to this business he has no one's respect, not to mention he's a liar."

The table fell silent and Dannie feared she had crossed some invisible line.

"I mean, I think he's a liar. Sunshine, at Langston's show Kent had me read something about his charity that said all the horses were housed at Forrest Equestrian. Is that true?"

Sunshine's look of confusion was answer enough, but she said, "Why no, he has no horses at our place. I need to speak with him about that."

"Please don't," said Dannie. "I mean, we need to get along leading up to the Silver Shores shows and I don't want to anger him. You can talk later, can't you?"

Sunshine agreed and Dannie didn't say that she really wanted to make sure he wasn't tipped off before she had the chance to speak with Miles. She left her knowledge of the actors playing soldiers completely out of the discussion.

The meal continued as the women heard from Sunshine regarding her mostly successful attempts to acquire sponsors and from Mary Jane about her favorite pastime, finding first place awards. Dannie could only hope this year's prizes would be an improvement over the stuffed red squid and sequined crab pillows from last year.

The clock was approaching quarter to three and Tootie suggested they retire to the library for the tea planned for three with Kent and Muriel.

"Ladies, I may ask you to repeat some of what we have already talked about here. As Dannie said earlier it is important we all get along right now and to that end I prefer my anticipated guests believe this was just lunch among four friends and nothing more. Alright?"

"Tootie, you sly fox," thought Dannie. She knew that Tootie had not reached her position in the world by being vapid and foolish and she had just proved she was much more aware of so many things than she ever let on.

Kent and Muriel arrived fifteen minutes late and firmly cemented a strike against them both in Tootie's book. She insisted upon punctuality but in this instance made no remark.

Just as she had cautioned, Tootie revisited their conversations from the lunch table as if they had never happened. She asked Dannie to explain the problems presented by Kent's version of the prize list and though he clearly wasn't happy he made no argument when told Dannie would be having a new draft produced. Sunshine and Mary Jane repeated their parts as well, and then it was Kent and Muriel's turn.

Muriel, obviously cowed by her surroundings and Tootie's presence, spoke meekly of her intention to take charge of the organization of ribbons and awards during the shows and she offered her help to all present in the room with anything they may need.

Kent spoke grandly of his plans for nightly events, the traditional exhibitor party held on Friday of the first week, and the amazing man he had hired just to announce each week's Grand Prix. It did not escape Dannie's notice that he uttered not a word about the actual administration of the horse show.

It was almost four-thirty when Tootie brought the meeting to a close while extracting a promise from everyone that they would meet once a week until the horse show began. She gave Sunshine a pass if she was not able, but it seemed she was up to traveling from Southern California to help any way she could.

Tootie pulled Kent aside for a one-on-one conversation and Dannie began to gather her things. She saw Muriel approaching out of the corner of her eye and wondered if it would be too noticeable if she grabbed everything and ran.

"Dannie, may I speak with you?" Muriel said sweetly.

"Sure."

"I wanted to talk about the last few weeks," Muriel said.

"What about them?"

"I feel as if we got off on the wrong foot, you and I, and I wanted you to know I gave a lot of thought to what you said about how we were treating Rebecca."

"Did you," Dannie said flatly.

"Yes, really, I did."

Dannie said nothing and waited.

"So I was just thinking, er, wondering, could we start again? It would mean a lot to me. I just think the stresses of a new situation, well; it didn't bring out the best in me. Could we?"

Dannie smelled a rat, but she had to admit it was possible that Muriel was sincere. It was very important to her that they all find a way to work together to make the three weeks of Silver Shores not only happen but to ensure they be a success so she said, "OK, I guess we could."

"Oh, wonderful!" Muriel exclaimed and lurched forward to hug Dannie.

Dannie however, stepped back and extended her hand. "How about we start with a handshake?"

"Oh yes, of course," Muriel said and nearly shook Dannie's arm off.

-15-

By Thursday morning, Dannie was beginning to recapture her routine. She dropped Robbie at school and then returned to the house to take Jake for a run on the beach.

After about forty-five minutes of dedicated play, she left him wet and covered with sand on his towel outside and went in to shower and dress for the day. By the time she was ready, Jake was somewhat dry and she was able to knock most of the sand from his fur. She let him in, fed him, and then left him to his morning nap while she drove in to the local grocery store in Silver Shores to buy what she needed for the night's dinner with Miles and his friend.

Jeff had been called to work sometime around two AM but had assured Dannie he would be back for their dinner well before six.

An hour or so later when she arrived back home, Dannie tidied up the house and the back deck, prepared her serving pieces, set the table and started her meal prep so the actual cooking would not take long.

Just before one-thirty she took a quick break to pick Robbie up from school then spent the afternoon finishing her preparation. She was dressed and ready for guests at just after four-thirty.

Dannie congratulated herself for a productive day as she headed for her phone. It was Bec's birthday and she had planned to be ready for their company early so she and Bec could have a talk without feeling rushed.

When she heard her friend answer, Dannie said, "Hey Miss Rebecca. Happy Birthday! My present to you is that I am NOT going to sing the birthday song."

Bec laughed and said, "Your flowers arrived and they're beautiful. Thank you so much."

"Of course. You sound great, how are you doing?"

"I've been feeling a little tired but Montana and my critters work on me just like the best medicine there is."

"As long as you are ready to come to Silver Shores in a few weeks; things are starting to come together."

Dannie and Bec talked about everything and nothing and had the sort of conversation friends often have. They laughed, told stories, and teased one another, compared dog antics and when Dannie hung up almost forty minutes later she was confident being home was the best thing for her friend right now. She sounded wonderful.

A quick check of the clock told Dannie she had enough time to feed Jake and Robbie before everyone arrived. While Robbie ate his chicken strips and corn-on-the-cob, Dannie told him about their company and suggested he could curl up in her bed and watch television while the adults talked. As he considered that a rare treat, he readily agreed and Dannie had just helped him into his pajamas and plumped up his pillows when the doorbell rang.

Dannie opened the door to a petite woman with shoulder-length auburn hair and piercing green eyes.

"Yes?"

"Danica?"

"Yes," Dannie said somewhat dubiously, suspecting a door-to-door solicitor.

"I'm Celia Prentice, Miles Wolcott's friend."

"Oh, come in! That wasn't very welcoming of me," Dannie laughed. "Why are you here by yourself?"

"Evidently Miles and your husband were having trouble getting away in time to pick me up. I drove here and told Miles I would drive him back to his car later tonight. He is riding over with your husband."

"Celia, Jeff isn't my husband...yet. We are engaged, but..."

"Well, Miles speaks of you both as if you're married so, honest mistake, I guess."

Dannie escorted her guest into the kitchen, poured a glass of wine for them both then led her out to the deck where the low flames in the fire pit swayed invitingly.

As they chatted, Dannie found she liked Celia immediately. She was unpretentious, warm, well-spoken and was very taken with Jake. It was a must that guests liked Jake, Dannie thought with a smile.

The big dog's wagging tail and alert demeanor announced the arrival of Jeff and Miles. They walked out through the opening in the glass door with beers already in hand, and it didn't escape Dannie's notice that Jeff looked exhausted. He'd been awake and working for nearly eighteen hours and she was sure the role of host was not high on his list right now.

"Hey, D," he said wearily. "Miles and I are going to get out of these jackets and ties, OK?"

"Of course. Miles, let me show you to the guest bathroom. You can freshen up there," Dannie said.

She introduced Jeff and Celia before guiding Miles inside. Before rejoining Celia on the deck Dannie checked on the rice cooker and started the oven to preheat for the main dish. She had decided to make chicken in a tarragon cream sauce with rice and asparagus. It was a good meal for guests but not labor intensive and the tarragon was from her herb garden.

She picked up the bottle of wine she had opened previously and took a small tray of simple appetizers out of the fridge and returned to the deck. Jeff had reappeared looking more comfortable and moments after Dannie came outside Miles returned as well.

"So, Celia, please tell us about your program," Dannie said.

"Well, we call it The Farmstead. We are a 501c3 non-profit and our mission is to offer therapy for PTSD to veterans and first responders."

"Equine therapy?" asked Dannie.

"Yes, but we also have a horticultural aspect to our program."

"Really? That's part of the therapy?" asked Jeff.

"Sort of. Many similar programs just focus on equine therapy, but we....oh, let me start at the beginning. About six years ago, my husband inherited a beautiful piece of property right on the coast."

"Husband?" Dannie said.

Celia laughed. "Surprised that I'm married, Dannie?"

"Oh no, I'm sorry. But had I known, well, he should have come with you."

"He stayed home to feed animals and clean stalls. We're on a shoestring budget and we want every cent donated to go to the program so we both have jobs and our early mornings and evenings are dedicated to our chores."

"You both work forty hour weeks and administer this program too?" asked Jeff.

"I work about twenty hours away from the farm and Mack, my husband, about thirty. Anyway, our property is a bit south of here. It's twenty acres, some of it clear, some wooded, with a lovely view of the ocean in several spots. Mack fought in the Middle East and the plight of many of our returning vets has been something we've felt strongly about for many years. When he inherited the property we just knew we could use it to do some good."

"Miles, you've been here such a short time. How did you meet Celia?" asked Jeff.

"I volunteered for a similar program near where I lived back East. The program director there referred me to Celia when she knew I was relocating."

"Do you have a background with horses?" asked Dannie.

"No, and I don't work with the horses. But I have, for lack of a better description, 'cred'," said Miles. "I was in Afghanistan, and now I'm a cop. When I go out to The Farmstead, I usually wear my hat with the 1st Infantry insignia on it and maybe a polo shirt that says Silver Shores P.D. I don't bother any of the clients, but if they want to talk, I'm there. I usually don't talk much, I just listen. Not as a therapist, of course, just an ear if they want one. I really like working in the garden, and living in an apartment I don't have much opportunity to do that."

"Tell me about the garden," Dannie said to Celia.

"Mack and I thought it would be a neat idea to use some of the land for a big community garden. It's not part of the official therapy, but we grow flowers, vegetables and even have some fruit; almost all the work in the garden is done by the clients. On the whole, The Farmstead is very peaceful and the clients seem to like working with the soil and being a part of the garden. We don't sell any of it, those that come to The Farmstead are invited to take home whatever produce or flowers they wish to."

"What a great idea," said Jeff. "I'd love to see it."

"You and Dannie would be welcome anytime. We don't normally give tours when our clients are there. Their comfort and privacy is our primary concern and we don't want them to feel as if they are on display," Celia said.

"Of course," Jeff said, nodding.

"No, I hadn't finished. Your job in law enforcement and Dannie's experience with horses would probably ensure you fit right in. Whenever your schedules permit let me know, if it's not convenient, I'll tell you," said Celia.

"The privacy aspect of the program is why I reacted the way I did at the Gala Horse Show. I was so surprised to see soldiers from Steeds 4 Soldiers at such a public event," Miles said.

"Well, Miles," said Dannie, "I think I have some information you'll find very interesting. If I don't finish my meal prep, however, we'll never have dinner."

"Need help?" asked Jeff.

"No, there's only about fifteen minutes left before it's downright cold out here. You stay out and talk and we'll continue this shortly."

Dannie had everything ready when the rest of the party came in from the deck twenty minutes later. They sat down to their meal and almost immediately Miles was back to the subject of the soldiers at the show.

"So Dannie, what did you learn?"

"Well, the Mallorys have been pushing Steeds 4 Soldiers at every horse show in the last several weeks. As you know, the soldiers were there to present the colors at the show you attended, Miles, and they were there at the show I worked last week in Fryetag. Well, it didn't register with me one way or the other until you said you got such a strange reaction from the one soldier at the Gala show, so when I saw the same guy last week in Fryetag I thought I'd see what I could find out."

"And?" said Celia.

"It would appear they are actors, all five of them."

"Actors!" Miles exclaimed. "How did you find that out?"

"The guy told me himself. I utilized a little blonde bimbo flirtation," said Dannie.

"Oh, did you now?" said Jeff with a wry smile.

"It worked, didn't it?" Dannie said with a wink. "But I don't see the harm, I mean; they are trying to fundraise without exploiting their clients, right?"

"I don't see it that way," said Miles. "They are being introduced as veterans, they are wearing the clothes to appear to be veterans, Mr. Mallory is deluding people into the belief they are donating to people like these men...actors. Who knows what these Mallory people are really doing? As far as the men; while it's not illegal to impersonate a soldier, we that have actually served call it 'stolen glory' and we feel very strongly about pretenders."

"There's more," said Dannie. "They gave me a flyer with information to announce and part of that information was the location where the horses for the program are housed. The problem is I spoke to the owner of the facility named and no animal belonging to Kent Mallory lives there."

"Do you have one of those flyers?" asked Miles.

"I do," Dannie said. "I'll get them when we finish eating."

She glanced toward Celia who had stopped eating and looked utterly dejected.

"Celia, what is it?" she asked.

"This doesn't sound good. I know a lot of people throughout the country that do great work with equine therapy and I've never heard of these people. I don't know everyone so I'll give them the benefit of the doubt until we learn more but if they are fake..." Her voice trailed off. "Well, Mack and I work so hard. The care and feeding of seven horses is not cheap and it's never-ending; stall cleaning, veterinary work, shoeing, feed, bedding. Every penny matters. If Steeds 4 Soldiers is a fraud, it makes it hard for all of us legitimately trying to help to find the needed funds because bad seeds affect the credibility of us all."

Miles reached out and touched Celia's arm. "I'm going to look into this. I'll talk to the lieutenant and if he's hinky about it I'll do it in my off-duty time. Don't worry."

"Dannie and I will help any way we can, Celia," Jeff assured her.

"It's funny. I haven't found either Kent or Muriel Mallory to be my cup of tea, but just yesterday she apologized to me and wanted to be friends," said Dannie.

"I don't believe her," said Jeff.

"Maybe not," said Miles, "but play along. We don't want to give her reason to suspect anything."

"Dannie scoffed. "I don't think she's bright enough for that."

Dannie stood to clear the plates and said, "How about we have our coffee and dessert by the fire. It's my favorite place on a chilly night."

Dannie took a moment to look in on Robbie and found him sound asleep. Jake was also asleep with his big head on the boy's shoulder. She wished she could just stand and watch as he slumbered; such a guileless, happy little boy. But she knew this was not the time and she headed to the kitchen to retrieve the tray with coffee and dessert for the four adults.

Settling in next to Jeff on one of the love seats, Dannie longed to lift the pall that had come over Celia. She was so animated and alive when talking about her own program that Dannie took that direction.

"Celia, can you tell me more about PTSD?"

"Oh, it's hard to describe in just a few sentences. It's an anxiety disorder in which a person reacts to trauma they have suffered. Not everyone that experiences trauma will develop PTSD and there is no time frame; one person may react within weeks of their trauma, some years after. There are some that say over 50% of PTSD cases are not treated."

"Wow," said Jeff. "How do clients come to you?"

"We take referrals; commanding officers, local mental health professionals, people that feel our program could have some benefit. We take military and first responders, you know, cops, firemen, paramedics."

"And they take riding lessons?" Jeff asked.

"Oh no! Some may eventually ride, but our program is based on the clients reacting with and using the nature of the horse to learn about themselves and to help us help them. We want to help them improve their communication and coping skills, to resolve some of their trigger factors and to regain a sense of more control over their life. We try to provide a non-threatening environment where our clients can take whatever time they need and utilize the therapy and professionals available to them to let healing begin."

"Well, it's no secret I love horses," said Dannie, "but how do they help here?"

"Some have said that our clients and the horses have a symbiosis, of sorts. Both of them are often hyper-vigilant to their surroundings, you know, the fight-or-flight-response. When we teach horsemanship skills; grooming and such, the clients learn the horses are mostly accepting and non-judgmental and we have a place to start. Oh, I feel like I'm leaving so much out," sighed Celia.

"No doubt you are," laughed Dannie, "but I look forward to learning more and it will give us a reason to get together again."

"I would really enjoy that," said Celia. "I really should be going though. Can I help with the dishes?"

"Oh no, I have Jeff for that," she said, giving Jeff a jab in the ribs for emphasis.

"Are you ready then, Miles?"

Miles nodded his assent and while they gathered their things the two thanked Dannie and Jeff.

"Dinner was delicious, this was a great idea," Miles said.

Dannie walked them to the door while Jeff excused himself to move Robbie to his own bed. Dannie stood on the porch until they were safely away and re-entered the house noticing a definite silence.

She walked to Robbie's room and found him tucked in and sound asleep. Jeff wasn't in the kitchen so she walked to the bedroom and found him on the bed, fully dressed and dead to the world.

Dannie removed his shoes and covered him with a throw she had handy. Then she returned to the kitchen to wash dishes and think about everything she had learned and wonder about all the questions she still had regarding Steeds 4 Soldiers.

-16-

The next two weeks passed at breakneck speed. Robbie's first school year was nearing completion and there were small projects to finish as well as preparation for the year-end program for parents. Jeff and Dannie saw very little of each other. As tourist season began in earnest, crime, at least in the town of Silver Shores, had increased and Jeff was putting in a lot of overtime.

Dannie was working tirelessly on the horse shows. As promised, she had delivered the corrected draft of the prize list to Tootie and Mary Jane and they in turn had made sure Kent and Muriel had copies.

Though both ladies clung steadfastly to the idea that Kent was the man for the job, with 'man' being the operative word, they hadn't consulted him further on the prize list and had given their seal of approval for it to go to print.

There had been two more meetings since the first at Tooties and the one thing abundantly clear to Dannie was that Kent was worthless. He liked to talk about doing things but he didn't seem to put his words to actions.

Aside from the prize list her first big project had been to tour local lodging establishments for staff housing during the shows. She even tried looking in to private rentals or alternative-type lodging but that had shown itself to be a logistical nightmare to coordinate so she abandoned that idea.

She finally settled on two separate motels as neither could accommodate the staff in total and with luck on her side, negotiated a reasonable price. Tootie and Mary Jane had agreed to the arrangements so now Dannie spent her evenings contacting judges, starters, ring crew, and any manner of support staff to verify their arrival and departure dates. She determined who was flying in, who was driving, who needed rental cars and began work on a budget for the staff per show week.

Truth be told Dannie felt this should have been done weeks ago but Tootie and Mary Jane had no idea where to begin and Kent couldn't, or wouldn't, accept any of it as his responsibility.

Their next meeting was scheduled for Wednesday at Tootie's home as the others had been. They were now just five weeks from the shows and Dannie was feeling the pressure. She was so anxious to have the shows go well and it seemed as if her list of to-do's just got longer, not shorter.

The Wednesday of the next meeting proved to be cold and foggy and as Dannie drove up the hill to the Bittler house she was thankful for the heated seat option in her car.

Just before Joe died, Dannie had been thinking of a new vehicle, but her inheritance had sent her in a different direction. Parked in the garage of the beach house were two lovely automobiles; Judith's luxury sedan and Joe's top-of-the-line SUV. Dannie sold her old faithful car to the son of one of Jeff's co-workers, sold Judith's car too, and decided to upgrade by keeping Joe's pride and joy. At no time was she more grateful for his penchant for every option available as she was on days like this that chilled you to the bone.

Tootie had planned today's get-together for two-thirty. Dannie entered the double doors of the library five minutes before the scheduled time to join Tootie, Mary Jane and Sunshine. There was no sign of Kent or Muriel.

"Hi, sweetie," said Sunshine. "You look positively frozen, come sit by the fire."

Dannie gratefully sat next to Sunshine and said, "So silly being frozen in California at the beginning of summer but that's the coast for you."

Tootie nodded her head in agreement while shooting a worried look in the direction of her foyer. "I'd like to get started, but I don't wish for everyone to have to repeat themselves when Kent and Muriel arrive." This had become a habit and she could barely contain her agitation.

"How about I start by telling you my progress with the staff lodging," Dannie said. "I don't believe Kent cares about that anyway."

The three women agreed and Dannie ran down the work she had done, the results, and what was left to do to check the task off the list. In total, she spoke for about five minutes at the end of which the Mallorys still weren't present.

Just about to continue regardless, the group heard a commotion outside the library and saw the Mallory's had let themselves in. Kent entered the room and sat in a large, leather armchair sporting an attitude as if he were the one that had been kept waiting.

Tootie spoke. "Kent, I feel I must protest your continued tardiness for these..."

"Couldn't be helped," he snapped. "Can we move along?"

Tootie was clearly taken aback but her good manners prevented her from continuing.

Dannie spoke again. "I'd like to go over our staffing. I have a list of positions for each week and if we run through them quickly we can potentially determine any gaps."

"Great idea," Sunshine agreed.

Dannie began with week one. She read staff names for the office, judges, ring crew, and then came to the starters. "For week one, actually for all three weeks, our starters are Logan Peters, Bill Roberts, Sylvie Andrews from the south, and Summer Stanton. I think..."

"You left out Mikey Gregory," bellowed Kent.

"No, I didn't. He is not hired as a starter here."

"What if I say he is?" Kent sneered.

"Say whatever you want, he is not going to serve as a starter at Silver Shores." Dannie could see Kent had come to the meeting with a huge chip on his shoulder, but she was determined to press on.

"If you have a job for him, Kent, that's fine but it will not be at a back gate. He is completely ineffective at the job."

Kent appeared ready to explode when Muriel spoke up, "That's OK, he can help with awards; my whole job actually. It's looking as if I may have to go home during week two to take care of some business that can't wait and Mikey will be a great help."

"Well, that's settled then," Tootie said. "Sunshine, would you like to fill us in on sponsorships?"

Sunshine ran through quite an extensive list of individuals and businesses that had agreed to sponsorships of classes, divisions, and events throughout the show. To no one's surprise she had done an amazing job.

When Sunshine finished speaking Dannie had one thing to add. "I guess this is just as good a time as any to let you know that I am offering a $5000 sponsorship for one of the classics, amateur or junior, but I want the sponsorship to be in the name of The Farmstead."

"Oh, thank you Dannie!" Mary Jane said enthusiastically.

Kent glowered. "The Farmstead? They are our competitors."

Everyone in the room save Muriel looked confused.

"The Farmstead is the local 501c3 serving veterans and first responders with equine therapy for PTSD," said Dannie. "I thought it would be nice to have a local sponsor and I am doing it in their name because they spend every cent donated to them on their program. As to competition, I wouldn't think that's a word that would be used regarding two organizations dedicated to meeting a need. All help is good. Besides, they're not fundraising; the money is going to the show simply to put their name on a class."

Kent looked blackly at Dannie and Muriel let a frown cross her face like clouds cross the sun on a windy day before saying, "Kent, dear, we, I mean the show, needs all the sponsors it can get."

Kent seemed to relax marginally and Dannie thought it may have occurred to him that if he went too far he was jeopardizing a good paycheck and possible future work.

The group continued to cover scores of details large and small in their preparation for the shows and Dannie thought more than once how sweet and helpful Muriel was proving to be. She hadn't forgotten the cautions from Jeff and Miles but it seemed as if maybe Muriel had actually turned a corner.

Just after four-fifteen, Kent stood and said he and Muriel had to leave. Mary Jane agreed that she should be heading home too. The three of them said their goodbyes and agreed to be present the following Wednesday for the next meeting.

Dannie began to gather her things and Tootie said, "Danica is it possible for you to stay just a moment or two longer?"

"Um, sure. What's up?"

Tootie glanced at her watch and said, "It's cocktail time, how about we move to the kitchen?"

It turned out Sunshine was staying until tomorrow morning so the three women walked to the kitchen and sat down on bar stools surrounding the large island.

"What can I get you ladies?" asked Tootie.

"Nothing for me," said Dannie.

Sunshine said, "Tootie, I'll have what you're having."

Dannie, was feeling restless and ready to go home. "Was there something else, Tootie?"

"Yes, dear, it won't take long," Tootie said as she prepared two drinks. "Mary Jane and I have realized there is so much about this that we don't know, more than we ever imagined."

"Uh-huh," said Dannie.

"Well, I told her that I would speak with you. We are beginning to understand your hesitation with our hiring Kent as the manager of these shows. He seems to have far more interest in his charity and in collecting donations than in helping the show to succeed."

"Yes, he does."

"Oh, Danica, don't make me beg. I realize we are asking a lot of you and you are taking on much more work than you should have to. But we agree with you, we have to 'get it right' this year or the exhibitors likely won't give us another chance. It just seems too late to eliminate Kent and we need him for the special events. I just wanted to tell you we understand and we hope you will continue to work with us."

"Did you think I didn't want to continue?"

"Kent called all three of us yesterday and said you had been quite vocal in your displeasure of your role with the show," Sunshine interjected.

"Vocal to whom?" Dannie asked.

"He didn't say," answered Tootie.

"I imagine he didn't," Dannie said, "because it is a complete fabrication. I told you all directly that I thought his selection was a mistake, but that it was done and I would help you in any way I could. I have never uttered a word about him running the show beyond that."

"Why on earth would he say that then?" asked Tootie.

Dannie longed to share what she, Jeff, and Miles had discussed regarding the questions they had about Steeds 4 Soldiers but she had given her word she would not. So instead she said, "I believe he was hoping the information would anger you enough to eliminate me from anything to do with the shows. Kent doesn't like me and the feeling is mutual I admit. I don't trust him and I don't trust his intentions when it comes to the three of you. Kent is not what or who he seems to be, please just be careful."

"I have to ask, Danica," Tootie said, "after last year and the things that happened during your time at Silver Shores, why do you want to help us at all?"

"The responsibility of what happened last year falls squarely on the shoulders of Jimmy Bittler and Darlette Simon; at least it would if they were still with us. I found myself caught up in their circus of a relationship and what can only be described as Darlette's mental breakdown. The Silver Shores Horse Shows were the backdrop, not the reason. I have a sentimental attachment to the shows here. I have great memories of showing here as a kid, coming here as a part of Brian's barn and showing during the time we were married, and even working here these last years. Now that I am a member of this community, I want to see the shows thrive again. So as I said, I'll help in whatever way I can."

Sunshine stood and hugged her. "I feel the same way about Silver Shores. That's why I'm here too."

Suddenly, there was a rapid ticking noise coming from one of the doors leading outside. The noise got louder and abruptly a tiny, bedecked and bejeweled Chihuahua, toenails tapping loudly on the tile floor, burst into the room. It was Queenie, the neurotic, quaking pocket dog belonging to Tootie's daughter, Shelaigh Bittler. Today Queenie was wearing a fleece coat in a zebra print with copious rhinestones at the neck and hip. She ran directly to where Tootie was standing and began shaking uncontrollably.

Following her overanxious mess of a dog into the room was Shelaigh herself. Dannie and Shelaigh had a long history of conflicts; some personal, some horse show related.

Dannie, seven years older than Shelaigh, first saw her competing in the Short Stirrup ring when they were kids; from that moment Dannie found Shelaigh to be spoiled, entitled, vain and frequently, ill-tempered to a fault. Shelaigh was an average rider and though Dannie had always believed the purpose was to enjoy what you were doing, somewhere inside you had to at least acknowledge your limitations. Even as a young girl, Shelaigh was of the belief that she was due a horse that would do the work for her, a blue ribbon every time she stepped in the ring and woe be to anyone within earshot if that didn't happen.

As they grew into young women, the divide did nothing but grow wider. Possibly in an attempt to garner the attention from other men she had found lacking from her father, Jumpin' Jimmy, her clothes became tighter, skimpier, and more outlandish and her makeup more dramatic. The horse world was full of thin, beautiful girls, each more educated and with larger trust funds than the next. Shelaigh had done herself no favors becoming a common housecat amongst a coalition of cheetahs.

Dannie could not have been more different. As a young girl she was shy, unsure of herself and her favored position in life was in the background. She did, however, have two parents that supported and encouraged her no matter her interests and in particular a father that stressed hard work, pride, and a never-say-die attitude. Added to this, she had horses. She spent time with them, groomed them, cleaned stalls, learned about them and from them. All this assured that Dannie and Shelaigh never saw eye to eye.

Everything finally seemed to come to a head the previous summer. Professionally, Dannie and Shelaigh butted heads often as Dannie's job was to efficiently get riders in and out of the arena and Shelaigh saw no reason to be timely about anything, ever. Shelaigh had also traded her adolescent rages for the occasional tantrum peppered with far more whining and mewling. Dannie, on the other hand, had found her voice as she became an adult and had no difficulty expressing her opinion which did not sit at all well with Shelaigh.

By far the most complexity had occurred in their relationship as it pertained to Dannie's ex-husband, Brian Rossi. That summer at Silver Shores. Shelaigh and Brian had been an item and Shelaigh was determined Dannie would not get him back. Of course, Dannie didn't want him back but Shelaigh was not one to let the facts stop her.

But something else had happened at the summer shows. Dannie knew that she and Shelaigh would never be close friends; in fact, their differences were likely too great for them to be any more than acquaintances. But Dannie had observed things about Shelaigh as an adult that she hadn't seen or understood as a girl.

Shelaigh was a product of a father that was convinced, and more importantly who convinced her, she was never going to meet his expectations...about anything. There was desperation in her repeated attempts to find someone to accept her as she was, to love her for who she was.

Of course her mother, Tootie, loved her, but as happens so often we don't seek acceptance from the person that has already given it, but from the person who never will.

Dannie had empathy for Shelaigh's plight and now that Jimmy was gone that problem could never be resolved to her satisfaction. Both women had lost their fathers last summer and that had placed them in a club no one wanted to join.

Dannie had not seen Shelaigh since her father's funeral, but was pleased to see that although Queenie, the Chihuahua, was still clothed outrageously; Shelaigh herself had toned it down...a little.

She came into the kitchen and placed what appeared to be a gym bag on one of the bar stools. She then unzipped her jacket, exposing a black t-shirt and zebra print leggings. At least, thought Dannie, they aren't two sizes too small and covered in rhinestones. She had to admit she sort of liked them.

"Hi Mrs. Forrest, hello Dannie," Shelaigh said, reaching for a wine glass and helping herself from an already opened bottle.

Both women returned the greeting and Sunshine said, "Shelaigh, are you helping us this year with the Silver Shores shows or will you be riding?"

"I'll be helping Muriel with awards and hospitality. I'm still riding, but I'm not showing right now." Shelaigh looked pointedly at Dannie as she said, "I'm looking for a new trainer."

Dannie nodded but didn't invite any more discussion, she didn't want to know. Shelaigh had been training with Brian while they carried on their relationship. It appeared that was over but Dannie had no interest in details.

"If you will all excuse me," said Dannie, "I need to head home. I'll be here for the meeting next week." As an afterthought she added, "Nice to see you, Shelaigh," only half meaning it.

Dannie had been home about thirty minutes when Jeff arrived. Tonight he had promised Robbie they would grill hamburgers and Dannie had made a potato salad to go with the meal.

Jeff took a beer from the refrigerator and opened one for Dannie as well. He gave her a kiss and the beer and as she sliced onions, tomatoes, and cheese they talked about their day.

"Miles contacted Kent Mallory by phone today to ask about Steeds 4 Soldiers," said Jeff.

"You're kidding. How did that go?"

"Well, it wasn't in an official capacity. Miles has been doing a lot of digging and it continues to look worse for the Mallory's, not better. Today he called and introduced himself as a veteran and said he was interested in the program. Kent's first question was, 'would you like to donate?'. Miles said he would like to learn more about the program first. He asked about where they conduct the therapy, who the therapists are and what their qualifications are, how veterans are referred..."

"And Kent said?" asked Dannie.

"He was very evasive. Didn't really answer one question. According to Miles he spoke in platitudes and generalizations and when pressed for details the line went dead," said Jeff. "Several moments later Miles received a text from Kent that said he was so sorry but he was out of town and in a terrible cell area and he'd lost the connection."

"Of course that's what happened," laughed Dannie. "But it surely explains Kent's foul mood when he arrived at the meeting."

Just then, Dannie heard her cell ring and it took her a moment to realize it was in the bedroom where she'd left it upon arriving at the house.

"Sorry, babe, let me go answer that."

"No problem, Robbie and I will get these burgers going."

Fifteen minutes later, Jeff and Robbie came back in the kitchen bearing a platter of perfectly charred burgers. Dannie was sitting at the island, eyes shining with tears.

"Dannie, what is it?"

"Jeff that was Rebecca Kirtlan's daughter on the phone. Bec passed away this morning. She's gone," Dannie said as the tears began to fall in earnest.

-17-

"Mommy, what's wrong?" Robbie asked with alarm.

Before Dannie could form an answer, Jeff set down his platter and said, "Mommy just got some bad news, buddy. One of her friends has died and she's sad."

"You mean like Papa Joe?"

"Yep, like that. How about I make you a plate with a burger and potato salad and you can watch the TV while you eat," said Jeff.

"But I'm not allowed to watch TV during dinner, Jeff."

"Tonight you are, Rob-ster. Go find a show and I'll bring your plate right in."

Robbie did as suggested and Jeff quickly made up a plate and took it to Robbie with a glass of milk. He returned to the kitchen, turned the oven on warm and put the platter with the burgers inside. He walked over and sat next to Dannie, pulling her stool close to his and enveloped her in a huge hug.

"I'm so sorry, D. What happened?"

"Her daughter didn't give many details. She said her neighbor stopped by to give her half of a pie she had baked and found her on the floor. She was already gone." Dannie dabbed at her eyes with a tissue. "I don't understand, we just spoke on her birthday and she sounded great."

"You said it was pretty clear she had a problem of some sort," Jeff said.

"But surely she would have told me if it was this bad, I mean, she was all alone, who would want that?"

"I think she did, D. She made her choices and from the little time I spent with her she seemed to be an independent woman. Some people just don't want the fuss, they know what's coming and they accept it."

"I just can't believe it, Jeff. And yet, when we said goodbye at Fryetag, she told me to be happy and that she would never forget me. I thought she was just saying that because I was leaving the starter job, but I think she must have known. But then why would she say she'd see me in Silver Shores?" Dannie asked.

"D, just because people accept their dying doesn't mean they hope it won't be too soon. I think Rebecca wanted to and hoped to be at the summer shows but the powers that be had other plans. I know she loved you and appreciated your friendship. Any plans for a service?"

"Her daughter said she would call. Oh, damn it!" she exclaimed as a fresh flood of tears started to fall and she buried her face on Jeff's shoulder.

He held her for a moment then said, "Why don't we have a bite of dinner?"

Dannie shook her head. "I couldn't eat."

With raised eyebrows Jeff said, "C'mon, give it a try? You go in the other room and assure your son you are alright and I'll put out the food and pour you a glass of wine. Please?"

Dannie relented and managed to keep her composure for the remainder of the evening but long after the rest of the house was asleep that night she laid awake thinking about her friend, Bec, and what life would be like without that million dollar smile.

The next few days were conducted mostly out of habit for Dannie. She couldn't shake the thought of Rebecca dying feeling as if no one cared. But what had she said to Dannie; she was happy in Montana where her dog and cat loved her and the only person Bec had to make happy was Bec herself.

Maybe Jeff was right. Rebecca made her choice and was happy with the place she had made for herself in the world but Dannie wished she had not witnessed so much unkindness going in Rebecca's direction. Well, it couldn't hurt her anymore; she shrugged, though she felt no better.

Rebecca's death had caused another problem for Dannie in regard to the Silver Shores shows. Bec had been hired to work as a Hunter judge the first week and a Jumper judge the second. Dannie needed to find a replacement, one that ideally could do both hunters and jumpers and work both weeks as Bec had been scheduled to do. But the show was just over four weeks away and it was often hard to find a judge that fit all those criteria and also one that was good at the job on such short notice.

It was Sunday; the next meeting for the shows was Wednesday and Dannie would like to be able to tell them about Bec, but also assure them the vacancy for a judge had been filled by then.

Dannie spent the next few days sticking close to the beach house. She ventured out to pick Robbie up from school, but that was about it. She made phone calls; arranging for the installation of the many portable stalls, trying to find a replacement judge, and continuing to check in with staff about travel and hotel arrangements. She and Jake walked the beach several times each day and at night she sat with Jeff and he listened as she grieved the loss of her friend.

It seemed she had experienced so much loss in the last year and she felt she could easily find herself mired in the sorrow, but Tuesday afternoon she received a phone call that gave her mind a different path to travel.

"Dannie? It's Tom Robinson."

Tom was Dannie's attorney as he had been for her father before his death.

"Hi, Mr. Robinson. How are you?"

"Can't complain, but I think you'll feel the same way when I tell you why I'm calling," he said.

"Oh?"

"I filed the papers today to start the process of finalizing your divorce from Brian. He returned everything we sent him in fine order so all that needs to be done now is to wait for the judge to do his part."

"How long do you think it will be?"

"Well, the six-month period began when we served Brian and though he had thirty days to respond he was much faster than that.. Today I submitted what he returned to me along with the agreement of how to resolve your property and child custody so we'll wait out whatever remains of the six months at which time the judge will grant the decree."

"Is there anything else I need to do?" Dannie asked.

"Nope, all we do now is wait," Tom said.

"Thanks so much for calling to keep me informed; as always, I so appreciate your help."

"No problem at all, hope everything else is going well. We'll talk soon." With that he rang off.

Dannie couldn't believe it was almost over. She also was amazed that her next thought was 'Bec would have been so happy to hear this'.

Dannie met Jeff at the door with an ice-cold beer. "Get comfortable and come in by the fireplace," she said.

Five minutes later minus jacket and tie Jeff joined her on the love seat.

"What's all this, D? Why the mystery?"

"A couple of things really. First, Tom Robinson called today and in less than six months I'll be divorced. It will probably be final sometime in October."

"Really?" Jeff seemed surprised. "I didn't even know Brian had returned the paperwork."

"I was afraid to jinx it. Until it was in the works I didn't want to say a word."

"So how do you feel about it?"

"The same," said Dannie, "it's what I've wanted but it's still a little sad, you know, for Robbie."

"And for you," said Jeff. "No one ever gets married thinking it will fail. But that being said, you're mostly happy, right?"

Dannie threw her arms around his neck, "Completely happy!"

"Me too! So it seems to me, Miss Dannie, we have some plans to make. But don't worry; I'll wait until the Silver Shores shows are over." Jeff's smile was from ear to ear.

"There's something else," Dannie said.

"Yes?"

"I know I've been moping around the house last week, you know, with the news about Bec."

"I understand, D," Jeff said.

"I know you do. But today, when I heard from Tom Robinson one of my first thoughts was how happy Bec would have been to hear the news. All of a sudden I realized how she would have hated me to brood like this. She didn't ask for sympathy and she didn't want any. She found happiness in the smallest things and she never dwelled on the negative. She wanted the very best for me...always. I can't say I won't miss her, I surely will but it's time I smiled when I thought of her instead of dissolved into tears. There's so much to smile about."

That evening after he was ready for bed, Robbie brought Dannie a book.

"Mommy, would you read me this story tonight?"

"Sure buddy, go climb in bed."

Robbie snuggled under his covers and Dannie opened to the title page of the book. It was there she saw the inscription from Bec and realized this was one of the books Bec had purchased when she and Dannie found the little bookstore in Fryetag. It said:

To Robbie from your friend, Bec. Think of me when you and your mom read this book

Mother and son read together and thought about Rebecca Kirtlan with every word.

The following day as Dannie got in her car to head to the weekly meeting at Tootie's she was feeling quite stressed. She had made so many calls to find a judge to replace Bec and had been completely unsuccessful.

As she was backing out of her garage, the console screen in the SUV showed an incoming call from an unfamiliar number.

"Hello? This is Danica Rossi."

"Of course it is, darlin' that's why ah'm callin'" said the owner of a smooth, Southern drawl.

"Sticks?"

"The very same."

The unmistakable inflection belonged to James "Sticks" Hansen; southern gentleman, extraordinary judge, consummate horseman and all-around nice guy. Rumor had it he swung a mean golf club every chance he got as well.

He had earned the moniker of "Sticks" from years of referring to the jumps that way; 'let's go jump over a few sticks', or 'the purpose of this exercise is to keep the sticks in the air instead of on the ground'.

"Miss Dannie, ah hear you might be in need of a judge out there in California," Sticks continued.

"Are you available?" Dannie asked incredulously. Judges like Sticks were usually booked solid from the beginning of February right through November. She had only called him because she was desperate, not ever believing he could do it.

"Ah heard the sad news about my friend, Rebecca. She liked you very much and ah just knew she would want me to help you. So ah made some phone calls, explained the situation, and found some people to replace me for the two weeks...therefore, ah am all yours," Sticks said.

"Oh Sticks, I don't know whether to laugh or cry. You are a life saver...thank you!" Dannie exclaimed.

"Happy to do it, darlin'. When and where?"

"I'm going to a meeting right now. Can I call you back in three hours or so and we'll go over everything."

"Yes, ma'am," said Sticks, "I'll talk with you then."

The meeting wasn't going any better than the one the previous week. Dannie had started by informing the group about Bec, information which brought a fleeting smile of triumph to Kent and a pleased look, however brief, to Muriel's face as well. How could anyone be that full of hate, Dannie wondered?

Tootie, Sunshine, and Mary Jane had much more appropriate reactions and Dannie could tell all three were quite sorry to hear the news.

She told everyone about her call to Sticks and his agreement to judge for them. She could tell Kent was unhappy, likely because he hadn't been consulted, but she wasn't worried.

The judge issue having been dispensed with, Kent spent far too much time talking about his grandiose plans for the week one exhibitor party; music and food selection, layout of the room.

Mercifully, Tootie said, "Kent, I really think these are details you and Mary Jane, as hostess, should hash out. We need to talk about the logistics of the show."

"I'm happy you said that, Tootie," Kent said. "I wish to hold a staff meeting the day before week one begins."

"To talk about what exactly?" Dannie asked, more sarcastically than she had intended.

"Everyone's job, of course, layout of the show, chain of command," Kent huffed.

"We've hired professionals to work here, Kent, they know their jobs. The best thing we can do is get out of the way and let them do those jobs. If there is a special class or something you need, everyone on this staff will be receptive to hearing from you but they don't need a meeting to do it. As far as chain of command, I think we'd all be a lot better off if we just stopped using the 'command' word; command respect, chain of command, it all sounds a bit authoritarian, don't you think?"

Though normally quiet as a mouse at these meetings, Mary Jane spoke up. "The day before the show is so busy for all of us; we can get by without a meeting, can't we?"

Kent stared down at his knee which was bouncing up and down in a quick and agitated manner. "Whatever, I guess."

Sunshine piped up too. "I could sure do with a five minute break. Everyone OK with that?"

The group stood up; some stretched and walked around a bit, some headed to the guest bathroom, and Dannie sauntered to the beverage cart near the large stone fireplace to pour herself a sparkling water. Almost immediately, Muriel was at her elbow.

"Don't mind, Kent. He's just feeling the pressure of the show being so close to starting," she said.

"As are we all," replied Dannie.

"Listen, I wanted to tell you how sorry I was to hear about Rebecca," Muriel said in a deferential tone.

"What?"

"Oh I know you think I didn't like her but that really wasn't true. I know you were close, you must be so sad."

"I am sad," Dannie said, feeling skeptical.

"It's so hard to lose a friend," said Muriel, touching Dannie on the arm. "The only thing worse is to lose a member of the family."

Muriel turned and went back to her chair leaving Dannie to stare at the spot on the carpet where she'd stood. What was that about? Had Dannie imagined that Muriel appeared happy to hear the news about Bec? Maybe she did understand what Bec's friends were going through. Dannie felt as if maybe she was judging Muriel too harshly. She had, of course, been awful in so many ways this spring, but people could change, right?

Everyone had returned to their seats and the group went back to business. Tootie reported that the crew in charge of general cleaning, painting, weeding, watering, and repair at the show grounds were making wonderful progress. Dannie filled everyone in on her continuing work on the stall chart.

"I'm getting close to getting everyone situated in a place they'll be happy, I think," she said.

"What do you mean? Isn't a stall a stall?" asked Mary Jane.

"Not exactly. A barn with primarily jumpers wants to be stabled near the jumper ring, someone with a stallion wants to be on the end away from other horses, and you have to make sure you don't put two barns across from each other where the member of one barn is the ex-wife of a guy whose new wife is housed across the aisle."

Everyone but Kent laughed. "So more rocket science," he sneered. "I have real problems. My guys aren't available to present the colors at the week one Grand Prix and I need them for my donations."

"Time for another call to central casting?" Dannie said and immediately regretted her words.

Kent's eyes narrowed to mere slits as he practically bore a hole through Dannie with his stare. "What do you mean by that?"

Dannie tried not to panic. "Nothing, Kent. Just a play on words, you know, find someone to fill in."

Kent stared at Dannie for a full five seconds more though it seemed much longer, and then slowly turned his attention to the rest of the group. "Anyway, I really need to get my donations up during week one so any thoughts in that direction would be helpful."

They spent another twenty minutes tying up loose ends and then set a time and date for their next meeting; the last before the show.

"Oh, I almost forgot," said Sunshine. "I won't be here next time. I received a call from an investigator with the state office of the Attorney General and he has scheduled an interview with me at home on that day."

There was just the slightest hesitation in Kent's movements as he heard Sunshine's news and he continued to gather his paperwork. It did not escape Dannie's notice, however, that his hands shook and his knuckles were smooth and white.

That night at dinner, Dannie relayed her slip regarding the comment about central casting.

"I'm so sorry, Jeff. It just came out. I know I promised not to utter a word."

"You may have covered it well enough. Just steer clear from now on, OK Nancy Drew?"

Dannie made a face and stuck out her tongue, but became serious again as she told him about Sunshine's pronouncement.

"I'm not surprised," Jeff said. "Miles is finding a lot of incongruities in all this and the lieutenant suggested he call the Attorney General. After all, they are in charge of compliance and enforcement when it comes to 501c3 charities."

"Has it really progressed that far?"

"I admit to being somewhat out of the loop," Jeff said. "My case load has been huge and I thought it would be better for you if I wasn't involved. It's just cleaner."

"I understand," Dannie said.

"I have no idea how long this investigation will take, but it doesn't look good for the Mallory's. Dannie, you have to stay out of it, no mention at all. Promise?"

"But I can't stand that he is bilking other horse people for donations if in fact this Steeds 4 Soldiers is bogus. Not to mention, like Celia Prentice said, the black mark it leaves on groups like hers even though they've done nothing wrong," said Dannie.

"To some extent it's 'caveat emptor', you know, buyer beware. Well, except it should be 'donor beware' and I don't know the Latin for that. Now enough of this, promise me you will stay out of it."

Dannie nodded.

"Excellent. Now bring your glass of wine and let's go sit by the fire, we have a wedding to plan," he said.

-18-

It was Monday and the first horses would be arriving at the show facility in just one week. The pre-entries for the show had been encouraging and Dannie was happy to think that after the debacle of the year before at least six hundred horses were giving them the benefit of the doubt and would be returning to Silver Shores.

The maintenance crews had finished most of the work on the grounds and had turned their attention to making sure all the jumps had a fresh coat of paint and needed no repairs. The company that supplied the portable stalls was just finishing the job of assembling over seven hundred 10' by 10' enclosures to house horses collectively worth millions and there was a steady stream of trucks belonging to countless shipping companies arriving with box after box of supplies.

Muriel and Shelaigh had the task of taking receipt of the parcels and either delivering them to their designated spot or sorting them for later. Mike Gregory was supposed to be helping with this but of course, he hadn't arrived and no one knew when he would.

Many of the boxes contained awards for the first place winners for the next three weeks as well as awards for the special classes. These needed to be sorted and divided and marked for disbursement each week. A large portion of the arrivals were designated for the retail vendors who would be setting up shop on Vendor Row. It was common practice for the merchants to ship to the facility so inventory was waiting for them when they arrived.

Dannie had designated a large shipping container, about the size of a single wide trailer, for the awards and had the maintenance crew install shelves for the staff. She had also made sure they had a designated golf cart just for their use which at the moment had barely stopped moving.

Robbie had completed his first year of school the previous Friday and he had begged Dannie to let him come with her and Jake to the grounds. She had worried he would be underfoot and lose interest quickly but to her surprise Muriel and Shelaigh had taken him under their wings and at the moment he was having the time of his life riding around in the golf cart.

Dannie saw the cart at the side of one of the access roads as a delivery driver loaded several large packages on the back. When he was done, Robbie shook his hand and then plopped himself on Shelaigh's lap as she drove toward Dannie. They were still about twenty feet away from Dannie's position when she heard the excited little boy.

"Moooommmmmmmmyyyyy, look...I'm driving!"

As the cart sped past, Shelaigh winked and moved her arm so Dannie could see though Robbie was holding the wheel with both hands, Shelaigh was in control. Muriel waved as they went by.

"Did you just see those two women? I think we're in the twilight zone, Jakey."

Dannie turned and headed to the show office, Jake at her side. It was already after lunchtime and she had yet to see Kent today.

She walked up the three front steps, through the area that next week would house Chelle, Jen and a plethora of computer equipment and office supplies to a side room that served as Darlette Simon's office last year. There she found Kent, sitting at a desk playing video games on his phone.

He jumped; as much in surprise as at having been caught, and nearly dropped his phone. Figuring his best defense to be a good offense he barked at Dannie.

"I expect you to knock when coming to my office."

"Knock?" she said. "You don't have a door; you have an opening in the wall."

Dannie looked at Kent's desk. It was exactly the same as it had been at Jamaican Farms; open laptop, pencil cup, business card holder and the red balloon bookends. There was not a paper, note or list to be seen.

Kent went on the attack again. "What do you want anyway, Danica?"

"I came in to see what you were doing. More importantly, I came to see IF you planned on doing anything at all to help this horse show happen."

"Well you're my assistant, aren't you?" Kent said, relishing every syllable of Dannie's title, "and you seem to be doing enough for both of us."

"That's not how this works, Kent. You're the manager; you ought to give actual managing a try. And just a hint, that doesn't mean putting plastic tablecloths on the tables at the gate."

"You really think you're something, don't you? You've spent a few years sitting on your ass at a back gate and you think you have it all figured out. I run a huge non-profit, I have a business in addition to that, I'm in demand," Kent taunted. "What do you possibly bring to the table to beat that? Not to mention I have the ear of important people, they listen when I speak."

"You are a phony and a liar and probably the most laughable thing in this whole mess is that you've been lying so long you believe your own hype," Dannie said. "Let's agree to steer clear of each other for the next three weeks and then I will be happy to never set eyes on you again. Just make sure you stay out of my way, Kent."

"How do you plan to prevent me from doing whatever I want?"

"Oh stop. You're far too busy filling your.....your charity's coffers to let a little horse show get in the way. C'mon, Jake."

Dannie made her way quickly out the door and walked around the office trailer until she was out of sight of any windows. She leaned against the building and closed her eyes, letting go of a huge stress-relieving sigh. She had almost accused Kent of collecting the funds donated to his charity for personal use. Of course, it was exactly what she believed to be happening but she had promised to steer clear of any discussion of Steeds 4 Soldiers. She pushed herself away from the building and expelled one more large cleansing breath.

"The only way for us to stay out of trouble, Jake, is to go back to work. Let's hit it, big guy."

At five Dannie decided to call it a day, at least at the show grounds. She had to get Robbie home, fed, and bathed, and Summer was arriving about ten.

With Jeff's blessing, she had invited Summer to stay in the guest bedroom at the house for the duration of Silver Shores. She was coming early to help any way she was needed and Dannie looked forward to her visit.

With an armload of things and Jake at her heels, Dannie walked over to the awards trailer. She could hear Robbie chattering a mile a minute as she neared the door.

"Mommy, I've been helping Miss Shelaigh unpack boxes and Mrs. Mallory says I'm the best helper ever," Robbie said.

"That's great, Robbie, thank you for being such a help. But we have to go now, buddy, get your things." Then, turning her attention to Muriel and Shelaigh, "You two have worked like dogs today. It will all be here tomorrow and remember this is a marathon, not a sprint. Go home and put your feet up."

"Are you coming to help me tomorrow, Robbie?" asked Shelaigh.

"I want to come every day," the little boy said.

"Oh, I don't know," Dannie said.

"Please!"

"I can't promise every day, Robbie, but you can come tomorrow. We'll just take it one day at a time."

Satisfied for the moment, Robbie grabbed his things and joined Dannie on the walk to the parking lot.

"See you tomorrow, Robbie," Muriel called after him.

Robbie was nearly asleep before his head hit the pillow. Dannie tucked him in and joined Jeff out on the deck where it was quite foggy and cool.

"Think I'll take a hot shower," she said. "I'm beat."

"I cut up some cheese, fruit and bread. Is that enough for dinner or do you want more?" asked Jeff.

"That's perfect, I'll be back in a few minutes," she said, kissing him on the cheek.

True to her word, twenty minutes later she returned to find Jeff in the kitchen retrieving a couple of platters from the refrigerator.

"Too cold to eat outside," he said. "C'mon."

She followed him to the small dining table that looked out on the herb garden.

"Robbie had a great time today. He spent all day with Shelaigh and Muriel Mallory," Dannie said.

"You're kidding, right? Why them?"

"What do you mean?" said Dannie, defensively. "They were driving around in a golf cart and unpacking boxes. He's a little boy, he was in heaven."

"He's your son, why did you dump him on them?"

Dannie could feel anger rising in her chest and she fought not to overreact. "Jeff, I didn't dump him. They were quite agreeable and he wanted to be there. He wants to go back and do the same tomorrow. What's this all about?"

Jeff ignored her last question. "I don't like him just being, well, loose, on the grounds like that. He's too little and you don't know who's around. And I don't like that Mallory woman and Shelaigh's an idiot."

"He's not loose, as you so eloquently put it," Dannie said sarcastically, "there are people all over the grounds that know Robbie and keep an eye out for him. I was raised hanging out on the grounds at horse shows and I was always fine."

"The world has changed, Dannie. I don't want him there tomorrow."

"Is that right? I've already promised him."

"Well, un-promise him," Jeff said.

She threw the napkin she had placed in her lap in the middle of the table. "You know, suddenly I'm not hungry at all. I'll be out to greet Summer when she arrives around ten." With that, she retired to her office to work on her list for the next day.

The only problem with her plan of putting pen to paper was that she could think of nothing else but her exchange with Jeff. She could count on one hand the number of times they had exchanged a cross word in the last year. She wanted to make it right, but taking Robbie to the show grounds was a non-issue and she had no idea why he had made it such a big one.

She folded her arms in front of her on the desk and used them as a pillow...maybe if she just closed her eyes for a moment.

Dannie woke with a start and tried to sit up but was stopped by a shooting pain in her neck and shoulders. She sat up slowly, realizing she had been sleeping for some time hunched over her big desk. She wiped the unfortunate drool from her cheek, tried to slowly stretch her protesting muscles and rubbed her eyes trying to focus on the clock on the opposite wall. One A.M. Summer!

She walked quietly to the foyer and looked out the window toward the driveway. Summer's car was there and all was quiet. She glanced across the great room to see the door of the guest room closed. What a loser I am, she thought, I can't believe I slept through her arrival.

Dannie started toward the bedroom and after a few steps stopped abruptly. Since the day Jeff had moved into the beach house they had not spent a night apart; at least not unless one of them wasn't taken away by work. At this moment however, their discussion had left her with a nagging unease that she couldn't put her finger on.

Jeff had been unflinchingly supportive, respectful and loving since the early beginnings of their relationship but tonight felt, well...condescending. His decree to 'un-promise' Robbie which followed a short but pointed discussion sent her a message that Jeff believed her to be a bad parent, and among other things incapable of making responsible decisions.

There was always the possibility that she was reading things into his words that weren't there, but...no, she was hurt and angry. She returned to the office and went to the couch, covering herself with a large, fluffy throw and eventually fell back to sleep.

Jarred from sleep again, this time Dannie was roused by the sound of a car engine. She stood from the couch and walked again to the foyer, this time still wrapped in the throw.

Through the window she saw the rear lights of Jeff's truck disappearing down the road. The clock over the fireplace showed four, he must have been called to work.

She turned to go back to the office before realizing she was fully awake. She might as well just get up and face the day; there would be no more sleep for her.

She took a hot shower and dressed, then went to the kitchen to quietly make a pot of coffee. She sat down several minutes later relishing the first cup and worked on the notes she had neglected the night before.

At just after six the door of the guest room opened and Summer appeared.

"Hi," Dannie said, "did I wake you?"

"Oh no, I'm normally an early riser."

"I'm so sorry I wasn't available, OK I mean awake, when you arrived."

"Don't worry about that, Jeff helped me with my stuff and got me situated in the guest room," Summer said.

"Um...yeah," Dannie said quietly.

If Summer was aware of any issues she didn't let on. "So, when do we leave for the show?"

"I planned to be there about eight-thirty, if that's too early for you just come when you're ready."

"Oh no," Summer said, "I'll ride over with you. After all, I'm here to do your bidding for the next couple of weeks. How's it been going?"

"You know all things considered it seems to be going pretty smoothly."

Dannie should have superstitiously knocked on wood when she had the chance because not five minutes after she, Summer and Robbie arrived at the show grounds it was evident things were anything but smooth.

As she was letting Jake out of the SUV, Wes Morgan, the thirty-something guy that Tootie had hired to be the feed and barn manager for the duration of the shows approached Dannie.

"Good morning, Dannie. So sorry to bother you just as you've arrived but we have a problem with the feed and bedding."

"What kind of problem?"

"The delivery trucks arrived about twenty minutes ago and they only brought seven hundred bags of shavings and fifty bales of alfalfa but no grass hay or bagged feed of any kind."

"That's impossible, I made the order myself. I ordered five thousand bags of shavings and," she dug in her pocket for a piece of paper, "here's the rest, you can see for yourself I ordered much more," Dannie said.

Wes said, "The driver told me he brought the total order. Would you come with me to talk with him?"

"Sure," Dannie said. She looked at Summer and then pointed toward the awards trailer. "Summer, would you take Robbie over there and make sure either Shelaigh or Muriel have arrived?"

Summer nodded and took Robbie by the hand while Dannie and Wes headed toward the large area that was designated for feed and bedding storage. It was separated from the show grounds by large sections of temporary chain link fencing and Dannie could see before they even reached the entrance the delivery was indeed woefully short.

She dialed the number of the feed company they had contracted with for the show and reached the owner right away.

"I'm afraid we have a real problem. We contracted with your company because we believed you could deal with the volume needed and if that's not..."

"Just one minute, lady," the owner said, "there's a problem but it's that I'm sitting on a crapload of inventory I brought in for these shows and you just changed the order with no advanced warning."

"I never changed the order," Dannie retorted.

"No, some guy named..." Dannie could hear papers shuffling. "Here it is, Kent Mallory, he called and changed the order."

"Is that right?" In that case, I apologize for taking it out on you and please, deliver the original order. We will use all of it and then some," said Dannie.

He agreed, but said before he disconnected, “Geez, don’t you people talk with one another?”

Dannie was walking back toward the office, intent on finding Kent, when she was stopped by Petey Anderson.

“Hey, Dannie, can you help me?”

“What’s up?” she asked.

“Kent just showed up back where we’re painting and repairing all the jumps and took three guys off the crew and told them they need to make signs that fit on every jump standard in each ring.”

“What kind of signs?” Dannie asked.

“Signs that say ‘Steeds 4 Soldiers’,” said Petey.

“Un-be-lievable!” Dannie sputtered and immediately took off toward the area where the jumps were being repaired. She was walking so quickly that Jake was trotting to keep up.

As she neared the jump storage she saw Kent get in his golf cart, with his passenger Tootie Bittler, and begin heading toward her. When he caught sight of her there was just the slightest hesitation in the forward progress of the cart before he looked down at his feet and floored the accelerator.

“Oh no you don’t,” Dannie said to no one in particular then she walked right in front of the cart and yelled, “Kent, STOP!”

He looked up with a somewhat sheepish expression but quickly steeled his gaze as he brought the cart to a halt.

“Yes, Dannie?”

“What in the hell do you think you’re doing?”

“I’m sure I don’t know what you mean,” Kent oozed.

“Where do I begin? First of all, why did you change the feed and bedding order?”

Tootie glanced at him in surprise as he said, “Your numbers were ridiculous. Someone has to be concerned with this show’s bottom line.”

"That's rich, Kent. You reduced the shavings order to seven hundred bales. We have seven hundred stalls here, if you ballpark that we will fill six hundred, just the first week how many bags of shavings do you think you'll need? How many bags do you think these grooms put in each stall?"

"Ummmm..."

"Roughly."

"Well....."

"I'll tell you, some as few as four, some as many as ten. Just for grins let's lowball it at four and multiply that by your six hundred stalls. That's twenty-four hundred bags of shavings. You reduced the order to less than a third of that. And while we're at it, you do know one of the best places for the show to make some money is on feed and bedding, right? Do you even know the profit margin on a bag of shavings?"

"You sell them for ten dollars a bale."

"Yes, but what do we buy them for?" asked Dannie.

"I...uh..."Kent stammered.

"My point exactly. Also, what are you doing taking three crew members off jump prep?"

"I need signs for the charity and..."

"We have signs; they are ready to be picked up at the sign company in town. They are not for Steeds for Soldiers, they are for various sponsors that have paid to have their name on a jump and they have been professionally done with logos and readable fonts. You haven't contributed to the show at all and therefore you do not get your name on a sign and certainly do not get to take three people off an important job to do your bidding."

Kent turned in the seat of the golf cart to face Tootie. Dannie thought he was looking for backup but none was offered.

"Why don't you go figure out what color napkins you should use at the party and stay out of the things I have already taken care of," Dannie finished.

Tootie frowned at her last statement but made no comment. She paused and then said, "Danica, there's a question I've been wanting to ask. I know nothing about this and I'm hoping you'll educate me."

"What is it?"

"I would like to know why you believe your...Summer, is it...to be a better choice to do a back gate than Mikey Gregory. She has had so little experience."

It didn't take a brain surgeon to dissect the reasons for Tootie's question, thought Dannie as she glanced at Kent smiling smugly as he sat in the cart. Coming from Tootie it was a reasonable question and Dannie would give her an honest answer.

"First of all, Summer is smart as they come. She learns quickly and thinks on her feet. She also has the advantage of understanding horse shows because of her many years riding. As far as experience, well, the first time I did a back gate was literally the first time. They threw me in to the job and I had to figure it out. I've spent several shows with Summer, but the best teacher is really just to do it. She has the instincts and she isn't afraid to ask questions if she's stuck. Maybe most notable; she wants to do the job, Mike Gregory doesn't."

"Thank you. That makes perfect sense. I look forward to meeting Summer," Tootie said.

Kent was clearly angry but had the good sense not to show it to Tootie. They drove away in the cart and Dannie went to find Summer and Robbie.

The remainder of Tuesday continued to throw challenges Dannie's way but she just kept tackling one at a time and things were getting done. Summer was amazing, she put her head down and went to work no matter what Dannie asked of her.

Just after one, Dannie asked Shelaigh to go into Silver Shores and pick up the sponsor signs at the printer.

"Sure, I'll go," she said. "Would it be OK if I took Robbie with me?" She exchanged a conspiratorial wink with the little boy. "You see, he's been such a help these past two days I told him I wanted to treat him at Big Top Ice Cream, you know, that new specialty ice cream store?"

"Please, mommy, please, please, please!"

"Well, OK but seat belt at all times and Miss Shelaigh is doing an errand for the show so don't pester her for ice cream until she is done. Understood?"

"Yes, mommy."

"I'm so glad he can go with me, I guess I'll have to try some ice cream too so he's not eating alone," said Shelaigh.

"It's only right," laughed Dannie.

Shelaigh and Robbie headed to the parking lot for her car and Dannie turned to Summer, "I swear, if you'd seen Shelaigh last year you wouldn't believe it's the same girl. I shouldn't say it but I must admit I'm just waiting for the explosion."

"I hope she surprises you," said Summer, "in a good way."

As the afternoon drew to a close Dannie felt she was checking a great deal off her list; the remainder of the first feed and bedding order arrived, the sponsor signs returned with Shelaigh and Robbie and they were beautiful and just what Dannie had envisioned. The awards room was taking shape and it didn't escape Dannie's notice that Mary Jane had outdone herself with this year's selection. There wasn't a stuffed squid in sight.

The tired, dirty group of three entered the front door of the beach house with Jake leading the way. He ran directly to the kitchen anticipating his dinner and happily greeted Jeff…and Miles.

"Miles is having dinner with us," Jeff said as if he expected a challenge.

"Great, happy to have you," Dannie said, meaning it.

Summer excused herself to clean up and Dannie ordered Robbie to his tub as well. She fed Jake and turned to Miles.

"Any more news on Steeds 4 Soldiers?"

Before Miles could answer, Jeff said, "I ordered Chinese."

Both Dannie and Miles looked inquiringly at him, not so much for his statement but for his tone.

"That sounds good," Dannie said. There was an awkward feeling in the room she couldn't shake. She didn't want to be fighting with Jeff and she couldn't for the life of her figure out what was going on. She wanted to talk with him, but this was not the time.

The doorbell rang and Dannie went to meet the delivery guy with the food, paid and tipped him and returned the large brown bag to the kitchen. Summer and Robbie had reappeared looking much better and Dannie excused herself to clean up too.

"What about dinner?" Jeff asked.

"I won't be long, I feel gross. Just a quick shower…go ahead and eat."

"Oh great," he said to the room in general, "we have permission to eat."

Dannie was hurt and embarrassed at Jeff's churlish attitude. She fixed a plate for Robbie and told him he could eat in his room if he wished then she went to take a shower and hoped that time with Summer and Miles would soften whatever rough edges he was feeling.

She unfortunately returned to a situation not much improved than the one she left. Summer, Miles and Jeff were already eating and Jeff's body language evidenced his agitation and annoyance as he stabbed at the food on his plate. He barely participated in any conversation at the table and with about half of his food still remaining on the plate he stood abruptly and said, "It's hot in here, I'm going out back to get some air."

Dannie looked at Miles and Summer but had no idea what to say.

Miles touched Summer on the arm. "How about you and I go explore the nightlife, such as it is, in Silver Shores?"

Summer looked doubtful, but Miles promised they would be back by ten so she agreed. She went into her room to grab a jacket and as she and Miles reached the foyer she shot Dannie a worried look.

Dannie smiled and waved but as the door closed her smile faded and she wondered what to do next.

-19-

About ten minutes after Miles and Summer left, Dannie walked out on the back deck. She had cleaned up the table and put away the food, but that was really just buying time as she composed herself to speak with Jeff. She found him staring out at the ocean to the west and watching the rapidly setting sun.

"Hey," she said softly.

"Hey," he replied though he didn't look up at her.

She sat in the large chair next to him and took his hand. "Please talk to me, Jeff. What's going on?"

"Don't you have somewhere to go or some calls to make or something?" he said sullenly.

"Let's not do that. Passive-aggressive, or sarcasm, or whatever that was isn't productive. Just talk to me."

"I'm frustrated, D. Do you have any idea that you and your entourage just blew in the door tonight with you sending Robbie and Summer to shower, asking Miles about the charity, feeding the dog, but at no time did you even acknowledge I was in the room."

"Well, I....no, I guess I was unaware of that."

"D, you have been completely enmeshed in this stupid show. You can't think about or talk about anything else. And when you're not talking about the show, you are taking about the people, going to meetings, making phone calls…have you forgotten you have a family?"

"That's really not fair, Jeff. Since we are clearing the air, let me remind you that you denigrate what I do every chance you get. Though you don't come out and say it, you make your position that my work is frivolous and really not work at all quite clear. Not to mention you as much as said I'm a bad parent which is fascinating coming from someone that has never been a parent."

"Now who's not being fair? I didn't mean to insinuate you were a bad parent. I know better and I'm sorry, truly, if that's what you heard from me. But I see things every day that would…"

"I know, that would horrify me," said Dannie, finishing his sentence. "You see terrible things with a regularity that is criminal, no pun intended. But I can't put Robbie in a bubble and I can't make him afraid of the world simply for what 'might' happen."

Jeff sighed. "I know you can't. But you are so wrapped up in this production of yours that I wonder if you can even keep track of him."

"First of all, I know where he is and who he's with all the time. Secondly, you have just made my point with "this production of yours". I'm aware that many people think this is all just folks playing horse show and that it's just fun and we call it work, but after your investigation into Jimmy's death last year I thought at least you understood that it is a business and to those producing the show it is important we treat it as a business. You know, Jeff, I have so much going on, I really don't need this."

"And that's it in a nutshell; you're Danica Rossi, strong, independent, intelligent, wealthy Danica Rossi. You don't need this argument, more money, more brains, hell, you don't even need me!"

There it was; the kernel of corn in acres of nothing. She stood and went to sit on the lounge with him, facing him. She measured her words before she spoke.

"I have lived through one bad, no, one terrible marriage and when you asked me to marry you, well, I had given lots of thought to whether I would marry anyone ever again. I said "yes" because it was you, Jeff Barnes, who convinced me that there was someone out there that 'got me'. First and foremost there is absolutely no excuse for not acknowledging you when we got home. I wholeheartedly apologize; you and Robbie are the two most important people in my world. And Jeff, I do need you. I need your strength and love and support. But if you thought I was going to be the clingy, needy woman waiting for your direction then you've made a mistake and I've been equally mistaken by believing you understood who I am and what I'm about."

Jeff took both of Dannie's hands in his and looked as if he would speak, but he didn't so she continued.

"I may not be catching bad guys and helping victims but I take my job as seriously as you do yours. To be me, everything attached to my name has to be as right as I can make it and that often means I take on more than I should. I know that about myself and I'm alright with it...I need you to be alright with it too when it happens every now and then. I love you, Jeff, don't give up on me."

Jeff opened his arms and drew Dannie into a hug, kissing the top of her head and stroking her hair.

She could feel there was still an open wound which would take more time to heal completely but she vowed to not be neglectful.

"So, I guess then a busy life gets busier. Your friend, Pat, called today. He is already in town and so I invited him to come over Thursday evening," Jeff said.

Dannie tried to stifle a laugh but found it to be useless. "So, the guy that feels left out added another social event to my calendar?"

"What can I say? Also, Celia and Mack Prentice have invited us for dinner Friday evening and for a tour of The Farmstead. Miles is invited too."

Dannie frowned momentarily but said, "I'll find a way to make it work. Should be fun."

Just then the slider leading to the kitchen opened and Robbie poked his head out. "Mommy, can I go with you again tomorrow?"

She thought she felt Jeff stiffen and was glad to reply, "Sorry buddy, no. Remember you're spending the day with Donte tomorrow. I think the plan is the aquarium, roller skating, and a sleep over."

"Oh yeah," he said brightly. "OK, will you tuck me in now?"

Dannie and Jeff followed Robbie into the house and considering the current climate in the house Dannie was pleased she'd had a reason to say no to Robbie.

The following morning, Summer tentatively approached her mentor on the way to the show grounds.

"Everything OK, Dannie?

"It will be. Listen, Pat Collingsworth is coming over for dinner tomorrow night and I want you to know you are welcome to join us."

"Well, um, I'm having dinner with Miles tomorrow night," she said shyly. "He also asked if I would go with you all when you go out to The Farmstead."

"No kidding, that didn't take long," Dannie said, winking at Summer.

"Oh no, it's much too early for "that" and he's too old, I think. But we had fun last night and I can't just sit in your house for the next three weeks staring at all of you." It occurred to Dannie that some of this attitude was borne from Summer's discomfort during Jeff's temper last night.

"Fair enough," Dannie said, "but you are always welcome to do whatever we are doing."

Other than small annoyances, mostly from Kent, the next two days felt like progress. Dannie and Summer pulled into the parking lot Thursday having just picked up Robbie from Donte's. Dannie had concluded it was a successful venture because Robbie was tired and listless; just what she would expect after any great sleep over.

As Dannie, Summer, and Robbie walked toward the large line of golf carts parked and charging for staff use, Dannie observed the surroundings were beginning to look like a horse show. The decomposed granite paths were pristine, the arena fences were gleaming white, Mary Jane had planted lots of half barrels of coastal vegetation and flowers that were grouped here and there throughout the grounds and the sky was a brilliant blue. She knew, of course, that no one at the show could take credit for the sky but it certainly contributed to the overall feel and look of the grounds.

"What's my job this morning?" Summer asked.

"I want you to take a cart and go to each judge or back gate booth. Take a broom, paper towels, whatever you think you may need to rid each booth of cobwebs and dust. Take some window cleaner too. When each is cleaned out make sure they have a chair and a wastebasket of some sort."

"No problem," Summer nodded.

"Mommy, can I ride with Summer?" Robbie asked.

For a moment, Dannie wondered what had happened to turn Robbie away from the awards trailer but it suddenly hit her that with Summer being the only other occupant of the cart, Robbie could easily catch up on the sleep he missed last night.

"It's fine with me, Rob-ster," said Summer and Dannie nodded in agreement.

Dannie started her morning with a visit to the jump area, Jake at her side. The painting and repair work was nearly complete and Petey figured they would finish tomorrow.

She headed from there to make sure everything was flowing smoothly at the feed and bedding area and that Wes Morgan had everything he needed, including the latest version of the stall chart for the first week. She was pleased to hear they hadn't seen Kent in several days.

Next she headed to the awards trailer. She didn't see their cart and she found only Shelaigh inside.

"Where's my best helper?" asked Shelaigh.

"Riding around with Summer. Listen, I feel I may be poking the hornet's nest but I have to ask; who are you and what have you done with Shelaigh?"

"What do you mean?"

"Don't misunderstand; Robbie has loved spending time with you. He's been having a blast. But you never showed any interest in him before not to mention you have never been able to stand me. What gives?"

"Do you remember last year when you found me in your house?" asked Shelaigh.

"How could I forget?" Dannie said dryly.

"Well, you told me to give myself a chance for happiness that day and I've been trying to do that. As for you, well, you intimidate me and even though you told me I had a brain I think you really believe I'm stupid, but I'm not."

"I said you had a brain because I meant it. I just hoped you'd make a bigger effort to use it."

"Don't pick on me, Dannie; I'm really trying to make my life better."

"Point taken, Shelaigh and you are to be respected for that."

"You asked about Robbie," Shelaigh continued. "I have to admit at first I thought him tagging along would be a pain in the ass, but it turns out he's a great kid. He's as funny as he can be, does his best to help and in some respects, he reminds me of me when I used to find all this exciting and fun. I don't want to see him become bitter and jaded like I have."

Muriel pulled up in the golf cart just then and Dannie had finished so she simply greeted Muriel and headed to the show office.

"What, too good to talk to me?" Muriel said to no one in particular. "Probably off to count her millions, she sure hasn't parted with any of it for Steeds 4 Soldiers."

"Donations can come at any time," Shelaigh said.

"Yeah, not from that one," Muriel said and turned in disgust to unload the golf cart.

Dannie had thrown together an easy pasta meal with a green salad and garlic bread for Pat's arrival. Jeff had called in the late afternoon to say he would be delayed and she knew that the meal itself was not the important thing for her and Pat.

As soon as he arrived she sat him down and brought him his favorite, an ice-cold sparkling water.

"Oh Pat, I'm so happy to see you. What brings you into town so ear...?" She stopped in mid-word, not believing she hadn't thought of it sooner. "You're here to see Mary Jane, aren't you? Are you staying at her house?"

"Absolutely not! I'm a gentleman."

"Have you forgotten who you're talking to? You are far more wicked than you let on."

"Don't make me blush. In all seriousness, I want a chance. Don't know if it will work but I have to try. Discretion, Danica."

"Of course, Pat," she said, squeezing his hand. "You know I want whatever brings you happiness."

They continued their meal as Dannie caught him up on life in the weeks since they had last seen each other. She told him about the "new" Shelaigh.

"It would be so incredible if she could just change like that, but I don't trust it. She's been crazy for far too long what with Jimmy Bittler's DNA running rampant through her and all. I just don't believe it."

"Aren't you being a little harsh? After all, she's young and you're not the same person you were in your early twenties. We grow up, we learn," said Pat.

"It's just too convenient," Dannie said dismissively.

They talked for at least another hour before Jeff arrived from work. Dannie gave him a kiss then excused herself briefly to return a phone call while he poured himself a glass of wine to go with the pasta Dannie had saved for him.

"Long day, huh?" Pat observed as Jeff lowered himself wearily into a chair at the island.

"Yeah, working on a couple of tough cases plus I haven't slept much the last couple of days. I'm sure Dannie told you about our issues," Jeff said, knowing how close they were.

"No, we haven't discussed you," Pat lied. Dannie had not gone into detail, but had mentioned the disagreement knowing Patrick was a loyal friend that would not make things worse for her by admitting their conversation. "What's up?"

"Oh, I shouldn't..." Jeff's voice trailed off. He paused, taking a sip of his wine and then briefly explained what Pat already knew.

"I see," said Pat simply when Jeff had finished.

"I have no idea why I just told you that," Jeff said.

"Would you like some unsolicited insight?" asked Pat.

Jeff nodded his assent.

"The very things that drew you to Dannie last year; her strength, her tenacity, even her heart, these are the very things frustrating you right now. These "horse girls", at least if they stick with their passion for any length of time, learn a life of solitude; hours of practice with no one but the animal for company, lots of traveling, days on the interstate in the wee hours or late at night. Think about it, how many women of your mother's generation would have hopped in a pickup with a trailer full of two or three thousand pounds of living, breathing animal behind them and driven to another town, or state? I know there are some but my mother sure wouldn't have, she didn't even want to drive over 40 miles an hour."

Jeff chuckled at the characterization.

"Anyway," continued Pat, "my point is they learn to do for themselves because their families stop helping in the hope it will prove too hard and they will quit....but they don't. They double their efforts; they work harder, whatever it takes. They are singularly focused on their compulsion to live in the presence of these animals. The only real understanding they find are from those that are just like them. Dannie carries that focus to everything she does."

"Maybe a little less focus wouldn't hurt," Jeff said wryly.

"Sure, and you could love her a little less than you do," smiled Pat. "But, I'm done. I've probably said too much."

"No," said Jeff, offering his hand to shake Pat's, "you and D are kindred spirits and you understand her in a way I can only hope to. Thanks for being her advocate."

"I love her, and you love her even more. I am glad she's found you and you'll be fine...both of you."

Shortly after, Dannie returned to the kitchen and the three talked for nearly thirty minutes more before Pat made his excuses and headed out the door.

As she washed the dishes Dannie thought, 'that devil, he never did say where he was staying.'

The next evening found Dannie, Jeff, Miles and Summer in Jeff's truck heading south down the coast road toward The Farmstead. Dannie was definitely in a Friday kind of mood; she'd left the showgrounds finally feeling as if this show would happen. Of course, it was always going to happen, but she felt prepared, the grounds looked great, and she was excited to see all her plans come to fruition.

Jeff turned off the road pulling into a driveway running alongside a white, two-story clapboard farmhouse.

"I love it!" Summer exclaimed while Dannie admired the seemingly effortless but beautiful garden beds around the house.

Jeff parked and the four walked up the front steps onto a large wrap-around porch. Miles knocked on the door but there was no answer. He knocked again and when there still wasn't a response he tried the knob and the door opened.

"Celia?" he called as he walked in, followed by the other three. "Celia, you home?"

"Ohhhh noooo," was the reply. Celia Prentice came into the hallway that appeared to lead to the kitchen carrying a dish towel in one hand and a paring knife in the other.

"Are we early?" Jeff asked.

"No, we are just horribly behind. Mack got home from work and the volunteer that was supposed to feed and clean never showed. He's out in the barn trying to do everything but I was counting on him to man the grill and..."

Dannie touched her arm. "Help has arrived, Celia. Summer and I are no strangers to barn chores and this guy right here, Detective Barnes; well he was born with a pair of barbeque tongs in his hand. You keep prepping the food, they'll get busy with the grill and Summer and I will stroll out and introduce ourselves to Mack, that is, if you point us in the direction of the barn."

Celia did just that and with Jeff and Miles in charge at the house, Summer and Dannie walked the short distance behind the house to a traditional red barn with gleaming white trim.

They could hear the sounds of some sort of work going on complete with inappropriate expletives and Dannie thought it might be wise to announce themselves before the language became saltier.

"Hellloooo. Mack?"

"Who's there?"

A bear of a man came out of one of the stalls near the door they had just entered. He had a pleasant face, dark hair and mustache, and was flushed but whether from temper or exertion Dannie was unsure.

"Mack, I'm Dannie Rossi and this is Summer Stanton."

"Your dinner guests," added Summer.

"Pleased to meet you ladies, I'd shake your hands but, well, you know," he said pointing at the manure fork he held in his other hand. "Our volunteer crapped out on us and..."

"We heard all about it," Dannie said. "This is your lucky day because Summer and I are long time barn rats and we're here to help. The three of us can knock this out in no time."

Forty-five minutes later they headed to the house with water buckets filled, fresh hay in the feeders, stalls cleaned, and seven horses happily munching their dinner, safe in their stalls.

They found the scene at the house under control as well with dinner being nearly ready to be put on the table.

"I planned for us to eat at the big table out back if that's OK with all of you," Celia said.

They agreed it was and each of them filled their hands with utensils, napkins, plates, glasses and platters. Dannie was the first through the door to the outside and thought possibly they had been too quick to agree because all she could see was illuminated by only one large utility light attached to a pole. As Celia stepped outside the house, however, she flipped a switch which lit what seemed to be hundreds of clear LED lights giving the large spreading tree and the table beneath it the appearance of a fairy garden. It was enchanting.

The meal consisted of grilled chicken and vegetables and fresh-squeezed lemonade. Celia proudly proclaimed that every vegetable as well as the lemons had all come from the labors of the people that visited The Farmstead. It was delicious.

"I can't thank you ladies enough for your help tonight," Mack said. "It's always wonderful having people around that prove to be good hands with a horse."

Jeff reached over and squeezed Dannie's hand. She didn't know why, but in that moment she knew he was done with whatever had been bothering him.

Dannie wasted no time sending the conversation in the direction of what Miles had learned about the Mallory's and Steeds 4 Soldiers.

"This thing is looking like the tentacles of an octopus reaching in many different directions at once," he said.

"I get so mad every time I think about it," said Celia.

"Um, excuse me," said Summer," can someone fill me in? I have no idea what you're talking about."

Miles ran down the background; the suspicions about Steeds 4 Soldiers, possible misuse of funds, Kent hiring actors to represent soldiers in the program and the lie he told regarding the animals in the program being housed at Forrest Equestrian.

"I tell you what," Mack growled, "just let me get my hands on those Hollywood wannabes and they'll stop impersonating soldiers. They make a mockery of real people struggling with real issues."

"Technically, Mack, they're doing nothing wrong," Jeff said.

"The hell they're not!" Mack roared.

"Jeff's right," said Miles. "As much as it burns my ass to say so they are just actors and they think they're just playing a part. I can't find anyone that has actually seen or heard any of these guys represent themselves to be part of a program dealing with PTSD. They are just portraying guys presenting the colors in a ceremony. It might be infuriating but what they're doing isn't illegal."

"On the other hand, Kent Mallory knows just why he hired actors to portray soldiers," Jeff said.

"Listen, I have to say this before we go any further. None of you are to utter one word about any of this. This investigation is in the hands of the State Attorney General and that's where it will stay. I am assisting them, and I may ask some of you for information but you are to speak to no one about this and do nothing without being asked. Am I clear?" Miles asked. "My career will not benefit from any of you acting as a lone wolf."

The group agreed and Dannie said, "It's just so frustrating to watch them continue and try to browbeat the show exhibitors for money. I overheard Kent tell Muriel today that he has arranged the raffle for next week's exhibitor party."

"A raffle?" said Miles.

"Yes, with two prizes to be drawn. Two separate parties produced by Kent's Events."

"Isn't that Mallory's company?"

Dannie nodded. "Is that a problem?"

"Could be," Miles said. If he uses the proceeds from the raffle to pay Kent's Events for the service, that's called self-dealing and it is illegal. But I'll let the AG's men know and they'll take it from there. Remember what I said...not a word from any of you. Now let's have that tour, Celia."

20-

It was Thursday afternoon of the first week of competition at Silver Shores. Dannie was knocking on every spare piece of wood she could find, afraid to jinx the overwhelming smoothness of the show so far.

Horses had arrived, moved into stalls and completed schooling on Monday with hardly a hiccup. The open divisions had been contested and show championships awarded the previous afternoon and trainers had been nothing but complimentary about the grounds, schedule, awards and overall feel of the show. Even the show staff from parking crew to judges seemed happy in their work.

Dannie knew something would happen, it always did, but she hoped it would be a minor inconvenience. She knew nothing was ever perfect. To that end she thought of the continuing saga of Mike Gregory.

He had finally appeared the previous Sunday; six full days after he was requested to arrive. If he'd had a reason, or more likely an excuse, Dannie hadn't heard it but then again he was completely Kent and Muriel's responsibility.

It hadn't escaped her notice, however, that upon Mike's arrival Shelaigh had been totally taken with him. In his presence she had returned to the loudly and tightly clothed, simpering, wheedling, needy young woman that Dannie knew all too well. Last year this persona of Shelaigh's had been an annoyance, but now that Dannie knew more about her life as the daughter of Jumpin' Jimmy Bittler, Dannie was overwhelmed by pity more than any other emotion.

All this was now occurring to Dannie she was sure, because she was on her way to the awards trailer and expecting to see Muriel, Shelaigh and Mike in full preparation for tomorrow's awards and ribbons.

She arrived at the trailer and asked Jake for a down and stay outside the door; he was just too big to be in the trailer with four and a half people, the half being Robbie, of course.

Dannie opened the door and stepped in to find only Shelaigh and Robbie. They were being entertained by Queenie, the Chihuahua, sporting this day's haute couture of a chartreuse corduroy jacket lined with an equally obnoxious chartreuse faux fur.

Queenie's ensemble was not what was entertaining the pair and Dannie noticed that while Shelaigh was giggling at the dog, Robbie was emitting deep belly laughs as only a little boy could do.

"She did it again," he said gasping for breath. "Did you hear her Mommy?"

"No, I,".....but then there it was.

Queenie was shivering, despite her jacket and the warm trailer. She was shivering so hard that when she was shaking almost uncontrollably she would snort; a very large snort, in fact, for such a little dog.

Robbie had dissolved into hysterics again but managed to gasp out the words, "I love Queenie, Mommy, she's the funniest dog ever!"

Shelaigh scooped up Queenie and held her close, probably to quell the shivering, thought Dannie. It hadn't escaped her that Shelaigh's cashmere sweater was chartreuse as well.

"You're all alone," Dannie observed.

"It's OK," Shelaigh said. "Kent has been at Mary Jane's all day getting ready for the exhibitor party tomorrow. He was anxious for Muriel and Mikey to join him. Everything is just about ready for tomorrow morning."

"Are you slated to go to Mary Jane's to help too?" asked Dannie. "If so, Robbie can hang with Jake and me the rest of the day."

"Oh no, I don't need to be there and I have to go decide what I'm going to wear to the party. Mikey is going to be my date. Muriel didn't even want to go. She is not impressed with Kent's theme for the party. She says it's way over the top and she wants no part of it. She told me today that Kent wouldn't know class and wealth if it hit him in the face but luckily she knew how to behave."

"What a strange thing to say," Dannie said.

"She's a little strange," said Shelaigh. "She pretends the charity is the reason for her existence but I was asking her questions about the raffle and she didn't know any of the answers."

"Probably just busy," Dannie shrugged. "Anyway, today's classes are just wrapping up so as soon as you pick up what's left at the rings and are set for morning why don't you go. Tomorrow will be a long day...and night."

All day Friday the show had been buzzing about the exhibitor party. All attendees and staff were invited which would make an unmanageable number if all appeared, but parents and kids tended not to come and the cocktail party ambiance meant a larger number could come and go all night.

The event started at eight, but Jeff and Dannie were just minutes from the Bittler home at seven-fifteen. Tootie and Mary Jane had been quite clear that Dannie's current position at the show required her to stand in the receiving line at the front door for at least the first hour.

On the way to the party, Dannie told Jeff the story of last year's fiasco from Jimmy's bad behavior, to her ex Brian's drunken spectacle, to the spectacle that was often Shelaigh, culminating in the coupling of Jimmy and Sunshine Forrest; unfortunate and regrettable, at least for Sunshine.

Dannie was sure this year would produce stories to tell too, but she was more interested in the plan about to be executed known only to her and her friends. Jeff was of course attending with her, Miles was to be Summer's date and Chelle and Jen would be escorted by two investigators from the Attorney General's office. Dannie had worked hard to get Chelle and Jen to agree. They thought it odd that Dannie was setting them up and she couldn't tell them why. The men planned nothing save observation and information gathering but it was exciting to see the net closing around Kent.

Jeff pulled his truck into the driveway of Mary Jane's home. "What. The. Hell. ?"

"Oh my God, Jeff, they're Bronies," Dannie was trying not to laugh.

"I'm sorry...they're what?"

"Bronies; adult men that dress in pony outfits similar to the little pony toys I played with as a child. Major creep factor," she said unable to hide the laughter any longer. "I don't think that was Kent's intent, he probably has never heard the word, but that's what he got."

It was evident that in the place of last year's parking attendants sporting black pants, white shirts and dark vests, Kent had opted for this quasi-horse theme. The clearly eager parking people were wearing all manner of plush full-body costumes in a large spectrum of colors with pastel and even rainbow manes and tails. Dannie suspected more central casting involvement.

One particularly enthusiastic man came prancing up to the driver's side of the truck, "I trotted right over to park your car," he said devilishly.

Jeff grabbed his wallet from the seat and flashed his shield. "No, just point where to go."

The Brony raised his hands in mock horror before saying, "Follow me!" then again prancing to an appropriate parking space.

"This guy's looking to get punched," said Jeff, but he too was laughing.

Jeff got out of the truck and went around to assist Dannie. The Bronies caught sight of her in the form-fitting red brocade dress she had selected for the party and sent appreciative catcalls her way. She had on matching heels and a diamond necklace Judith, her stepmother, had left her all of which set off her blonde hair perfectly.

"Isn't that considered tasteless and harassing behavior these days?" Jeff asked.

Dannie eyed him in his faded denims, white button-down shirt minus a tie and navy blazer and said, "Well, we both look hot, maybe all that noise was for you."

He made a face and took her hand for the walk to the door. As they drew closer Dannie couldn't believe her eyes. Evidently

Kent had settled on some sort of carousel unicorn theme, but it had all gone wrong.

Framing the door were two gigantic figures appearing almost like the retro flocked animals of yesteryear with their close-cropped fuzz already down to smooth plastic in places. The attempt had been made to hide this with gauzy, cotton candy-like filler that appeared closer to the popular spider web material sold at Halloween. They were gaudy and amateurish at best.

Walking through the front door Dannie had no words for what she saw. There were more of the flocked horse figures everywhere; some rearing, some bowing, some frozen in a high-stepping trot. They all were clumsily wrapped in the same web-like substance found at the front entrance but additionally there was lots of gauzy pastel material and glittery ribbon...yards of it.

Mary Jane came hurrying from the back of the house looking beautiful though her facial expression was full of worry.

"Oh, Dannie, isn't it just awful? What he's done to my house, I just can't believe it and I will never get rid of all this glitter! "

"Mary Jane, you should have called me."

"It was too late. By the time I saw all this being unloaded yesterday there was nothing anyone could have done."

"Surely when Muriel arrived yesterday you could have asked her to intervene for a bit of, shall we say, restraint?" said Dannie.

"Muriel wasn't here yesterday, Dannie."

"But I thought...."

"She called Kent to say she was stuck at the show."

Dannie excused herself and went to find Jeff to pass on that bit of news.

"Why would she do that, and where do you think she was?"

"From what you've said these past couple of days, it sounds like maybe Muriel is reaching her limit with Kent. Not for good, I'm sure, but as to her trip south next week to take care of "personal business"; my guess is she just wants to put some space between Kent and herself for a few days. Wouldn't you?" Jeff asked. "But why would she take Mike Gregory? A little May-December?"

Dannie pretended to gag. "Oh gross! No Mike Gregory is totally averse to work, so if he thought he could tag on to the 'have to help Kent' story and go back to the hotel instead that would have been his plan."

Dannie spent the next hour in the formal receiving line sandwiched between Tootie and Mary Jane. She greeted trainers, staff, and exhibitors and thanked them for their support of the Silver Shores shows. Tootie had taken charge of the line right before eight and had placed Kent and Muriel at the end. It was evident they were not happy with her decision.

Summer and Miles had arrived and so had Chelle, Jen, and their escorts. All of the men had, as expected, faded in to the background to observe and ask unobtrusive questions.

The rainbow pony-clad people had invaded the house too, only this time it was the servers working for the caterer. Many were women so Dannie figured she should adjust her Brony opinion to simply note them as ridiculously costumed staff.

But perhaps the best visual of the night involved the bar set up in one corner of the spacious living room. Two large, bowing unicorn figures flanked either side of the bar and because their heads were lowered in a submissive attitude, their horns were positioned, for many, just at crotch height. As the large crowd around the bar would readjust, patrons stepping forward as one left with a beverage, the one stepping away backed up or turned to allow access to the next in line and often received a horned unicorn "greeting" that was quite unexpected.

As the receiving line neared its one hour requirement, Dannie was amazed to note the appearance of Barb Snowden. She greeted Tootie then moved to face Dannie.

"Barb, this is a surprise."

"Muriel invited me. I came for the Grand Prix tomorrow but she said I could come tonight."

"Of course, you're welcome to be here," Dannie said, wishing it was not so.

"The weather here has been just beautiful, hasn't it?" asked Barb.

"I thought you just got here," Dannie said.

"Er, I did. I mean, I've just been checking online. Mrs. Bittler, thank you for hosting," said Barb, quickly moving down the line.

Shelaigh had begun her party early. Her date, Mike Gregory, was a no-show so Shelaigh had opted for her stand in date, vodka. Dannie noticed her talking with Jeff; he was looking quite amused. Dannie's intent was not to torture Jeff too much this evening as he was coming to the Grand Prix tomorrow night also.

"Tootie, what else do you need me to do?"

"Oh, in a few minutes I wanted you, Mary Jane, Kent and me to speak for just a few moments. Is that alright?"

"Of course, whatever you need."

She wandered over to Jeff, who kissed her briefly before shaking his head.

"Where's Shelaigh? She's vanished," Dannie teased.

"She hit on me," said Jeff.

"What?"

"She hit on me, drunk, slurring-her-words-hit on me, wanted me to meet her in the gazebo outside."

"Oh, poor girl," Dannie sighed.

"What? She could do worse," Jeff said, feigning outrage.

Dannie elbowed him lightly, "You know exactly what I mean. On another subject the good news is we can get out of here soon. Tootie just wants me to be part of the group that formally addresses the guests."

"I'll be waiting," Jeff winked.

Tootie waved at Dannie and she walked to join the group in front of Mary Jane's grand piano.

Mary Jane spoke first and shyly thanked everyone for attending the party. Dannie noticed Pat, who was standing just to the side give her a thumbs-up for encouragement. Tootie was next and she covered the sponsors, staff, and community partners that were supporting the show. She introduced Kent.

"I am so humbled by the support and encouragement I have received here as your manager, not to mention the support for Steeds 4 Soldiers. Please don't forget the raffle. You can purchase tickets tonight and tomorrow at the Grand Prix. Two winners will be drawn at the end of week two. You should know that every dollar makes a diff..."

Tootie interrupted, "And Dannie?"

"I want to add my thanks to those of everyone else. This show is a tradition for so many of us and has a special place in our hearts. Thank you for giving it one more chance and thank you for coming tonight, please enjoy the rest of your evening."

After a few moments of small talk and party-goers approaching to offer their thanks, Dannie and Jeff said their goodbyes and headed back to the beach house. As the truck passed beneath a street light Dannie noticed a shimmer coming from the front of her dress.

"Amazing!" she exclaimed. "I am covered in glitter and I was nowhere near those damned ribbons."

A crazy Saturday began the moment Dannie fetched her radio from the show office.

"Dannie?" came Patrick's voice.

"Go ahead, Pat."

"Do you have a moment to come to the judge's table at the Main Jumper?"

"Sure, what's up?" she asked as she began walking in that direction.

"It involves the decorations for the party tonight."

"Yeah, they planned to do most of that last night."

"Uh-huh. I'll see you when you get here," Pat said cryptically.

As she neared the large tent, she could see not one, but several significant problems.

The special section for sponsors and VIP spectators was under a large white tent nearly as long as the side of the arena. The judge for the Main Jumper ring sat at a table under the tent as did the announcer but the two were tidily blocked from the people traffic and noise. Today, Dannie found, they were blocked from even more.

The designers for the evening soiree had taken their job of transforming the space quite seriously. Hanging on both sides of the tent where the roof joined the straight sides were curtain after curtain of white billowing fabric. Dannie was sure that the intent was to create a bright, yet intimate space for the party and fundraising but they had done so much more.

She motioned to Sissy, one of Kent's designers. Sissy flitted over smiling from ear to ear.

"Don't you just love it, Dannie?"

"Actually, no Sissy."

Sissy appeared crestfallen. "Why not? What's wrong?"

Dannie knew her irritation was showing. "Do you see all these glorified bedsheets hanging down here? Well, we have a problem...a big problem; they are obstructing the view of the ring. Right here at this table," she said indicating Pat, "I have a judge. The good people that have paid large sums of money to enter this show are expecting the judge to actually view them as they do what they came here and paid large sums of money to do. Not to mention, all day and early this evening, there will be things going on in this ring that people wish to watch and they can't see through the sheets."

"Well, Dannie, they aren't actually sheets, they ar..."

"I get it! Now you need to get it. The first horse is going to step into this ring in twenty-five minutes. Horses don't like big, billowing pieces of material waving in their space and Mr. Collingsworth needs a view of the ring, the whole ring, therefore you have twenty-five minutes to raise, tie-back, or whatever else you can manage so these things won't be in the way."

As if for emphasis, a gust of wind blew one of the drapes straight back at Pat covering his face and head.

"Sissy!" said Dannie as she pointed.

"Oh I can't, they'll wrinkle," Sissy whined.

"You will, or you will have such bigger problems from me than wrinkles in that material."

As she turned, leaving Sissy to her problem-solving her radio called to her again. This time it was Summer. Her back gate was near the awards trailer and as such she was the first to be aware of the next problem.

"Dannie, could you go to the awards trailer? There seems to be some sort of altercation going on."

"What now?" Dannie muttered to herself, jogging with Jake at her heels.

Approaching the trailer she could hear Shelaigh screeching and Mike Gregory grumbling in return though she couldn't make out the words. Coming around the corner, she caught a glimpse of Shelaigh, holding Queenie, and yelling in heated fashion at Mike.

"You stood me up, you bastard! You said you'd be my date."

"No, you said I'd be your date, Shelaigh. I never agreed."

"Why couldn't you have just come anyway?"

"I had stuff to do."

"You didn't have to be Such. An. Ass." With each of the last three words, Shelaigh shook her fist at Mike for emphasis. The only problem was her fist was at the end of the arm holding Queenie and therefore the dog was jarred with each resounding word.

"Enough! Both of you stop...now. Shelaigh, you take the golf cart and go take breakfast or drink orders from the staff at the Hunter rings. Mike, you walk over and do the same at the Jumper rings. After you order the food, wait for it and deliver it when the orders are complete. I don't want to hear another word about last night."

They took off sullenly in opposite directions and Dannie turned to Muriel who had been working unassumingly in the corner of the trailer.

"Shelaigh's hungover," she said.

"No doubt," said Dannie, "but not my problem."

"Listen, I'm glad you're here," Muriel said. "About tomorrow, I plan to be out of here about noon to beat the traffic heading south. I'll make sure and have everything for tomorrow's special stuff ready to go but I have a rental car to pick up."

"A rental car?"

"Well, I have to leave the RV for Kent and I thought a little sedan would be better anyway for a quick trip there and back."

"You're probably right," Dannie agreed, "noon should be fine."

"I'm sure I've set up everything to make next week easy," Muriel said.

"Great, but if there's a problem, well, my mom is coming down late tomorrow. She's going to watch Robbie next week but she could fill in in a pinch. She's been around a horse show or two in her time."

"Your mom, huh? That's good to know," Muriel nodded.

She walked away from the trailer happy that since it was Saturday Robbie was home with Jeff. He didn't need to be in the middle of the Mikey and Shelaigh show.

The Grand Prix was scheduled for a six PM start with the party following. Everything was well within schedule; the day's classes had finished several hours ago and as the crew completed the course build and the tractor and water truck made the jumping surface pristine, Kent's minions put the finishing touches on the party area.

Dannie's only hope was for there to be an improvement over last night's flocked, mythical creatures but approaching the tent she was reminded to be careful what she wished for.

It appeared tonight's theme was to be the circus. There were already performers trying out the areas set up for them; a scantily-clad woman hanging from a modified trapeze suspended from the top of the tent, a magician using grand gestures to pull a huge bouquet of flowers from a walking stick, and a man looking as if he modeled his costume from a story Dannie read as a child, Ali Baba and the Forty Thieves. 'What could possibly go wrong here?" she thought sarcastically.

She tracked down Kent who was busily adjusting chairs, straightening floral arrangements and checking wine glasses for fingerprints; just the thing a show manager should be doing an hour before the biggest class of the week.

"Kent, I don't know what all these people will be doing, but they can't do it during the class. You know that, right?"

"They've been contracted to begin their acts at six."

"No. The class is the show to be seen at six. They can do...whatever, when the class is over."

"I don't have time for this," Kent snapped, "my skills at management have been well proven so far this week, haven't they?"

"You're delusional," said Dannie and walked away from the circus.

They were just moments from the Grand Prix being underway. Under the tent, Dannie saw Jeff and Robbie. They had been invited to sit in the sponsor area of Forrest Equestrian with Sunshine and Blimpy. She went over to give Robbie a hug and get a kiss from Jeff when Sunshine pulled her aside.

"I know you're crazy busy, honey, I'll just take a minute. I wanted you to know that Blimpy and I told Kent he was not welcome to bring his show dates to Forrest Equestrian."

"Really?"

"Yes, after my interview with the man from the Attorney General's office, Blimpy and I don't trust Kent. He amended his original paperwork with them regarding Steeds 4 Soldiers to reflect that his animals for the program were housed at our facility, as you know. Of course they aren't, but he made that amendment a year ago, before out facility even existed."

"I think you made the right decision," Dannie said squeezing her arm. "My advice to you now would be to send in applications for his three dates yourself. I don't think he'll hold on to them much longer. Gotta go."

Dannie checked with all the people that made the class go; judges, back gate, crew, and announcer, and the first horse crossed the plane of the gate at exactly six PM. The crowd was huge with not a spare seat anywhere.

She walked past Tootie Bittler's seating area and saw that the judge, "Sticks" Hansen, was one of her guests. He motioned to her and when she neared said,"Miss Dannie, ah declare ah'm so happy I was able to join you this week. Top notch, darlin', top notch. The only thing better is ah'll be here next week too, after I play a few rounds of golf, that is."

Dannie kissed him on the cheek and smiled at Tootie who blew a kiss in her direction. She felt as if she could begin to relax, but as usual she was so wrong.

Her aim was to head to the other end of the tent and make sure all was well throughout. Her glimpse of the trapeze artist made Dannie cringe but she supposed she could live with her dramatic spins and poses. She took another few steps and looked at Ali Baba. He had a torch, a lit torch. She watched him draw a great breath through his nose and it suddenly struck her that he was a fire-breather!

She yelled, "Nooooooo," but it was too late and he sent the fuel out of his mouth in a fine mist. It connected to the flame on the torch and with a great roar a horizontal column of flame shot out from under the tent and just thirty feet in front of the horse approaching the jump on the near rail.

The horse nearly sat down, locking all four of his legs so committed was his effort to go no closer to the flame. He threw his head up, his eyes large and showing white all the way around, his ears pointed directly at the fire-breather.

The rider, caught completely by surprise lost his balance and fell off; that was automatic elimination.

There was a stunned silence throughout the crowd. The rider wasn't hurt, nor was the horse, but an audience of riders and horsemen were mystified that anyone would have thought fire near the arena was a good idea.

Logan Peters, the announcer, did a great job of getting the crowd once again focused on the ring by running down the leader board as it currently stood and reading the biography of the next rider.

Dannie marched over to Ali Baba and said, "You're done. Right now, you're done." She then turned to the girl on the trapeze. "You too, off you go."

She noticed Kent quietly working his way toward the exit of the tent. "Oh no, you need to stay and face the music, Kent. I told you they needed to stop during the class and you showed complete disregard for the sport and the safety of the competitors. "

Jeff appeared at her side, "Need help, D?"

Just make sure he doesn't leave," she said waving in Kent's direction.

The trainer of the fallen rider began by demanding a re-ride, but it was out of the question based on the decision of the show committee. In the end, they agreed the horse needed to save the jumps for another day and graciously accepted Dannie's offer of a refund of their class fees and stall charges for the week, not to mention her sincere apology.

The two investigators for the AG's office had taken over babysitting Kent. Dannie hadn't even been aware they were in attendance.

Kent was mumbling, gesturing wildly and his agitation only increased as Dannie drew near.

"You have tried to undermine me from day one, tried to discredit my charity, tried..."

Dannie could stand it no longer. "You have no charity. You have a therapeutic program involving horses but you don't have one horse. You continue to badger people for donations for something that doesn't exist. You insult good, hard-working people that do provide a service to those in need and you make it harder for them to accomplish their mission. I don't need to undermine you, you do it to yourself every time you open your mouth or hold out your hand for money. You disgust me and you deserve everything that's coming to you."

"We have some questions for you, Mr. Mallory," said one of the investigators as he took him by the arm and led him away from the tent.

Dannie looked around and realized the class had continued, in fact, was almost complete. The horse show had gone on, as horse shows always did. She had an award to present and so that's what she went to do.

Sunday was a quiet, happier day. Exhibitors were raving about the week just finishing and the next week would have even more horses attending.

The biggest issue today was what was called turnover. Some horses were staying for another week and those stalls were fine, all they needed was a guaranteed feed and bedding order to carry them through Monday before the next week's show started again Tuesday. But some people were leaving and bright and early the next morning new horses would arrive to use the same stalls, therefore, in a small window of time the stalls had to be stripped of any bedding and 'turned over', or made ready for the new arrivals.

Dannie had a crew hard at work on that turnover. As soon as a barn finished showing and loaded up for their trip home, the turnover crew moved in and went to work.

Kent had not made an appearance today. Dannie was fairly certain he was humiliated at the events of the past few days and was saving face. She expected he would be back with a vengeance next week.

Shelaigh and Muriel had worked like dogs to prepare for the first show day of week 2. Mike Gregory was nowhere to be found but Dannie thought he might have been tapped by Kent for some help. Jeff had to work early that morning so Robbie had come with Dannie and Jake and spent all day in Shelaigh's company, happily doing as he was asked.

Dannie was busy, but contentedly so. She checked in at the office where Chelle and Jen were swamped but efficient as always. She went by the feed area and Wes Morgan assured her they were in great shape for the turnover as it related to deliveries of feed and bedding to new arrivals. She had paychecks, completed by Tootie and Mary Jane she planned to deliver to all the staff well before they finished for the day and her last trip was to the awards trailer.

She crossed paths with Tootie who was just leaving the trailer, visiting with her daughter Dannie was sure. When she entered the trailer though, she found herself to be completely wrong.

"Mommy, look what I got!" said an excited Robbie, holding up a wad of cash.

"Where did you get that, buddy?"

"Mrs. Tootie just paid me, she said everyone that works as hard as I did deserves to get paid. She paid me ten dollars a day for last week and this week."

Dannie took the bills from his hand and counted them; one hundred dollars.

"That's a lot of money for a little guy."

"I worked hard, Mommy. I'm going to treat Miss Shelaigh to ice cream at Big Top Ice Cream."

"I don't know, Robbie," Dannie said.

"I was going to treat him," Shelaigh said, "I promised at the beginning of the week. But it's OK if he wants to be the big spender." She ruffled his hair in an affectionate gesture.

"OK, well I should be done here at about five; will you be back by then?"

"Before then, I'm sure," said Shelaigh.

The remainder of the afternoon flew by. Muriel, as planned, had left around noon but the awards trailer was in great shape for next week. Shelaigh and Robbie were off for Big Top Ice Cream and Sticks, ring completed, was heading for at least nine holes of golf.

With all rings done, Dannie stopped in to check once more with Chelle and Jen. They would be working tomorrow checking in week two entries and Dannie wanted to make sure they had everything they needed. She, of course, would be working too, but everyone's start time would be closer to nine than six-thirty.

Dannie glanced at her watch. It was four forty-five and she was sure Shelaigh would have called when they returned from their ice cream "date".

She walked to the awards trailer but it was locked up tight and there was no sign of Shelaigh's car. She called Tootie, thinking they may have just gone there after their visit to town but Tootie hadn't seen or heard from them.

Becoming a little concerned she called Jeff, wondering if Robbie had been in contact with him. She told him the story and he had a cruiser stop by Big Top Ice Cream.

At five-thirty he called her back saying the store remembered them coming in but they had been gone for hours.

Dannie dialed Shelaigh's cell number which went immediately to voicemail. She dialed three more times with the same result, then called Tootie again but she knew nothing new.

Dannie's heart was pounding though she tried to remain calm. Even Jake was becoming anxious, no doubt feeding off Dannie's nerves. She wanted to go home, surely at this point Shelaigh would just bring him there believing everyone was gone from the show grounds but she was afraid to leave. Why didn't Shelaigh call?

At eight-thirty, Dannie's world shattered into a million pieces of panic, fear, and terror as she accepted the reality that Robbie and Shelaigh had vanished into thin air.

-21-

Jeff and Summer found Dannie and Jake sitting in the dark in her SUV, the only car in the parking lot at Silver Shores. They had both been at the beach house when the horror of the situation began to unfold; Jeff having returned from work around four and Summer from the show an hour before that.

Jeff pulled his truck next to the SUV, got out and went immediately to Dannie. He opened the driver's door and she turned to look at him but it was as if she had no idea who he was.

"D, I'm going in to work to see how I can help. I brought Summer to drive you home. D? Are you hearing me?"

Her nod was barely perceptible. She didn't move so Jeff gently took her by the arm and said, "Let's move you to the passenger seat and let Summer drive."

Dannie stood and walked with Jeff around the car, stopping briefly to weakly ask, "Jake?"

"Right here, he's right with you in the car."

They reached the passenger seat and Dannie sat, staring straight ahead. Jeff reached in and buckled her seatbelt and then directed a small nod at Summer.

"I'll be in touch," he said as he headed back to the truck.

Summer guided a virtually unresponsive Dannie into the house and said, "I'll feed Jake."

A few moments later, she put the bowl down for Jake and turned to find Dannie gone. She walked to the bedroom and the office and found nothing then heard a small noise on the other side of the house and went to peer inside Robbie's room.

Dannie was sitting on the edge of Robbie's bed, holding his little down jacket and the plastic T-Rex she had bought him at the truck stop in the spring. She smoothed the jacket on her lap, silent tears cascading down her cheeks and then barely above a whisper said, "He'll be cold, he should have his jacket. Why would she do this?"

"Who?" asked Summer.

"Shelaigh, of course. I thought she was changing, that she liked Robbie. It's my fault. She sucked me in, I believed that bitch!" The tears began to fall anew.

"Dannie, we don't know who did this..."

"Of course we do!" Dannie snapped.

"Listen, let me make you a cup of tea, maybe some toast. You probably haven't eaten in some time." In truth, Summer had no idea what to do. How did you console someone that was inconsolable? With no further exchange she went to the kitchen.

In town at the Silver Shores Police Department every part of the station was on high alert. Many officers had been called back in for additional help and it was a very uncharacteristic Sunday evening.

The moment Jeff had arrived the Captain had called him in to his office. "Barnes, you know you can't work on this."

"Cap…"

"Not negotiable. I don't need some defense lawyer down the road making a case for improper police work because you are engaged to this kid's mother. Every step of this must be documented and clean as a whistle. Have I made myself clear?"

"Yes, sir."

"I've made Wolcott the lead detective, everything will go through him."

Jeff nodded, excused himself and walked down the hall to his desk. Miles walked by and paused.

"Hey, I've called a briefing in five in the conference room."

"Cap says I'm out," Jeff said.

"He didn't say you couldn't listen in, did he?"

Jeff jumped up and followed Miles and in minutes the briefing was in full swing.

"So, I want to bring all of you up to speed. We are looking for a five year old boy, Robert Rossi. He'll be six in the fall and he goes by 'Robbie'. Most of you also know that he is the son of Barnes' fiancé. We are also looking for Shelaigh Bittler, twenty-three, daughter of long-time Silver Shores resident, Tootie Bittler. We don't know if she has abducted Robbie or if she too could be in danger."

Miles continued to lay out what they knew so far which at that point was precious little. He gave a timeline for Shelaigh and Robbie's movements up until they reached the ice cream store and he introduced the two FBI special agents that were working side by side with Silver Shores on the case.

He wrapped up the briefing by saying, "We issued an Amber Alert for Robbie at ten PM which includes details and the license number of Bittler's car. We are also waiting on the owner of Big Top Ice Cream. There are surveillance cameras in and around the shop but the kids that work in the store don't know how to recover the recordings. The owner's been called but has not yet called back. We have a lot of ground to cover. Go to work, guys."

It was four-thirty in the morning when Jake heard noise at the front door causing him to emit a low, threatening growl.

"Hush," said Dannie as she took a sheet of chocolate chip cookies out of the oven. "Probably one of the neighborhood cats."

The front door opened, however, and instead of a cat revealed Beth Hoffman. Jake ran to greet her and she set her bags in the foyer.

"Mom, what are you doing here at this time of the morning?"

"Jeff called about midnight and I threw my stuff in a bag and drove right down."

"Perfect! You're just in time for a warm cookie."

"What?"

"When Robbie gets home he's going to be hungry, I've been making his favorites."

"Oh Dannie, have they found him?"

"Not yet, but I wanted to be prepared."

"Danica, you're scaring me with this," she waved her hands toward the mess in the kitchen, "all of it."

Dannie smiled, then in an instant her face crumbled and she grabbed the island for support. Beth rushed to her and pulled a chair close for Dannie to sit in, another for herself right next to her daughter. She drew her into a tight embrace and rocked back and forth slightly.

"It's going to be alright, honey."

"Oh Mom, he's scared and probably cold, I just know it. It's my job to protect him, to take care of him. He'll be wondering why I'm not there." She dissolved into great, racking sobs and Beth held her and let her cry.

At seven AM Miles had called another briefing to insert some additional information into the general consciousness. Jeff sat down with an enormous travel mug of coffee as dark as black shoe polish. He had caught a couple hours of fitful sleep and now he ran a hand through his hair and rubbed his eyes as he waited, along with everyone else, for Miles.

He blew through the door at five after the hour, followed by the FBI men.

"We've got the car."

Now Jeff was wide awake. He asked what everyone wanted to know.

"Robbie?"

"No, it was empty. They're towing it in to the lab to be processed now. They found it on a dirt road out in the valley, about twenty miles from the equestrian center. Also, the owner of the ice cream store is on the way down with a zip drive with the info from the cameras yesterday. Finally, I want to get Robbie's mother and Shelaigh's mother in today to question them. Do-able?"

Jeff's cell phone rang. He held up his hand as a form of apology and stepped outside to take the call. It was from Beth.

"I'm sorry to bother you. Any news?"

"A little, are you with Dannie?"

"She's in with Summer. Jeff, I'm so worried, when I got here she was making cookies...at four-thirty in the morning. There's something else. When I got to your front door, there was an envelope stuck in the crack of the door with Dannie's name typewritten on the front."

"Did you touch it? Did you tell her about it?"

"I knocked it into my bag with the sleeve of my jacket. And no, I didn't tell her."

"Beth, here is what I need from you. Bring Dannie down to the station, the sooner the better. She will be interviewed, but it's purely routine. When she is occupied with that you can give me the letter and we'll talk about what we know so far. OK?"

"Absolutely."

"While she's here I will have my friend Scott talk with her. You remember him, Chaplain Henderson?"

Jeff ended the call and returned to the briefing to update Miles and the rest of the team on what he suspected was a ransom letter.

Word had reached many of the show staff and Pat, Chelle and Jen had mobilized the crew. They had called everyone and asked them to give up their day off to come in for a meeting at eight on the dot. To a person, they agreed without hesitation.

They were all sitting in the patio area near the show office and had helped themselves to the coffee, tea, and pastries Pat had provided. They now listened as he told them the news.

"We have no idea when, or if, she will be back, and we can't count on seeing Tootie either. What I... I mean, we," he said indicating Chelle and Jen, "are asking is that everyone here can step in and take care of one of Dannie's pieces of the puzzle."

Mary Jane said, "I'll take care of the awards, no need to worry about that."

"Jen and I will oversee any schedule changes," said Chelle.

"I'll work with Wes on feed orders and the stall charts for move-in today and the stalls for next week," added Logan Peters.

It was overwhelming. Every person attending thought of something they could do to contribute to the show and keep it running smoothly.

"Pat, what about that Mallory fella?" asked Sticks.

"As far as I know, Sticks, no one has seen him since he was escorted away Saturday evening. And one more thing everyone, it was so important to Dannie to have a drama-free show after last year. I know we can't change what has happened and I know you are all hoping for the best. I also know it is natural to be curious and you will talk with each other about it, just please don't involve the exhibitors or answer their questions. Dannie would hate to be the subject of horse show gossip."

The group agreed and set off to their respective jobs determined not to let their friend down.

At nine, Miles was called to the front by the desk sergeant to meet the owner of the ice cream store. He immediately escorted him back to the briefing room.

All available men working on the case joined them. Miles asked the owner to please identify the areas they were seeing in the various camera angles.

The group saw Shelaigh pull up in her SUV, watched her get out from one side and Robbie, with Queenie on a leash, from the other. They seemed relaxed and happy as they walked in the store.

Inside, they both ordered and received an ice cream cone and Robbie paid as he had promised. It was then that a man seated at one of the tables in nondescript pants and shoes and wearing a hoodie, approached Shelaigh and struck up a conversation.

The trained eyes of the watchful officers discerned she did not seem threatened and in fact, might even have known the man. Shelaigh and the hoodie talked for a few minutes more during which time he ordered a cone as well. Receiving his order, all three walked with Queenie toward the door of the shop.

To this point the unknown man had only been seen from the back and was unrecognizable. Jeff, who was standing at the back of the room watching the footage, hoped as the group approached Shelaigh's car they would have a glimpse of his face.

To everyone's surprise, Shelaigh went to the passenger side of her car and got in, Robbie and the dog entered the rear passenger door. Mr. Hoodie walked to the driver's side and as he pivoted to open the door there was a crystal clear view of his face.

"Who the hell is that?" asked Miles.

Dannie and Beth walked through the front door of the police department and were instantly greeted by Jeff. He had been pacing nervously for the better part of fifteen minutes after Beth's text alerted him they were on their way.

Dannie hugged him but it was almost ceremonial it was so lacking in emotion.

He pushed her back gently holding her at arm's length and searched her face for some idea of how she was feeling.

"Go ahead," she said dully, "say it."

"Say what?"

"Say 'I told you so'. Go ahead, say it."

"No, D, this isn't..."

Miles appeared at Dannie's elbow and said, "Great, you're here; let's go in one of the interview rooms."

Beth and Jeff watched Dannie disappear down the hallway with Miles. Jeff put his arm around Beth's shoulder.

"Oh Jeff, I've never seen her like this. And Robbie, I can't bear to think of it."

"Beth, everyone here is putting every fiber into finding Robbie. As for Dannie, it isn't unexpected for her to go through stages; sort of like the stages of grief but then again not the same. People who've had loved ones kidnapped go through shock, anger, guilt, feeling completely helpless and trying to find something to do, and often they come out fighting. It's a roller coaster of emotion."

"Aren't you feeling any of that?" she asked. "I'm sorry to say this but you seem, well, detached."

"I feel all of it, but I'm trying to fall back on what I've been trained to do. Now, I'm going to arrange for you to have a comfortable place to wait. Did you bring the letter?"

She held up her bag and he placed a thin, protective glove on his hand before retrieving the envelope. He motioned to a man standing near the officer at the desk who walked closer to Jeff.

"Beth, this is Special Agent Frugoli of the FBI. Frugoli, this is Robbie's grandmother, Beth Hoffman."

"I'm sorry to meet you under these circumstances, ma'am," he said and Beth nodded.

Jeff told him about the letter and the two excused themselves after another officer came to take Beth to a waiting room.

Miles held a chair for Dannie then walked to a small refrigerator in the corner of the room to retrieve a bottle of water, which he set on the table in front of her.

"Can I get you anything else?"

She shook he head.

"OK, we'll get started then."

Dannie glanced at the other man that had been waiting in the room when she and Miles entered.

"Dannie, this is Special Agent Baker of the FBI," Miles said.

"FBI?" Dannie said in alarm.

"Let me assure you it's perfectly normal, Mrs. Rossi, that we are involved when we suspect a child under the age of twelve has been kidnapped. I am so sorry for what you are going through right now."

"Dannie, we have an extensive list of questions and this will probably take a while. Some of them may seem silly, but often things will seem normal to you but we will find significance in them, OK?"

Biting her lip she nodded again and took a deep breath, waiting.

Jeff left the envelope from Beth with an evidence tech, but only after the tech opened it and showed it to the FBI's Frugoli.

"Ten million. They want ten million," he told Jeff. "We have to share this with Mrs. Rossi."

Jeff knew he was right, but Dannie was still being questioned by Miles and Special Agent Baker. So for the time being he and Baker went back to the briefing room.

Jeff had sent a text to Summer after seeing the footage from the ice cream store. He felt sure Summer could ID the man in the hoodie. He thought Dannie could too, but he was expecting Dannie, the fighter, to return to herself at any moment and they needed to retain the element of surprise. He was afraid Dannie would take off like the cavalry to the rescue.

Summer was escorted in to the briefing room and Baker explained what they were looking for. They had printed a still photo from the flash drive and they placed it on the table in front of Summer.

"Do you recognize that man?"

"Sure, that's Mikey Gregory."

Back in the interview room it was evident Dannie was losing patience with all the questions from Miles and Special Agent Baker. She was fidgeting in the chair having already peeled the label off the water bottle in miniscule shreds now scattered across the table.

Miles said, "Now, yesterday afternoon..."

"Oh my God!" Dannie's temper erupted. "Why are you asking me these ridiculous questions? Why is no one trying to find her?"

"Find who?" asked Baker.

"Shelaigh Bittler. Anyone with half a brain knows she's kidnapped my son."

"We don't know who has kidnapped Robbie, not yet," Baker said.

"Why does everyone keep saying that?" Her voice was rising in frustration. "I know."

Miles stood and walked to Dannie's side, turned her chair to face him and knelt down to look her in the eye.

"Dannie, you're an intelligent woman. I see it every time I'm around you so I know you will understand when I tell you that I am a good detective. The reason I'm good is because I let the evidence come to me, let it speak to me, I don't try to make it fit where I want it to go. It may turn out you are right and it's Sheleigh that has abducted your son, but it may not. I'm detailed, I'm thorough, and I'm doing everything I can to find your son for you. Fair enough?"

Special Agent Frugoli had wasted no time with the ID of Mikey Gregory. He called the horse show office and got the staff hotel information from Chelle, then sent officers to pick up Mikey for questioning. While they waited for word, Jeff accompanied Frugoli into the room with Miles, Baker and Dannie.

Frugoli spoke to the room. "There's been a ransom demand. It's for ten million dollars."

"I'll pay it," Dannie said.

"No, that's not wise," Miles said.

"The hell it's not! Let me see the letter. This is my decision, not yours. It's my money. Jeff, you agree, right?"

"D, I can't be involved with..."

"Not involved!" she shouted. "We're your family, he's a little boy, my little boy."

Jeff's shoulders drooped as he closed his eyes and turned and left the room.

The hurt in her eyes shone like a beacon. She directed her attention back to Miles and tried to focus.

"I want to see that letter."

"It's being processed as evidence right now, Dannie. I will let you see it when they are done."

The door to the interview room opened and Scott Henderson, Silver Shores PD chaplain entered.

"Gentlemen, if you are done, may I have a moment with Mrs. Rossi."

A handcuffed Mike Gregory was escorted through a back door that led to the large bay where Silver Shores PD cruisers disgorged their most recent occupants.

Just inside the door, Miles and Special Agent Frugoli met the officers that detained Mike and guided them into the nearest interview room. As one of the officers removed the handcuffs, Miles asked Mike if he wanted water or soda. When he declined, Miles indicated a chair and asked him to sit down.

Mike sprawled in the chair, his body language speaking of arrogance and bad attitude.

"Mike, my name is Miles Wolcott. I'm a detective with the Silver Shores Police Department. Also in the room is Special Agent Frugoli with the FBI. Do you know why we've brought you here?"

"No, and by the way, it's Mikey."

"Great, Mike. You're here because we believe you were the last person to see Robbie Rossi and Shelaigh Bittler before their disappearance yesterday afternoon. You are not under arrest; you've been detained so we can ask some questions. Where did the three of you go in Ms. Bittler's car after you left the ice cream shop?"

Mike threw his head back and flashed his characteristic mega-watt smile, "What ice cream shop? You guys are whacked."

Miles calmly opened a file folder on the table in front of him and removed a piece of paper which he placed on the table in front of Mike. It was the photo of him that Summer identified earlier. Mike forgot his attitude and sat up straight in the chair, staring at the photo, mouth open in disbelief.

"Big Brother's everywhere, eh, Mike?" said Miles.

Frugoli spoke up. "Mr. Gregory. I can assure you we are not playing frat boy games. These two people have been missing for," he checked his watch, "now just shy of twenty-four hours. We believe you are involved with their disappearance and because we have evidence and third-party identification putting you in the company of these two individuals at the ice cream store, unless you start telling us what you know we are prepared to charge you with two counts of kidnapping and one count of extortion for the ransom demand. That's for starters."

"I don't know anything," Mike said. "I want a lawyer."

-22-

Chaplain Scott Henderson sat alone with Dannie in the interview room. He had been listening for nearly twenty minutes as she poured her heart out; her guilt, her fear, her anger, and her hurt at Jeff's refusal to address the ransom issue.

"I can't believe I was so consumed with a stupid horse show," she said. "How shallow could I be? And Jeff, I thought he loved Robbie, loved me, he doesn't seem to even be working on trying to find him. And tell me, why isn't anyone trying to find Shelaigh?"

"That's a lot of questions, Dannie," smiled Scott, "and I'm sure you have more. Will you let me try to answer at least some of them?"

"Of course."

"First, let's talk about that big guy that loves you, and he does love you, Dannie. He was ordered by the Captain to steer clear of this investigation." Scott proceeded to tell her why. "If he disregards the order there could be consequences; problems with the investigation possibly, but frankly, it could also jeopardize his job. Your guy loves his work and he helps the citizens of this community every day. If you ask him to choose between his job and you, I predict he would choose you but at what cost? Is that really what you want?"

Dannie shook her head.

"Now about your work. When events like Robbie's disappearance occur, we are polarized by them. We become hyper-focused and suddenly everything else seems trivial and ridiculous. But no one can exist in such a heightened state forever and we all must return to what is normal in our lives. You are not a bad mother. You have to understand that none of this was caused by you. There is someone out there, maybe several someones, that systematically planned to do evil and you and your son were caught in the crosshairs. He is a victim, you are a victim."

"But Scott, I should have seen it coming, I don't know how but there must have been something that Shelaigh said or did..."

"We don't know yet if Shelaigh did this,"

"Oh, not you too."

"Dannie, we have far less control over the world and our lives than we think we do. It is comforting to think we have it all handled. We don't. You can't stop evil but what you can do is not allow it to defeat you, do whatever you can to prevent it from taking hold, no matter how small the gesture seems."

"I'm so scared, Scott. What if he's...?"

"I know you don't follow an organized religion, but you have expressed to me you do hold faith in your heart. I want you to call on that now. Have faith in Jeff, in his colleagues, in your mother, your friends; trust they are there for you and will help you in any way they can. Believe that Jeff loves you and loves Robbie and that you are loved by all of the people I just mentioned. I know you would expect a chaplain to say this but I do believe that love can move mountains."

Dannie managed a weak smile.

"Now if this was a movie the soundtrack would swell with an inspirational song and the happy ending would come. I am a realist and know I can't promise where we go from here and I know that prayer is not in your wheelhouse. It is, however, in mine and I hope you won't object if I pray for Robbie, and for you."

"No objections, I believe if anyone has an "in" it's you."

"I'll take you out to meet your mom. You can go home now."

Dannie stepped through the doorway of the interview room and almost ran directly into Tootie Bittler. Tootie threw her arms open and stepped toward Dannie, but Dannie immediately stepped backward, arms folded.

"Dannie, I've been thinking about you all..."

"Yeah, I've thought about you too. How does it feel to have raised a kidnapper, Tootie?"

Tootie looked as if Dannie had slapped her. Scott Henderson took Dannie by the shoulders and pushed her gently away and in the direction of Beth and her ride home.

It was after six Monday evening and Mike Gregory's attorney had arrived. Mike had called his father who had in turn made sure his son was well represented by more than a court-appointed public defender. His father had left his home in San Francisco and come to Silver Shores too, but since Mike was over the age of twenty-one his father would not be present at the questioning.

Most of the principals in the investigation had had almost no sleep, but they would not stop now. Miles and the two FBI men entered the room to speak with Mike.

After nearly three hours of interrogation with very little progress one of the officers with Silver Shores stuck his head in the door. "Hey, Baker, your idea paid off. We found someone at one of the local rental management companies that remembers renting a house out in the valley to a woman that wanted "remote and quiet". He's digging up the paperwork now and should be sending the address shortly."

Miles had an idea. "So, the noose is tightening, huh Bud? You are running out of time to get in front of this. When the others are caught, it's possible the deal goes to the one that talks first. How much of the ten million ransom were you promised for all this loyalty?"

"Ten million? The bitch was giving me ten thousand."

Mike's lawyer tried to rein him in, but Mike Gregory began squealing like the rat that he was.

At the beach house, Dannie was still beside herself. She'd had no sleep, had been unable to keep anything down except water or weak tea and was beginning to feel the anxiety that helplessness created once again.

She had been distracted in the afternoon by visits from friends; Pat, Chelle, even her ex-husband, Brian. She could hardly hide her amazement at seeing him.

"Dannie, I may have failed as a husband and a father and no one would argue with the idea that I'm pretty screwed up, but I'm not heartless. I don't like the thought of such a little guy out who knows where without the people he loves. You're a great mother; thank goodness he's had you. You've never let him down. I just wanted to come by to let you know I was thinking of you."

Before evening fell, the final visitors to the beach house were Dannie's attorney, Tom Robinson and her financial advisor, Jerrold Ryan.

"Originally it was our intent to speak with you about the final details regarding the plan you and Jeff had, but we both feel that isn't appropriate right now. We just wanted to come and offer our support and prayers for the return of your son," said Robinson.

"Thank you, but I'm just on hold now. Why don't you go ahead and tell me what you came to tell me."

She listened and gave them the go-ahead to execute the final pieces of the plan.

Dannie's phone rang about seven. "Muriel?"

"Dannie, I just heard on the news down here. Who could have guessed Shelaigh would do such a thing?"

"You're the only one besides me that believes it was her," Dannie said. "I can't thank you enough for calling."

"You take care, dear, and remember, anything I can do."

About ten-thirty, Summer was ready to go to bed. It had been a long day but everything for the start of week two tomorrow was in place. Everyone had worked tirelessly to make all things right and they had done it!

She had wanted to tell Dannie about it and about what her friends had done, but she knew right now Dannie didn't care. Dannie hadn't even mentioned the show and Summer completely understood. Still, she wanted to tell someone; maybe she would call Miles, she thought.

She dialed his cell and made sure he had time to talk. He said he had a moment so she told him briefly about her day before asking a question that had been nagging at her.

"So some of us were wondering...no one has seen Kent since he was taken away Saturday. Do you think he could be involved in Robbie's disappearance?"

"We're fairly certain he's not. The investigators from the Attorney General's office were keeping close tabs on him and Saturday in the middle of the night he just pulled up stakes on his RV and drove away. We got word the RV was sighted in New Mexico this afternoon."

"Why didn't they arrest him before he left?"

"The AG's office wants to make a case that will stick and then a complaint will be filed. I have no doubt it will happen. In the past several years he has collected thousands, if not more, for a charity that exists in name only. There are no horses, no facility, and no soldiers have benefitted from anything associated with the Mallory's. They have used those thousands to pay personal bills, take trips, wine and dine prospective donors, and Kent has done what's called self-dealing. By offering parties by Kent's Events for raffle prizes, then paying himself from the raffles proceeds for the "donation", he has participated in self-dealing. He's in trouble, no doubt about that but he wasn't around when Robbie disappeared. Plus it appears he falsified all the financial statements he was required to file."

"And he even left Muriel behind," Summer said.

"Yeah," replied Miles, "a real bastard."

At quarter past midnight Dannie's cell trilled. She'd finally fallen asleep on one of the love seats from pure exhaustion with her head on Beth's lap. She jumped and almost screamed into the phone.

"Jeff?"

"We've got him, D, he's safe."

She began to shake, the tears cascading down her face. "Let me talk to him...please!"

"He's not here yet, he's in a cruiser with two officers and they are on their way back to the station. They've assured me he is safe and unharmed."

"We're leaving right now." She hung up without waiting for a response and ran for her shoes and car keys.

Jake, who had also been on edge the last thirty-six hours because of the odd behavior of Dannie, his heart, seemed to sense a change and was up, standing at the door excitedly wagging his tail.

Dannie practically sprinted past Beth heading to the garage but Beth managed to wrest the car keys from her grasp. "No driving for you. You let me drive and you can tell me what he said on the way."

Dannie and Beth ran through the front door of the station house with Jake in tow. Dannie was sure Beth couldn't have gone slower if she tried, but they were here, it didn't matter now.

Miles met her at the desk and said, "Come with me, we just got a call they're about five minutes out."

Dannie practically pushed him down the hall as he led the way to the same door Mike Gregory had entered earlier that led to the large bay where the cruisers came and went.

Jeff was waiting there and Dannie threw her arms around him. "I'm so sorry, I…."

"No matter, D, I understand. I understand." He held her until they heard a car's tires squeal on the smooth cement.

Dannie turned, straining to see inside the police car. It stopped opposite the little group and Miles opened the rear door.

"Mommy!"

Dannie sank down to the cement and grabbed Robbie in an embrace. Jake was excitedly licking his face.

"Too tight, Mommy," he said, "and why are you shaking?"

"I'm just really happy, buddy."

A second police car parked behind the one that brought Robbie. Miles again opened the rear door and helped Shelaigh, carrying Queenie, out. Tootie, whose arrival Dannie hadn't noticed, ran to her and hugged her tightly.

Dannie remained seated, holding Robbie, but turned to look at Shelaigh who was smiling at her; a smile that faded as soon as Dannie began to yell.

"How could you do this? What kind of psychotic bitch would do this to a child? I hope you…"

"Mommy! STOP!" Robbie had placed the palms of both his hands on Dannie's mouth. "Miss Shelaigh took care of me, she told me stories so I wouldn't be scared, she let me hold Queenie so I wouldn't cry and when the bad people wanted to hit me she stood in front of me." Not until that moment had Dannie noticed Shelaigh had a black eye.

That was when a third cruiser pulled into the bay. Miles didn't welcome this one, two officers did and they removed two handcuffed individuals from the back, Muriel Mallory and Barb Snowden.

-23-

Three nights later, on Friday evening, the beach house was awash with light, thick with the smells of good food and filled with the laughter and happiness of good friends.

Dannie and Jeff were playing hosts to Beth, Miles, Summer, Pat, Mary Jane, Chelle, Jen, Scott Henderson, Sunshine, Blimpy and Raine Forrest, Celia and Mack Prentice, and nearly twenty other show staff and friends. Even Sticks had asked to be included and Dannie had welcomed him.

It was a celebration and Robbie, the guest of honor, had already gone to bed exhausted but happy. He had been invited to select the menu therefore pizza was the main dish but everyone had tried to bring salads and sides to fill in any gaps.

Dannie had not returned to the show grounds since the previous week but had plans to go there tomorrow after one stop first thing in the morning. She wouldn't stay at the show, but had a few things to take care of.

She hadn't actually planned to go back at all, but with coaxing from Jeff, her friends, and primarily Robbie, she agreed to return for week three.

The group was out on the back deck around the fire pit when Pat spoke up.

"Detective Wolcott, I don't mean to ask you to jeopardize your investigation but do you think you could tell us what you've learned about why Robbie was taken?"

"First of all, it's Miles. And yes, I'll give you the basics but Dannie and Jeff, only if it's OK with you."

"Everyone here is more family than friend," Dannie said, "Of course you can."

"Well, in a nutshell Muriel Mallory and Barb Snowden were two miserable, fed-up women. Barb was tired of running around behind some balding accountant that thinks he's from Jamaica," there was a smattering of laughter, "and Muriel was tired of being Muriel. She felt she was married to a pompous windbag who fraudulently took money based on other's generosity. She didn't mind the money but in her words, 'he spent most of it on himself'. She believed she deserved better than living in a beat-up RV and following Kent around like she actually liked him. Add to this, neither of them were fans of Dannie. In the interrogation, Muriel said Dannie had looks, brains, and a good-looking man, at least I guess some people think he's good-looking," Miles said under his breath, "but she couldn't stomach that she had that and money too.."

"How did Shelaigh figure in?" asked Chelle.

"Barb and Muriel decided they were going to get enough money that they could both disappear and live the good life. I don't even think they were going to disappear together. They decided that they could extort even more money from Tootie if they also took Shelaigh and no one would ever see them again."

"Barb came down to Silver Shores ostensibly to watch the show, but was spending her days renting and setting up a house to hold Robbie and Shelaigh. Muriel continued to work in the awards trailer and learn what she could about the normal comings and goings of the two."

" When Robbie and Shelaigh made the trip for ice cream a thing and made their plans known, Muriel knew Mike Gregory was a sucker that lived to make a quick buck and she promised him ten thousand in return for chatting up Shelaigh and finding a way to drive them out to where we found her car."

"Muriel met the car wearing a hood and neither she nor Barb were ever without a hood in the presence of Shelaigh or Robbie and they never spoke."

"Their plan had a hiccup though when Barb suggested that helping to send suspicion Shelaigh's way might help them get away cleanly. At that point they couldn't ask Tootie for ransom."

"But how did you find them?" asked Sunshine.

"We found a property rental manager that had dealt with Barb and he gave us an address, but almost at the same time we gave Mike Gregory the information that the women stood to walk away with almost five million each and he was getting a measly ten thousand. He flipped like a pancake and told us everything he knew, and then we caught the two ladies with Shelaigh and Robbie blindfolded and bound in a room of the house they rented. Slam dunk!"

Sticks said, "So if ah understand, now the two women will indeed disappear for a while, and someone else will pay all their livin' expenses. It just won't be the resort they were hopin' for. What happens to the boy?"

"Well, that's up to the DA. He cooperated with the investigation and wasn't as involved as the women. We'll just have to see what the District Attorney decides to do."

The guests talked in small groups for a moment as Jeff, Dannie and Beth refilled glasses with beverages of choice. When

Dannie reached Celia and Mack, she took a moment to propose an idea that had been germinating in the back of her brain. She was pleased when they agreed. Then glasses full, Dannie stepped forward.

"I have a few things I'd like to say. First, thanks to each and every one of you that supported me through several of the worst days of my life. I appreciate everything you did to pick up the slack in my absence. I now know what my father meant when he told me 'everyone is replaceable'. I'm sure most people this week haven't noticed anything amiss at the show."

"Second, my undying gratitude to Detective Miles Wolcott, Chaplain Scott Henderson, the two FBI Special Agents, the other men and women of the Silver Shores PD and especially to my guy, Jeff Barnes, for putting up with my incredibly bad behavior as they did nothing but try to help me and do their jobs."

"Finally, I must eat crow, a very large crow. When this show season started, because that's how we all measure time right, by the show season? Anyway, I was deep in the belief that we women can't possibly worry about how we are treated by men when we treat each other so horribly. I believed 'you' needed to work on that, it wasn't a lesson I needed. But like so many other things I was wrong. Every one of us should be vigilant about how we treat each other. Shelaigh Bittler did her best to protect my son when I wasn't there to do it. She didn't have to but she did and I couldn't see it because I didn't want to see it."

"I treated her abominably for no other reason than I felt like it. I was cautioned repeatedly to wait for the facts, to keep an open mind and I did none of it. At least I have learned in my life to admit when I am wrong. I will offer her an apology and ask her to forgive me but will understand if she doesn't. But I don't need to just tell her which is why I bring it up tonight. It is an apology I want to shout from the rooftops."

Jeff joined Dannie in front of the group. "Believe it or not, we didn't bring you here to talk you to death," he joked. "Just two more small bits of information and then back to the celebration."

"Dannie has informed me that our new friends, Celia and Mack Prentice, have graciously agreed to host a special exhibitor party at The Farmstead. It will be next Thursday evening during week three of the show. This is a beautiful facility; the Prentices work tirelessly for the mission of their charity and take impeccable care of their animals. Staff and exhibitors alike are invited and we promise...no felted unicorns," he winked.

"Now to end the lecture portion of our evening," he joked again, taking Dannie's hand, "something of a more personal note. You are our close friends and family and we wanted you to be the first to know. We have set our wedding date. In the spirit of new beginnings, we wish to be married on January first as the sun rises on a new day, a new year and our new life. We realize this is a bit different than most weddings, but for those of you that are able and willing to get out of bed at that hour we hope you will join us. Every one of you has played an integral part in one, or both of our lives and it wouldn't be right any other way. Now, there's plenty of food and lots more celebrating to do so let's get to it."

The following morning Dannie drove up the winding driveway to Tootie Bittler's home and again parked in front of the fountain across from the large portico. She sat for a moment, taking a deep breath and gathering her courage, then walked to the entrance.

The door was opened by Tootie herself, though she was uncharacteristically stone-faced.

"Hello, Tootie. May I come in?"

Tootie stepped aside to allow Dannie into the foyer but invited her no further into the house.

"Is Shelaigh here? What I've come to say involves her too."

"You've said enough, I think."

"Please, Tootie."

Tootie relented and summoned Shelaigh, who came down the stairs to the entry but was no more welcoming than her mother. Dannie could still see the greenish cast of the fading bruise around her eye.

Dannie began by saying nearly what she had told her guests the previous night but continued beyond that.

"Shelaigh, we have had our problems through the years and I have always blamed you. After all, I couldn't conceive it would be me. But everything in this life takes two and honestly you tried to explain the efforts you were making to live your life differently and I paid very little mind to it. But my dear friend who has always been more tolerant of me than I deserve reminded me that I am not the same person I was seven or eight years ago."

"People can change. We are very different and though I don't know that we would ever be close, you have not deserved my treatment of you this year and I was wrong. And Tootie, I can never apologize enough for what I said to you. You have never been anything but kind and helpful to me and I embarrassed myself speaking to you that way."

"I hope that at some point you can find it in your hearts to forgive me, though I understand if you cannot. And Shelaigh, I will be forever grateful to you for doing your best to protect and reassure Robbie."

"Well," she said when there was no response from mother or daughter, "thank you for your time. I'll go now." She turned and left without another word.

When Jeff and Dannie arrived at The Farmstead Thursday evening Dannie couldn't believe her eyes. There were twice the clear lights she remembered and every decoration was perfect. Mary Jane had spearheaded the party set-up and had done an amazing job.

Dannie had paid Celia and Mack to rent the facility, had rented tables, chairs, glasses, and plates, and had hired a caterer so the only work for the Prentices to do was to make sure The Farmstead put on its best face.

Mary Jane had gone with the currently clichéd country theme but had done it in such a tasteful manner it was beautiful. There were huge baskets of sunflowers placed everywhere, round tables were covered with white tablecloths accented with yellow napkins and arrangements of daisies, marigolds, and zinnias. It was the perfect setting for Dannie and Jeff to announce the plan they had been working on with Tom Robinson and Jerrold Ryan for so long.

Dannie and Jeff arrived early so as to be able to greet the guests. Even though this was an exhibitor party for Silver Shores, it was so much more.

Dannie had chosen a royal blue, beaded dress and as Jeff helped her from the truck he took a moment to admire the picture once again.

"You are stunning, D."

"There will be lots of good-looking women here tonight. I needed to make sure you didn't consider changing your mind."

"Not a chance."

Celia and Mack met them near one of the tables and thanked them again and again for wanting to have the party at The Farmstead.

Dannie said, "I hope later in the evening you will be willing to give interested guests a quick tour."

"I'll be happy too and I have a few ex-servicemen that live in the area that have volunteered to help."

"Perfect!" Dannie said.

"Where's your mom?" Celia asked.

"She opted to stay home and do popcorn and a movie with Robbie. I'm glad; I think I'd have a hard time leaving him with anyone else right now. To tell the truth, even with Mom was a little hard."

One of the first cars to arrive bore Tootie and Shelaigh Bittler. Dannie clenched Jeff's hand a little tighter when she saw them. It had been nearly a week since she had apologized to them both and there had been no communication from them even though Shelaigh had been at the show working on awards every day.

Jeff greeted them first and was his usual charming self for which Dannie silently thanked him. Then Tootie moved to face Dannie and took both of Dannie's hands in hers.

"Danica, I would be a liar if I told you I was not hurt by the way you spoke to me in the police station."

Dannie nodded.

"I am still hurt, but the hurt will fade. I want you to know I forgive you. You were raw and scared and lashing out, it was a terrible time for us all. But I thought about all the things you have done in your life and in our friendship that are good and kind, and I just wanted you to know that I accept your apology. We both do," she said, drawing Shelaigh closer.

Dannie looked expectantly at Shelaigh and she confirmed her mother's sentiments.

"Thank you so much," Dannie said. "I know you didn't have to but I'm so glad you did."

Summer approached Dannie shortly after. "Do you need any help?"

"No, we're good. Did you come alone?"

"No, Miles is over getting drinks. But get that sparkle out of your eye," she laughed. "He's really a nice man, but the jury's out on any kind of serious relationship right now," said Summer.

"In other words, 'mind your own business, Dannie, right?"

The Farmstead was full of people; they drank and ate and talked and were having a wonderful time. There would be a band and dancing, but Dannie and Jeff took the stage first.

"Wow, it's been a roller coaster three weeks. Thank you all so much for coming. We hope you appreciate this beautiful venue," Dannie said and the crowd applauded enthusiastically.

"We had a couple of reasons for bringing you here tonight," said Jeff. "The first involves the man that, if things had gone as they should, would have become my father-in-law. Joe Hoffman. I never had the honor of meeting Joe, but I have come to know him through all of his friends and family and learned that he was a man that valued hard work, championed education, and believed a helping hand should be given whenever possible. To that end, Dannie and I have created the

Joe Hoffman Memorial Scholarship Fund. Grants from this fund will be available to people from Dannie's world and mine; what I mean by that is people from the horse world or the world of law enforcement. Need is key, we will accept applications from young people looking to advance themselves in their lives. It could be college, trade school, practical experience; if our committee receives a compelling application, it will be considered. We hope as time passes, we do not have to limit ourselves to one recipient a year but because we wanted to kick this off tonight, the inaugural recipient of the Joe Hoffman Memorial Scholarship is Summer Stanton."

A cheer went up from the crowd and Summer sat, dumbstruck at Jeff's words.

"Summer had to leave her studies this year through no fault of her own and we want to make sure she has the opportunity to finish what she started," Jeff said, motioning Summer to come forward.

She stepped up on the stage and hugged Dannie and Jeff tightly, tears falling freely. "No words are thanks enough," she whispered in Dannie's ear.

Dannie spoke next. "A wise man told me recently that we have far less control over our lives than we think we do and he was, of course, right. Add to that, my grandmother's warning to me many times in my young life when I was likely to complain; 'light a candle, don't curse the darkness'. Jeff and I decided we would worry about what we could control, namely ourselves, and work toward helping others do great work. We have established the Candleglow Foundation, and the first recipient of a foundation grant is The Farmstead. This charity combines part of Jeff in that it helps veterans and first responders, with my love and the love of many of you here by using our beloved horses to provide that therapy. Please take a moment to speak to Celia or Mack Prentice. They will tell you about their heart, their dedication, their mission, and they are happy to provide a tour of the facility. I hope you find their efforts as worthwhile as we do."

Dannie and Jeff left the stage to such enthusiasm and happiness. The band started to play and the dancing began in earnest. Dannie and Jeff were inundated with well-wishers and congratulations and were quickly separated by those wanting their attention.

Dannie was happy to see so many people talking with Celia and Mack and nearly an hour later Celia rushed up to her, flushed and excited.

"Dannie, I never dreamed of something like this. We have received some incredibly generous donations tonight including some from Mrs. Bittler, the Forrests, and so many other wonderful people. I can't believe it! Thank you for what you and your friends have done."

Jeff, standing twenty or so feet away, had been watching Dannie. She was positively glowing. She was in her element; no matter how she struggled with this horse world these were definitely her people. He thought back to last year and the loss of her father, as well as her challenges this year. Dannie was like a phoenix rising once again; every time she seemed defeated she found the strength to come back and triumph over the demons. He loved this woman and still couldn't believe she'd said 'yes'.

That night as he closed the bedroom door he turned to Dannie and said, "Ma'am, it was my honor to watch you and your blue dress own the room tonight, it will now be my even greater pleasure to help you out of that dress."

This is a work of fiction. All of the characters, organizations, and events portrayed in this novel are either products of the author's imagination or are used fictitiously.

PROS AND CONS
Book 2 in the Silver Shores Series

Cover photo credit: Yvonne Miller
Author photo credit: Clarke Miller